PRAISE FOR
THE BIRTH OF A MOVEMENT

"A notable new book."
—*Boston Globe*

"A remarkable look at the power of mass media and the nascent civil rights movement at a pivotal time in American history."
—*Booklist*, starred review

"Lehr's fascinating portrait of simmering American racial tensions moving into the early twentieth century, and his spotlight on men and women who, intentionally or not, helped galvanize painful and necessary conversations about civil rights, race relations, and the power of mass media for decades to come."
—*Library Journal*, starred review

"A powerful rendering of an enduring conflict."
—*Kirkus Reviews*, starred review

"D. W. Griffith's 1915 film, *The Birth of a Nation*, may have been billed as the 'Most Wonderful Motion Picture Ever,' but to African Americans of the Jim Crow era, it was a grotesque reminder of how invisible their true lives—their history and their dreams—were across the color line. Speaking out against the white-hooded nostalgia the film inflamed, William Monroe Trotter, Harvard's first black Phi Beta Kappa graduate and a leading newspaper editor, revived a protest tradition that would set the stage for the civil rights movement to follow. Distinguished journalist Dick Lehr's account of this racial debate is not only enthralling to read; it reminds us of the singular importance of 'the birth of' Monroe Trotter."
—Henry Louis Gates, Jr., Alphonse Fletcher University Professor, Harvard University

THE BIRTH OF A MOVEMENT

THE BIRTH OF A MOVEMENT

HOW *BIRTH OF A NATION* IGNITED THE BATTLE FOR CIVIL RIGHTS

DICK LEHR

PUBLICAFFAIRS
New York

First published in hardcover as *The Birth of a Nation* in 2014 by PublicAffairs™, an imprint of Perseus Books, LLC, a subsidiary of Hachette Book Group, Inc.

PublicAffairs books are available at special discounts for bulk purchases in the U.S. by corporations, institutions, and other organizations. For more information, please contact the Special Markets Department at Perseus Books, 2300 Chestnut Street, Suite 200, Philadelphia, PA 19103, call (800) 810-4145, ext. 5000, or e-mail special.markets@perseusbooks.com.

Book design by Trish Wilkinson

The Library of Congress has cataloged the original edition as follows:
ISBN 978-1-58648-987-8 (hardcover)
ISBN 978-1-58648-988-5 (hardcover e-book)
ISBN 978-1-61039-823-7 (paperback)
ISBN 978-1-61039-824-4 (paperback e-book)

10 9 8 7 6 5 4 3 2 1

For my daughters, Holly and Dana

CONTENTS

PART IV: 1915

PART V: VICTORY AND DEFEAT

AUTHOR'S NOTE

This is a work of nonfiction. The people are real; no names have
been changed; no changes have been made in the chronology of
events. Dialogue is based on letters, journals, newspaper reports,
and other archival records. Regarding terminology, I made the decision to use the terms *Negro* and *colored* that were commonplace
during the period when this story occurred—the early twentieth century. When I read narrative histories I find the use of present terms
African American or *black* jarring; they take me out of the historical
moment. Besides, terminology is fluid. For example, the journalist
Ray Stannard Baker, in a 1908 article titled "An Ostracised Race in
Ferment," made this observation: "Many Negroes who a few years
ago called themselves 'Afro-American' or 'Colored Americans' and
who winced at the name Negro now use Negro as the race name with
pride." It is also worth noting that the Associated Press, long the ar-
biter of style in journalism, in December 1914 issued this comment
about usage: "We have a broad rule to the effect that the word 'Negro'
should be capitalized in our service, but we do not control the typo-
logical appearances of the word as it appears in the newspapers."
The latter part of the comment was the AP's way of dealing with the
fact that many newspapers using its service either changed *Negro*
from upper to lower case or substituted derogatory terms in its place.
Finally, Monroe Trotter's preferred term changed over time; early
on he favored *Negro*, but he later came to think that term suggested
separatism and so he switched to *Colored* or *Colored Americans*.

PROLOGUE

January 2, 1915

David Wark Griffith watched intently as curious residents of Riverside, California, filed into the Loring Opera House for a Saturday evening preview of a new movie promoted as the "Most Wonderful Motion Picture Ever." The moviegoers crowded the ornate thousand-seat theater, which first opened in 1890 to showcase opera and musicals and had only just begun to present the new medium of film.

Excitement was building. Griffith, the motion picture's director, had personally arranged the eight p.m. screening. He had even persuaded many of the film's stars to attend the sneak preview: among them the enchanting Lillian Gish, doe-eyed Mae Marsh, and popular leading man Henry B. Walthall. The director had wanted to get away from the hubbub of his Hollywood studio, choosing this young city sixty miles inland from the expansive, big-sky locations in the California hills where he'd filmed some of the movie's panoramic battle sequences.

As was his custom for test screenings, Griffith settled into a seat at the back of the theater, not far from the booth where projectors were hand cranked. The operator had to find a frames-per-second speed that would satisfy Griffith: The pace had to suit both the fury of galloping horses and the solemnity of a death scene. His secretary and film editor—then called a film cutter—by his side,

Griffith was at once studying the film and gauging the audience's reaction, dictating notes for additional edits. "Every single subtitle, every situation, every shift in scene or change in a sequence that is made in editing a film, has to go before an audience for its test before being accepted as part of the complete product," the director said about his process. Griffith was fanatical about his finishing touches. He was preparing for the premier in Los Angeles the next month, with even bigger things to come afterward, including a trip to Washington DC, to show the movie to President Wilson in what would be the first-ever film screening inside the White House.

The Kentucky-born director was to celebrate his fortieth birthday in three weeks, but the personal milestone paled in comparison to the impact his film was going to have on the history of American cinema. For Griffith, 1915 marked the culmination of a professional journey that had begun in earnest at the turn of the century with his arrival in New York City as a raw, aspiring actor. He turned to directing in 1908, but nothing he'd made so far came close to the production quality of his new movie that took up twelve reels, or about 12,000 feet of film, consisting of more than 1,300 shots and 230 separate titles.

For the most part, films had previously consisted of a series of long shots. The camera would stay in a fixed position, recording actors as though they were on a stage. Griffith moved the camera around, shooting a scene multiple times from various angles and then editing the footage to assemble a sequence of action shots that was more compelling, intense, and intimate. With his work, Griffith did more than any other director to legitimize film as art. He insisted that critics and the public move past the conventional view that movies were unworthy "spectacles" and recognize "photo-plays"—the term he preferred—for the sophisticated forms of artistic expression that they were. It was a campaign Griffith started in earnest with his new work. Titled *The Clansman,* this photo-play had been adapted from a popular novel about the Civil War and Reconstruction by southern author Thomas Dixon Jr. In Griffith's hands, the story was transformed into a titanic piece of filmmaking, a game-changer in the making, marketing, and public appreciation of cinema.

Griffith planned the hype for the film's launch himself. Ever his own best publicist, he stretched facts in ways that would have made the innovators in the infant field of public relations proud. In the very first notices that announced the special preview in Riverside newspapers, Griffith called himself "The World's Foremost Motion Picture Producer," and published outright falsehoods to embellish the film's feats. Ads reported the movie cost $500,000 to produce and employed "25,000 soldiers in action on battlefield." Both numbers were not even close to being accurate.

The ads lured Riverside moviegoers to the Loring Opera House, where Griffith delivered a three-hour feature film the likes of which no one had seen before. The crowd heartily "gave its stamp of approval," a local reviewer wrote afterward. The hooded Klansmen riding across the screen to defeat rioting Negroes comprised "a beautiful piece of motion picture photography splendidly acted." Griffith, the reviewer concluded, "has given the world a masterpiece. There is not a flaw in the production." But, of course, there was one major flaw.

Griffith had produced the country's first blockbuster movie, one that has become the centerpiece in college courses on film history. I was taking such a course when I watched the movie for the first time. My second viewing was not as typical; in fact, it had nothing to do with filmmaking history but had everything to do with its racist content. In the fall of 1979, as a reporter for the *Hartford Courant*, I was assigned to cover a recruiting drive the Knights of the Ku Klux Klan had launched in Connecticut. The organization was based in Metairie, Louisiana, and its Grand Dragon was a man named David Duke. In December 1979 Duke traveled north to meet with members in a rented grange hall in Danbury. I attended the meeting using a false identity so as to infiltrate the group. (The deception was part of the newspaper's effort to expose the Connecticut klavern's local leadership.) D. W. Griffith's silent film turned out to be Duke's prop. At the screening, he read aloud its subtitles, adding his own bigoted commentary, while standing between the reel-to-reel projector and an American flag. When a group of Klansmen on horses dumped the corpse of a black man they had murdered on the doorstep of the governor's mansion Duke began to clap his hands, a firm clap that grew louder as others joined to applaud the death of a black man on-screen.

The KKK meeting took place in a darkened grange hall doubling as a classroom for Duke's course on white power—with the film his main teaching tool. The next week Duke sent me a Christmas greeting—a bright red card picturing robed Klansmen holding a fiery cross, with this inscription: "May you have a meaningful and merry Christmas and may they forever be White." It was clear that the Grand Dragon of the modern Klan fully understood the value of Griffith's film as propaganda—just as civil rights leaders understood a century ago as they reacted in horror to its initial release. The film's 1915 debut coincided with a precipitous decline in civil rights, when post–Civil War hopes for blacks in America had taken a terrifying turn.

Nearly 1,700 miles away, on the same day in 1915 that Griffith's film was previewed in Riverside, California, William Monroe Trotter strode across the polished marble floors of the La Salle Hotel, which, with its twenty-two stories and one thousand rooms, held bragging rights as the largest and most luxurious hotel in The Loop, Chicago's fast-developing downtown. Had any of the midday guests seated in the lobby's overstuffed chairs taken notice of the visiting newspaper editor from Boston they would have observed the following: He was dressed impeccably in a dark suit, he sported a neatly trimmed mustache, and he was Negro. They would have noticed, too, that Trotter carried himself confidently and with a sense of purpose—"the splendid individualist," as one historian later described him.

Trotter was navigating his way through the hotel's mostly white clientele to find the grand Red Ballroom, where he was due to speak at a crowded gathering of the Irish Fellowship Club. Trotter had only been in the Windy City a few days, arriving on December 31 at the invitation of longtime friend Ida B. Wells. He was forty-two, a decade younger than the civil rights leader who had been born a slave and, as a young woman in Tennessee, had waged a crusade against lynching in the newspaper *Memphis Free Speech* and then later in the *New York Age*. Trotter and Wells shared certain traits, most notably an aversion to "the restraints of organization."

For his part, Trotter had been the first black man to graduate Phi Beta Kappa from Harvard and, in 1901, was cofounder of a radical weekly newspaper that challenged Booker T. Washington's get-along, go-along approach to civil rights. He had become a national figure, mentioned in the same breath as Washington and W. E. B. Du Bois. "We need leaders, let us have more William Monroe Trotters," the *Chicago Defender*, an influential black weekly, had said about him.

His prominence at an all-time high, Trotter was in great demand to talk about "the Negro question," a sought-after speaker before Negro audiences in Chicago and, in the weeks to come, in Pittsburgh, Pennsylvania; St. Paul, Minnesota; Omaha, Nebraska; and St. Louis, Missouri. But on this day, January 2, as he reached the entry to the La Salle's Red Ballroom—the same day the US Senate was passing a sweeping new immigration bill that would exclude anyone of "the African race" from entering the country—Trotter received the coldest of cold shoulders.

He presented his business card, expecting to follow a brief speech by the Cook County clerk with his own. But when word of his arrival spread through the hall, trouble erupted. Fellows shouted, "No, no!" and the club's secretary and president left the rostrum to confer with the Negro visitor from Boston. Others throughout the ballroom cried out, "We don't want him here!"

The tangle made news. "Negro Kept Out of Irish Club," reported the *Chicago Tribune* on its front page the next day. Trotter had not taken the rejection lightly, according to the story, and had angrily tried to push his way into the meeting until a doorman managed to block him. Trotter disputed the account; he said a club member had invited him to speak if a scheduled speaker proved unable to attend. Told the speakers were all present, he said, he had taken the news cordially and simply left.

Either way, it was a moment that captured the disparate view of the crusading Negro newspaper editor who made his name as an outspoken challenger of the status quo, both in the civil rights movement and in society at large. Many saw Trotter as a distasteful provocateur, while his followers believed he was simply and forcefully demanding his race's rightful place at the table.

Buoyed by the reception in Riverside, California, D. W. Griffith returned to his Hollywood studio, a maze of projection rooms, open-air stages and dressing rooms, to continue tweaking his new movie. For him, 1915 had opened on a positive note. Meanwhile, Monroe Trotter's year had begun discordantly. Unknown to either, they were on a collision course over the director's film adaptation of *The Clansman.* It was as if Trotter grasped the enormous power of the new medium—that he might circulate a year's worth of newspapers and still not come close to reaching the mass numbers of people filling theaters in Boston, New York City, Los Angeles, and elsewhere. So he embarked on a crusade against D. W. Griffith that would define his lifetime, knowing full well that to protest the new film might have the unintended consequence of actually fueling its publicity and ticket sales. But Trotter decided that to *not* speak out—and to let stand the movie's racism—would be worse.

The story that follows reconstructs Monroe Trotter's violent efforts to halt the spread of the movie that was at once a masterpiece in filmmaking technique and a virulent brand of hate speech. The battle was waged on every possible stage across the nation, one that embodied a big bang moment of sorts—in mass media and marketing; in free-speech protections that we now take for granted; in an increasingly diversified nation struggling to define its identity; and in a still fragile civil rights movement forced to adopt ever more militant direct actions that would set a precedent for the future of the fight for equal rights.

And at its heart were two passionate, driven, and flawed men—each determined to fight for the cultural and political soul of the still-young America.

PART I

Fathers and Sons

Lt. James M. Trotter   Lt. Col. Jacob "Roaring Jake" Griffith

— 1 —

Guns, Bayonets, and
Cannon "Grapes"

William Monroe Trotter's father—James Monroe Trotter—was born in 1842 in the Deep South in Grand Gulf, Mississippi—a tiny town near the Mississippi River about twenty-five miles south of Vicksburg. He was of mixed race. His mother, Letitia, served as the slave mistress to a plantation owner named Richard Trotter, and James was born "light complected" but with black hair and black eyes. When he was ten, James and his mother left Mississippi. Little is known about his early boyhood, so it isn't clear if he and his mother fled or if Richard Trotter had set them free. They moved north about 750 miles to Cincinnati, Ohio—passing through Tennessee and Kentucky—where a blustery southerner named Jacob Wark Griffith happened to be plotting a run for the state legislature.

Soon after their arrival in Cincinnati, Letitia enrolled her son in the Gilmore School, a college preparatory school for Negro children on the east side of the city that a wealthy Methodist minister had opened during the prior decade. James displayed a keen musicality and sang with his classmates during vacations and summers throughout Ohio, New York, and Canada to raise money for students in need. One of his favorite songs was "The Captive Knight," a widely popular tune about valor and chivalry, with lyrics by the English poet Felicia Dorothea Hemans and music by the poet's sister, Harriet Mary Browne.

Although as a teenager Trotter worked as a bellboy in a downtown hotel and as a cabin boy on a steamer traveling the Cincinnati–New Orleans route of the Ohio–Mississippi River system, he continued to focus on music until he headed off to the Albany Manual Labor University. This integrated work-study college was located on three hundred acres of farmland in Albany, Ohio, a town that served as a key station for slaves traveling the Underground Railroad. Tuition for each ten-week term was $4.00; weekly room and board, $1.90. He graduated in 1862. The South had seceded the year before, and the country was in the midst of the Civil War, but James had his sights set on a career in education.

He took a job as a teacher in communities east of Cincinnati, where he met two persons who would prove crucially important to his life—William H. Dupree and Virginia Isaacs. Both lived in Chillicothe, Ohio, a small but bustling town that welcomed free Negroes migrating from southern states. Three years older than James, Dupree was a freed slave and the manager of the Union Valley Brass Band. The two men quickly discovered a common interest in music. Virginia and her sister Elizabeth lived a wagon ride from town, on a family farmstead featuring a big house atop a central hill shaded by tall locust trees, with a grassy front yard and shrubbery all around. Fruit trees covered the hill to the east, and a stream used to water the horses ran at the foot of the hills. The sisters were attractive, popular, and known for their wit and hospitality. James Trotter had his eye on Virginia, who worked as a schoolteacher in Chillicothe.

In a way, the Isaacs family belonged to American royalty. They had ancestral ties to one of the country's Founding Fathers. The family's oral tradition had it that Virginia Isaacs's maternal great-grandmother's stepsister was Sally Hemings, a slave at Thomas Jefferson's Monticello plantation in Virginia whom Jefferson took as a lover. The second link to Jefferson was more direct, resulting from the marriage of the eldest Isaacs sister, Julia Ann, to Thomas Eston Hemings, one of the sons born to Sally Hemings and Jefferson.

The spark between James and Virginia had little time to catch, however. By early 1863, recruiting agents were canvassing Ohio in search of men for an all-Negro Union regiment being mustered in Massachusetts. Negroes had been barred from enlisting during the first two years of the Civil War, but wartime necessity had softened opposition. Massachusetts governor John A. Andrew, a champion of Negro soldiery from the start, had been authorized to round up troops of African descent. But in a state long identified with abolitionism there were, in the early 1860s, only about two thousand free Negroes—hardly enough from which to create a one-thousand-man regiment.

Recruiters, working on a commission basis, were dispatched. They spoke at rallies in Ohio and other states and enlisted the Negro press to spread the word. Listening to the call was William H. Dupree. He enlisted in Ohio on June 5 as a private. Six days later, James Trotter, now twenty-one, followed suit.

Immediately the two were shipped out to Boston, where they were taken to Camp Meigs, a military encampment in the Readville section of Hyde Park, just south of the city—a lowland location less than two miles from where Trotter would eventually settle.

When the men arrived at the base, they found it humming with activity. Recruits drilled out in the open on level fields ideal for mustering troops. During heavy rains, the grounds turned into "bleak and cheerless" mudflats. The barracks consisted of barnlike wooden structures built in rows. One regiment—the 54th Massachusetts (Colored) Infantry—was already filled, so Trotter and Dupree were placed in the newly opened 55th Massachusetts Volunteer Infantry, also comprising Negro recruits.

Training was intensive, including practice marches up and down the roads of Hyde Park. But Trotter quickly stood out to the white officers who commanded Negro units, for his leadership potential. Unlike the majority of the battalion, which consisted mainly of farmers and laborers, Trotter was literate and educated. Eleven days after he enlisted, he was made a sergeant and assigned to Company K, one of the ten companies, each with about a hundred men, which made up the 55th. Dupree, too, became a sergeant.

The men trained hard, under pressure to pull together and be ready to ship out the next month. They also developed practices that white officers were unaccustomed to seeing in their army. The very first night at Camp Meigs, after officers had dismissed them to their barracks, the recruits gathered on their own, said a prayer, and then, as one white officer later wrote, "joined in singing one of their peculiar hymns." When possible, the men of the 55th made a practice of ending their day this way. They also organized a regimental band. No surprise that William Dupree emerged as manager.

James Trotter believed the 55th's band eventually became the best in the entire Union army, providing necessary relief to soldiers in war. "In camp-life it often enlivened the dull hours and gave, by sweetest music, a certain refinement." Morning services were held on Sundays.

Once, during war service, the 55th was camped next to a Negro regiment commanded by Colonel Thomas K. Beecher—a minister and the younger brother of Harriett Beecher Stowe, author of *Uncle Tom's Cabin*, and Henry Ward Beecher, also a minister. That particular Sunday, Colonel Beecher led the service, and James Trotter sat enthralled, "listening with deep, thrilling interest to the inspiring words of this fighting parson."

At Camp Meigs, Trotter was instrumental in creating "improvised schools" in the regiment so that he and others with formal education, including some of the white officers, could teach the other soldiers to read, write, and sing. They set up school tents. Books were scarce, so the instruction given was entirely oral. Trotter took particular interest in tutoring a corporal named Alonzo Boon, a recruit from Boston. Trotter explained that literacy was a prerequisite for advancement because of the daily paperwork sergeants had to submit. He said he'd help Boon to win that rank, and shortly after becoming Trotter's student, Boon got the promotion. Sergeant Boon was not only able to fill out all the paperwork required but also surprised his family when he wrote three letters home.

The regiment conducted daily drills at the camp and embarked on grueling four-hour marches, but the men also found time to meet a handful of prominent Bostonians—supporters of Negroes in the army and in society at large—who traveled to Hyde Park to see the mustering of the new units. Trotter met William Lloyd Garrison, the bespectacled abolitionist and editor of the *Liberator*—the anti-slavery weekly newspaper he'd been publishing in Boston for more than three decades—and Garrison's youngest son, Francis. While writing letters from the battlefield to fifteen-year-old "Franky," Trotter quickly warmed to the boy's father as a "friend of my race." Trotter also served in the 55th under another of Garrison's sons, George, who was commissioned as a second lieutenant on June 22, the same day Trotter himself had been promoted to sergeant.

On July 30, in the pouring rain, James Trotter and Company K boarded a schooner, aptly named *Recruit*, in Boston Harbor and sailed to South Carolina, the first state to secede, where the regiment joined the mission to conquer a city at the heart of the Confederacy: Charleston.

Trotter was now a full-fledged member of one of 116 Negro regiments—known as the "Black Yankees," the "African Brigades," and the "Black Phalanx"—that only began mustering two years into the bloody War Between the States. The Union army's initial thinking at Camp Meigs had been that Negroes, believed unfit in terms of courage and manly makeup for combat, would serve as auxiliary backfill—armed mostly with shovels rather than rifles and performing "fatigue duty," the grunt work of digging out rifle pits and protective batteries for artillery, or building the fortified, breast-high trenches known as breastworks: an insult to the new soldiers that the 55th would quickly prove wrong. Negro troops were paid $10 a month, three dollars less than what white soldiers earned.

Battling headwinds, the schooner carrying James Trotter and the 55th took ten days to reach South Carolina. They arrived on August 9 at Folly Island, which lies eight miles south of Charleston, with its more than forty thousand residents, one of the South's largest cities, at once cosmopolitan and a munitions stronghold. In the coming twenty months, except for a short swing into Florida, the 55th made camp in this region. By the end of 1863, James Trotter was promoted to the most senior of noncommissioned ranks—sergeant major in Company G.

In late June 1864, Union commanders were putting finishing touches on plans for yet another attack on Charleston. The 55th joined two other infantry regiments to try to break through Confederate defenses just south of the city on James Island. Trotter and

the others started out on the hot and muggy morning of July 2, using small boats to make the crossing from Folly Island. He recalled
afterward that the landing was so swampy "some of the men sunk
nearly up to their necks." But he added, "We were at last in Rebel
Territory, and although much fatigued and all wet and muddy began our march toward the enemy and his numerous forts."

The soldiers struggled to make headway through the swamp,
"plunging, wading and part of the time almost swimming." The
55th took up the rear, behind one regiment from New York and
another from Connecticut. Suddenly, Trotter heard gunfire. Explo-
sions erupted as the regiments ahead ran into a small fort armed
with two cannons. The enemy "threw solid ball and shell" on the
troops, which hit "like hail scattering death and destruction all
around." The Union soldiers panicked. The New York and Connecticut regiments turned and retreated, running toward Trotter
and the other 350 Negro soldiers who made up the 55th that day.
Confederate forces were emboldened at the sight of bluecoats rac-
ing past commanding officers unable to restrain them. At the same
time, Trotter and his comrades in the 55th realized it was up to
them to save the Brigade.

In its coverage of the Battle of James Island, the *New York Herald* highlighted the 55th's battlefield response to a turn of events
where Negro soldiers suddenly had to dodge fleeing comrades as
well as incoming fire and "never flinched." The 55th was determined to capture the fort. Its men advanced steadily along the narrow trail the enemy had made nearly impassable by cutting down
trees, fighting their way forward and facing a "pouring of grape
with deadly effect," until they got within two hundred yards of the
battery and began screaming in a desperate rush.

Now it was the enemy's turn to run. Confederate soldiers jumped
on their horses. "By the time we gained the parapet [they] were far
down the road," Trotter said. "O how they did fly!" The Union soldiers found two cannons still loaded, which they turned and fired.
But the 55th was too tired to give chase. "We had no support, the
other regiments having failed us." Instead, the troops took stock
of their accomplishment, and eventually hauled the cannons back

to Folly Island as a trophy. "You may imagine how proud we felt when we found ourselves masters of 'Johnny's fort' and with what satisfaction we looked upon *our* pieces of cannon which now looked innocent enough but which a few minutes before had dealt death to so many of our brave fellows."

The 55th had indeed suffered—nine men killed, nineteen wounded. Fatalities included two of the regiment's sergeants; one was the man Trotter had taught to read and write. "Poor Sergt. Boon!" Trotter wrote in a letter he sent the next month from Folly Island to young Franky Garrison in Boston. "Do you recollect him?" Boon couldn't carry a rifle due to an arm injury but had managed to convince his commander to let him participate in the battle anyway. Outfitted with only his sidearm, Boon was "wounded by a large grape in the leg, which was amputated, causing instant death." They buried the sergeant on a hill "near to where stands the cannon out of which hurled the ball that caused his death." The loss hit Trotter hard. "No one's death has made me feel so sad," he confided to Garrison. "In truth I loved him."

The 55th would suffer worse losses four months later in the biggest battle in its regimental history. Two days after Thanksgiving 1864, the regiment boarded two steamers at Folly Island and crossed over to Hilton Head to join a larger Union assault on Charleston once again, and its assignment was to cut off the railroad running from the city to Savannah, Georgia.

Trotter and his comrades were ferried up the Broad River to a point called Boyd's Landing. There they assembled with other Union troops. When dawn came on November 30, this force of more than five thousand soldiers broke camp. They headed west on foot through forest and swamp, and after marching about five miles, encountered enemy gunfire. The Union army kept going, pushing the enemy back and advancing a few more miles. Then, at around eleven o'clock in the morning, the men looked up at a ridge known as Honey Hill, where a Confederate earthwork, fortified with seven cannons, was built blocking the only road through the wilderness. On either side of the road was an impassable marsh. There was only one direction for an army to go, and the Union general commanding the force ordered the 55th to lead the way. "We rushed cheering and yelling," Trotter said. "The cannon on the hill opened. Shot, shell, grape and canister was hurled down." The Negro regiment didn't stand a chance.

"The men could only go by the flank—4 men in a breast," Trotter said. "It was like rushing into the very mouth of death going up this road." The commander of the 55th, Colonel Alfred S. Hartwell of Massachusetts, was one of the first to be hit in a hail of gun- and cannon fire that also saw his horse shot from under him. "The Colonel, though wounded in two places and nearly crushed by his horse falling on him was bravely rescued by the men." The fighting continued through the afternoon, the "unavailing bloodshed" all around Trotter, as casualties mounted for the 55th and the other Union troops.

With dusk approaching, and after repeated surges failed, the Union forces had had enough. "We fought," Trotter wrote, "until dark, when under its cover we silently withdrew." The men retraced their steps to Boyd's Landing. More than seven hundred Union soldiers were killed or wounded during less than five hours of combat. The 55th was hit the hardest. "Our loss is about 30 killed," Trotter wrote, "and 108 wounded. We went in with 502 muskets." Trotter was one of the injured. But whatever the nature of the wounds, he was not out of action for long. On December 18, 1864, less than a month later, he was back on duty.

The mission to cut off the railroad to Charleston ended in defeat at the Battle of Honey Hill. The 55th Massachusetts Volunteer Infantry finished the year a battered and weary bunch. But the Union forces were taking control, propelled in large part by General William Tecumseh Sherman's famous "March to the Sea," the decisive campaign that began in November in Atlanta with Northern troops' moving inexorably south, capturing enemy strongholds and destroying the Confederate rail transportation system, and ended in December with the capture of Savannah, Georgia.

By the start of 1864, James Trotter had been serving for eight months as a second lieutenant, just not officially. After promoting Trotter and two others, Colonel Hartwell was told by his superiors in Washington he had no business doing such a thing. "There is no law allowing it, they being colored men," a general said.

Issues of Negro pay and promotion, while rarely interfering with the troops' conduct in combat, was of paramount concern to the 55th and other all-Negro units. James Trotter was in the thick of it as a leader and activist, insisting their pay be increased to equal the $13 a month given white soldiers. "We gladly peril our lives," he said, and so deserve "Manhood and Equality." In 1863 Governor Andrew of Massachusetts had offered to appropriate money to make up the difference. But Trotter and his comrades rejected the well-intended gesture. It was a matter of principle—either equal pay from the US government or no pay at all. "We'll never take it," Trotter said when the compromise was presented. "We are soldiers, we will accept nothing less than the soldier's pay."

Trotter was crushed by the situation. He felt that a "deep injustice" had been "meted out by the Government." Morale suffered, with one officer's April 1864 regimental fitness report making this observation: "The non-payment of the men produces in some a marked feeling of insubordination." In June of that year, a private named Wallace Baker protested violently and was charged with mutiny. The soldier was convicted at trial and then, by men from his regiment, executed. But the 55th still fought bravely that July 2 in the Battle of James Island.

After sixteen months without pay, the matter was resolved. The men were aided by their white commanders' persistent lobbying of Congress. "You cannot imagine what a day of rejoicing this event occasioned," Trotter told a friend in a letter several months later, on November 21, 1864, a week before the Battle of Honey Hill. The men celebrated with a parade, Dupree's brass band, singing, and speeches. But rejoicing was not just about the money. "No," Trotter said, "it was because a great principle of equal rights as men and soldiers had been decided in their favor—that all this glorious excitement was made."

He was twenty-two years old.

Then there was the matter of Trotter's, Dupree's, and a third Negro's so-called promotions—a more personal grievance than the pay dispute affecting every soldier. "This *acting* Lieutenant business is not all pleasant when you reflect that no other thing stands in the way but our *color*," Trotter wrote in July 1864.

Trotter felt most white officers gave Negro officers the cold shoulder. Even those few who seemed supportive were awkward about it. One told Trotter he was not against Negroes becoming officers, only that it was happening too fast. White lieutenants needed more time "to get rid of their prejudices" and to get used to the idea of sleeping "in a tent with a colored one." Trotter was quick to mock the white-centric bias, and its assumption that "decent colored officers would never object to sleeping with [a white officer] whatever might be his character."

The double standard, Trotter said, was simply a "painful and burning wrong." He even sought press coverage at one point from William Lloyd Garrison. "Please tell Mr. Garrison about the refusal of the Government to muster as officers colored men duly commissioned, so that it may be referred to by him in the influential *Liberator*," Trotter wrote the editor's son Franky.

Trotter continued coping with "Colorphobia," as he called it, over his rank until the end of his service. In the winter of 1865, following his recovery from his wounds, he and his company briefly headed south into Georgia to perform garrison duty outside Savannah. Trotter was quick to note the locals' worried looks. "Ours is the only colored Regt. so near Savannah and, of course (we) create much sensation among the Georgians." In February, Trotter returned to South Carolina and joined thousands of Union soldiers converging on Charleston for the Confederacy's last stand, as remnants of its forces from all over raced to the area, including a rowdy bunch of fighters from Kentucky led by a swaggering, sword-wielding lieutenant colonel named "Roaring Jake" Griffith. Griffith's vastly depleted Kentucky brigade slogged through the swamps, trying to help stop the Northern troops' inexorable advance.

Trotter's 55th marched into Charleston on February 21, 1865, to finally topple the citadel of slavery, but the Union troops were bivouacked outside the city when word came that Richmond, Virginia, had fallen. On April 9, General Robert E. Lee surrendered to General Ulysses S. Grant at Appomattox Court House.

The momentous and bloody Civil War, which cost 625,000 lives, had ended—and with it, the dispute over Trotter's rank. Within weeks, the 55th's commanders received word from the Union's secretary of war that Trotter, Dupree, and the third Negro could be made second lieutenants—although the appointments were not official until July 1. Some white officers threatened to resign in protest, but Trotter was ecstatic, grateful he'd be discharged at the rank earned the previous year and generously noting, "Our *best* officers do not manifest any Colorphobia." In Boston, the *Liberator* mentioned him in a story about Negroes who had been promoted to officer ranks, "in the service of their country."

Trotter did not leave the South immediately after the war ended. From late spring until his discharge in September he became part of the transition force overseeing the early days of Reconstruction. His job was to ensure that slave owners signed labor contracts with their freed slaves. Under the new rules, no plantation owner was allowed to have Negroes working the fields without such contracts. "The former slaveholders wince under the new order of things," Trotter observed. "It seems to hurt them sorely—having to treat as intelligent free men and women . . . those whom they have tyrannized over with impunity, treating them as so many cattle."

Armed with a Colt revolver, he'd ride alone on horseback to war-torn plantations that had lost much of their antebellum luster and grandeur. "The Chivalry all treated me with respect and were very skillful in concealing whatever bitterness they may have felt when seeing a 'nigger' with shoulder straps riding along the road to Columbia visiting their plantations in order to see that they were treating properly the colored people." But he could see the defeat etched in their faces. "The people of South Carolina who have been in this wicked Rebellion are now completely cowed down," he said. "They are whipped."

James Monroe Trotter certainly understood Carolinians' role in history—"They began the Rebellion," he wrote a friend. Fifty years later, a Kentucky-born filmmaker would agree, when he chose to set his dramatic Civil War epic in South Carolina. But the courage, book smarts, and eloquence of the young second lieutenant would always expose the lie that Negroes were heathens, as David Wark "D. W." Griffith, son of Confederate officer "Roaring Jake," would portray them in *The Birth of a Nation*.

2

The Trotters

As a boy, Monroe Trotter learned his Civil War history from a father who, as one family historian said, "had just enough of the war to make him know and properly value manhood and freedom in its truest sense." When Monroe was ten, the senior Trotter was one of the keynote speakers at a reunion of the 55th and 54th Massachusetts Infantries. James Trotter recalled the Negro soldiers' unity in their refusal of unequal wages, the suffering of their families back home, and the shared honor of standing together against racism. "In their struggle for equal pay and recognition," he said at the gathering November 8, 1882, "the Massachusetts colored troops finally won for themselves, for all other colored troops, and relatively for their race and its friends, a complete and glorious victory."

Following his official discharge from the army in September 1865, James Trotter had returned briefly to Ohio, where he renewed his acquaintance with the Chillicothe schoolteacher Virginia Isaacs. Then, at age twenty-three, he moved to Massachusetts. He and his best friend William Dupree settled into a tenement at 18 Blossom Street with four other bachelors. They were staying in the Boston neighborhood where most Negroes lived—on the back side of Beacon Hill, a crowded area of narrow side streets and alleyways in the West End that some referred to by the slur "Nigger Hill." Both men began working in 1866 for the post office—Trotter as a clerk and Dupree as a letter carrier. Both also stayed in touch with the Isaacs sisters. Two years later, Trotter and Virginia Isaacs, both twenty-six years old, were married in the Chillicothe Colored Baptist Church, and two years after that, Dupree followed suit, marrying Virginia's older sister Elizabeth.

The Trotters' first two babies were stillborn sons. Virginia's third child, William Monroe Trotter, was born on April 7, 1872, at her parents' farm outside Chillicothe. Returning to Boston seven months later, the Trotters moved into a brick house on Kendall Street in the city's South End. They remained close to the Duprees as well as to other Negro families that, like theirs, were relatively new to Boston, in addition to socializing with some whose roots in the city were long standing. For example, Charles Pindell's family lived just a few blocks away. The Pindells belonged to the so-called Negro elite in a Negro community that made up only about 3 percent of the city's overall population during the late 1800s. Before the Civil War, Pindell's uncle William had lobbied to end school segregation in the Boston courts and state legislature. Charles Pindell was himself an attorney. He had a daughter, Geraldine, nicknamed "Deenie," born in 1872, seven months after Monroe Trotter was born, and as youngsters the two became acquainted during their parents' get-togethers.

Monroe's boyhood was rich intellectually, and his family's circumstances comfortable. The Trotters moved out to Hyde Park when their second child, Maude, was due in 1874. Growing up there, Monroe saw his father commute to Boston each morning on a horse-drawn streetcar to his job at the post office's registry section. During that period, James also found time to complete a book that captured his enduring passion for Negro music: published in 1878, the 508-page *Music and Some Highly Musical People* was the first of its kind—a historical survey of Negro music, covering every region and every type of music. "It should find a welcome to every library," wrote New York's *Baptist Outlook* in its review. The opus featured a huge section of mini-biographies of Negro musicians and composers, along with a lengthy appendix of songs by twelve Negro composers.

More than five thousand copies sold within three years of its release. By the next year, the book's royalties proved a welcome source of income. Chafing about discriminatory practices at the post office

James M. Trotter's likeness in his book, *Music and Some Highly Musical People* (Boston 1880; New York 1881).
COURTESY OF BOSTON UNIVERSITY'S GOTLIEB ARCHIVAL RESEARCH CENTER.

and mulling what to do after a white colleague—"his inferior both in rank and ability"—got a job ahead of him, James Trotter at last made up his mind. In 1883 he quit in protest. It had become a matter of principle. To date, young Monroe had witnessed his father's intense work ethic. Now he tasted the independent spirit that was the true measure of the veteran's Civil War service.

Out of a job for the first time since his discharge from the army, the senior Trotter cobbled together a living from his book royalties and his modest success with dabbling in real estate. But the family did not go wanting for too long. Trotter's independence of mind, asserted in politics, brought him an unexpected return. He had grown increasingly wary of the assumption that the Republican Party owned the Negro vote. In 1883 he broke rank during a statewide gubernatorial race to support the Democratic nominee, a war veteran and lawyer named Benjamin Butler, and Butler was elected. During the 1884 election, Trotter campaigned vigorously for Grover Cleveland, and Cleveland won, becoming the only Democrat to serve as president during the fifty-two years between Lincoln's win in 1860 and 1912, when Woodrow Wilson was elected.

James Trotter left the family behind in Hyde Park—his son, Monroe, just entering high school there—to become recorder of deeds in Washington, DC in 1887. The federal post was the highest a Negro held at the time, and Trotter succeeded the first-ever Negro recorder, the famous abolitionist and orator Frederick Douglass. His start proved difficult, however; bedridden from tuberculosis or pneumonia, he was so weak at one point that a Negro newspaper in DC reported Trotter was "on death's door." Although he never regained full health, Trotter did recover enough to resume work. His tenure as recorder turned out to be short, anyway—ending after two years once the Republicans regained the White House with the election of Benjamin Harrison in 1888.

Financially, however, the timing of Trotter's brief stint in Washington couldn't have been better. Recorder of deeds was not a salaried position; his wages were based on fees paid to the city, which was in the midst of a building boom. Trotter earned more than $10,000 annually (an income exceeding $200,000 in 2014 dollars). He had few monetary concerns, although, conscientiously, he continued to add to his real estate portfolio back in Boston. Trotter spoke occasionally at Civil War reunions and civic events, where he stressed racial pride and manhood. "I greatly value the uplifting of the colored race," he said at one such event.

James Trotter was forty-seven, weakened in health, when his wife and family welcomed him back to Hyde Park in 1889. His son was then a high school junior who now stood about the same height as his father, at five foot eight, although his build was thicker. The senior Trotter set a high bar for him in every way, including which combatant he expected to prevail in schoolyard tussles: Monroe was instructed that he "could expect two beatings if he lost one to a white boy." The teenager indeed became skilled with his fists, but he was also fun-loving and popular with his classmates, most of whom were white. He thrived on the competition of such sports as baseball and hockey.

If he seemed less sensitive than his father when it came to issues of race, Monroe had certainly inherited James's intense work ethic. In grammar school, he was valedictorian. When he graduated from the Hyde Park High School in 1890, he was first in his class and had been elected class president by the twenty-one white seniors. The Negro minister at the local First Baptist Church, which the Trotters frequented, was hoping to recruit Monroe into the ministry, but his father strongly objected on the grounds that the church was all Negro—and thus segregated. It took the graduate a year to sort out his next move—but few were surprised when Monroe Trotter headed off to Cambridge in 1891 to attend Harvard College.

Richard T. Greener was the first Negro to earn an undergraduate degree at Harvard in 1870, which meant Monroe Trotter's arrival on campus, while not typical, was not odd. Trotter certainly didn't seem hesitant, forming fast friendships with several of the 376 freshmen—John A. Fairlie, a dorm mate, went on to become a political scientist, professor, and lifelong friend. While getting settled into College Yard, a gated area next to Harvard Square where redbrick dormitories for freshmen were located, Trotter would have noticed the fashion shift in student attire, as the baggy trouser popular for the past few years was replaced on campus by a pant neatly creased at the tailor's—or, as some enterprising students looking to save money had discovered, pressed between their mattresses at night. For Sunday outings, the updated look for the stylish Harvard man was completed with a frock coat, silk topper, and cane.

Trotter continued his record of academic excellence, applying himself in his courses—English, mathematics, foreign languages, and philosophy. He attended lectures given by some of the foremost thinkers of the time, including George Santayana and William James. One talk that the internationally acclaimed James was known for centered on the observation that "few men live at their maximum energy," and that this failure to function at full potential cheated both the individual and the community. James called the lecture "The Energies of Men," and in it exhorted the unleashing of an intellectual "second wind" so that a man could break "the habit of inferiority" and achieve his "*full* self." Trotter—at least in terms of his academic energy—certainly stayed on task, even as his family suffered a monumental loss halfway through his freshman year.

James Trotter died of tuberculosis just before midnight on Friday, February 26, 1892. He was fifty. Monroe had been summoned home in time, and although the next morning he was grieving and helping to plan the funeral, he was also thinking about his homework. "Please send me my Latin, Greek, French and German books with dictionaries by express today," he requested of his new friend John Fairlie in a telegram sent before lunchtime at the Western Union station in Hyde Park.

That Sunday, Trotter sat down and wrote his classmate a more formal note: "Dear Fairlie, My father died last Friday night. The funeral takes place from the house, 68 Neponset Ave. Tuesday at one o'clock P.M. It would please if you could be present. Your Friend." Fairlie was indeed there the afternoon of March 1, the Trotter home filled with friends and family as the funeral service began with the beat of a drum and the marching arrival, in uniform, of members of a war veterans' post. Many officers of the 55th attended, including its former captain, George T. Garrison, who served as a pallbearer, carrying Trotter's casket to Mount Hope Cemetery. William Lloyd Garrison spoke, recalling how, when they'd first met at Camp Meigs, Trotter had been "conspicuous among the soldiers of the 55th Regiment for his intelligence, activity and interesting personality."

Despite James Trotter's passing, his son refused to be thrown off track. He finished his freshman year ranked third in his class. On the first anniversary of his father's death, when coincidentally he was home sick, Trotter wrote a chatty letter to Fairlie in which he said nothing about his loss of the previous year. Instead, he gossiped about school, described the oyster stew his mother had made him, and worried about missing his classes.

When Trotter went home the summer after his freshman year in 1892, the foremost thing on his mind was making money. He paid little attention to events beyond Hyde Park, such as those in Memphis, Tennessee, where the murder of three Negro businessmen in March was both national news and the tipping point for another young Negro—Ida B. Wells, a writer for a Negro paper in Memphis called *Free Speech*. The men, one of whom was

Wells's friend, were shot and lynched following their arrest for defending a grocery store against a ransacking mob hired by a white competitor.

Wells's fiery editorials condemning the murders led angry white mobs to storm her office and destroy the printing presses. She became targeted for abuse and death threats, and by spring had fled Memphis for New York City. Undeterred, she launched an anti-lynching campaign, and by summer was hard at work on a pamphlet, *Southern Horrors: Lynch Law in All Its Phases.*

Trotter, meanwhile, was working as a door-to-door salesman, selling inexpensive, portable Chautauqua Industrial Art Desks, which upper-middle-class families liked to buy for their kids. He would lug several of them strapped together as he made his way around Boston. He liked to haggle over the price but refused to ever go below $3.25. "No house is too poor for me to call," he wrote to his pal Fairlie late in the summer. "My being a student helps me a little. I always manage to let them know it." Day after day Trotter honed his pitch, discovering "affability and good lungs are essential to success—and success means money!" He was proud that he made at least one sale each day, with a personal best of seven sales a day. "It takes pluck, grit and hard work"—and yet he still had time for reading, bike trips, tennis, and twice going on outings to the beach with family.

The summer that followed his sophomore year was spent mostly in Ohio on his grandparents' farm. "Leading a happy-go-lucky sort of life," he wrote Fairlie in a letter signed affectionately, "Mon." The city-bred Trotter did some farmwork, romanticizing the country life and its health benefits: "The scenery about here is grand." But most of all, he boasted about the turf tennis court he'd built in the yard. "The afternoon I finished the court I played with everybody in the place," he said. Word of his court spread, and neighbors flocked to play a game that was new to them. "It is more fun than a goat to see two stiff jointed old farmers with their big clumsy boots, slipping and sliding and missing the ball!"

That summer climaxed with a visit to Chicago and the 1893 World's Fair, the Columbian Exposition, which celebrated the 400th anniversary of Christopher Columbus's 1492 arrival in the New

World. Trotter urged Fairlie to attend, calling the spectacle a must-see, "great, magnificent and grand." The rave review completely ignored the controversy at the fair that concerned his own race. Prominent civil rights activists were threatening to boycott the exposition because there were no exhibits on Negro life in America. Leading the protest was the crusading journalist Wells, now a Chicago resident. Together with Frederick Douglass, she drafted an eighty-one-page booklet to spotlight Negro exclusion from the fair, and to detail some of that history, covering both emancipation and the scourge of lynching. Supporters handed out the pamphlet, called *Reasons Why the Colored American Is Not in the World's Columbian Exposition*, to visitors flocking into Chicago. Trotter apparently never read a copy.

Matters of race and civil rights, whether in the South or in his own Harvard Yard, were not particularly on the radar of handsome young student. He was oblivious to the fact that he could never join his college's exclusive social clubs. Not that he wanted to. Nor was he perturbed by the commotion in the spring of his sophomore year, involving Negro football star William H. Lewis, the son of former slaves who had left Virginia for higher education in the north. Lewis twice walked into a barbershop in Harvard Square to get a haircut, only to be ordered each time to leave the premises. Instead, Trotter navigated college life with a certain ease and élan—a quality other Negro students at Harvard noticed. One in particular was William Edward Burghardt Du Bois.

W. E. B. Du Bois, four years older than Trotter, grew up in Great Barrington, Massachusetts, and earned a bachelor's degree from Harvard in 1890. He began his doctorate studies in sociology in 1891, when Trotter was starting his freshman year. The two became friendly in a relatively small circle of Negroes that also included Lewis. In fact, before Lewis had started at Harvard Law School, Trotter, Du Bois, and a group of friends crossed the state to attend Lewis's graduation from Amherst College. Du Bois noticed that Trotter didn't "seek other colored students as companions" and, at times, acted "curiously aloof." But Du Bois did not begrudge Trotter for this. If he felt lonesome as a minority surrounded by so many whites, he admired the way Trotter exuded the attitude that "colored students must not herd together, just because they were colored." Trotter was "no hanger-on, but a leader among them." But Du Bois might well have begrudged Trotter's luck in courtship. For a time, Du Bois had a crush on one young woman in their crowd who was taking courses in bookkeeping and stenography at a business college in Boston: the silky-haired Deenie Pindell, whose family had lived near the Trotters when she was a toddler. She was a "fine, forthright woman," Du Bois said, "blonde, blue-eyed and fragile." The two dated for a bit, "but in the end I had no chance." Monroe and Deenie had rekindled their friendship and soon turned what had been a long-standing family acquaintance into a full-fledged romance. "Monroe Trotter found his love for once and for all time," Trotter later wrote, describing the first time he and Deenie kissed after a lawn party in Revere, north of Boston.

However, grades mattered most. In four years, Trotter would never rank lower than eighth in his class. He was the first Negro ever elected to Phi Beta Kappa—not as a senior, but during junior year, as one of the so-called First Eight chosen. But in those days, he still showed no interest in the bigger civic ideas that had been his father's passion—politics, civil rights, and race. His sister Maude, who attended Wellesley College, once called her brother a "jolly, fun-loving, affectionate and merry" student, although sociability for him did not include even a hint of alcohol. Trotter was a member of the Prohibition Club as well as a founding member of the Total Abstinence Club, and once insisted to Maude's future husband that "beer-drinking students were headed straight for Hell."

By Class Day on June 21, 1895, Monroe Trotter was awash in academic honors, set to receive his bachelor of arts degree magna cum laude as a proud member of Phi Beta Kappa. "Unexpected was my A in English 6," he proudly told Fairlie, in a note thanking his friend for "four years of fellowship." Deenie, ill in the weeks leading up to graduation, recovered in time to watch Trotter receive his degree on his big day. Harvard was a special place for him, "an inspiration," he wrote later, a "place of freedom, equality and real democracy."

Others in his circle—Du Bois and William Lewis—might not have shared his misty-eyed sentiment, but Trotter had experienced

William Monroe Trotter (top row, left) with fellow members of the
Phi Beta Kappa fraternity at Harvard in 1895. Trotter was the fraternity's
first African-American member. COURTESY OF THE BOSTON PUBLIC LIBRARY.

the college as a meritocracy. He had succeeded in a big way, earning the credentials to fulfill his dream of a career in international
business, even if that vision was narrowly focused compared to the
accomplishments of his father, a man who had achieved his full
potential—teacher, Civil War officer, post office supervisor, writer
of a musical history, and more. Monroe Trotter did not yet seem to
possess the senior Trotter's wisdom. In a way, the young Harvard
graduate was entering the real world acting as if he didn't know he
was a Negro. That would change soon enough, as he discovered for
himself the kind of big ideas and new energy to propel him toward
what William James had called "the full self."

3

The Griffiths

David Wark Griffith was a just a child when he first began tiptoeing out of the bedroom he shared with his siblings to hide under a table in the parlor and listen to his elderly father, Jacob, hold forth in the evening. "He had a voice of terrific power," the filmmaker said later. Eavesdropping became a way for a boy hungry for connection to get closer to a father he'd not gotten nearly enough of during his short life. In fact, from the time when David was two and until he was four, Jacob Griffith had lived separately in a boardinghouse in Frankfort, Kentucky, the state's capital, while serving a term as state representative.

The family homestead was named Lofty Green—a title invoking the image of a grand southern plantation. As an adult the younger Griffith romanticized the site, located in Oldham County about twenty miles outside of Louisville, as a "lovely palace, the true Kentucky estate," although its 260-odd acres of farm country, where a handful of former slaves continued living in their old slave cabins, were not close to the dimensions of true southern plantations. The house itself was a plain-looking structure with four rooms on the first floor and an additional room, or garret, under a sloping roof above. One notable feature was the front porch, another venue where family patriarch, nicknamed "Roaring Jake," liked to hold court within arm's reach of the bourbon barrel.

It was the early 1880s—the post–Civil War years—when David Griffith hunkered in the parlor on "reading nights," the flickering candles that adults used to illuminate the room doubling as magical enhancements for the eager boy. He was, in effect, a child in search of a bedtime story, and he got plenty. The thunderous voice had the impact of a preacher upon a worshiper, even if the senior Griffith's reputation as a southern gentleman was chock-full of blemishes. Jake Griffith was a hard-drinking barroom swashbuckler and loafer, a man of property—through marriage, not through the fruits of his own hard work—who ultimately ran the family's holdings into the ground under massive debts.

But those failings aside, he was indisputably stellar on two fronts—as Confederate soldier and raconteur—and these were what young David Griffith soaked up while hidden under the table. It's hard to imagine that a boy crawling like a puppy into the room would go undetected, and so the grown-ups likely simply let it go, allowing him a ringside seat for his father's various performances, be they readings from Shakespeare, poet Edgar Allan Poe, or romantic novelist Sir Walter Scott; lectures on Griffith family history; or, most important, theatrical retellings of heart-pounding moments and heroics from the Civil War that the film director later said, "were burned right into my memory."

Most of the time during these performances, the truth wasn't enough and was instead like clay, something for Jake Griffith to work with in the molding of a more impressive narrative. This was especially the case when he was covering the family's ancestral history. The way young Griffith heard it, his lineage was a mix of English and Welsh aristocracy, tracing to an Englishman identified as Lord Brayington, first name unknown, who arrived in Maryland in the early 1700s. For reasons unknown, the aristocrat began going by his wife's maiden name of Griffith, which Jake further reported was the anglicized version of Gruffydd, a line of powerful Welsh chieftains, the point being the Griffiths were descendents of Welsh lords.

Next in line came Jake's grandfather, Salathiel, whom Jake portrayed as a Revolutionary War hero; and then his father, Daniel, whom he described as a captain who valiantly fought during the War of 1812 in New Orleans alongside Andrew Jackson. Later in

life, D. W. Griffith hired genealogists in a bid to entangle fact from
fancy, but he could never fully sort it all out one way or another.
His biographers had better luck peeling away some of the embel-
lishments, revealing that while Salathiel Griffith did enlist in a
Maryland volunteer unit during the American Revolution, there
was no evidence of heroism. As for Daniel Griffith, he was never
a captain and never fought alongside Andrew Jackson, but was a
corporal who served for only a month in the Virginia Militia that in
August 1814 was unable to repel a British force from burning down
much of Washington, DC. But none of these facts got in the way of
Roaring Jake's accounts of impressive Griffith manhood that showcased breeding and bravery.

Jacob Wark Griffith was a fourth-generation American, born
on October 13, 1819, in Virginia's Jefferson County. In 1836 his
father, Daniel, moved to Kentucky, where he began working farmland north of Louisville. In 1839 twenty-one-year-old Jake joined
him there. With no trade and barely more than an elementary
school level of education, Jake began a medical apprenticeship
with a local doctor. In a couple of years he had his own practice,
making his rounds on a horse. On September 18, 1848, he married
Mary Oglesby, from one of the more prominent families in Oldham County. The Oglesbys had a history and assets that would
have caught Jake's attention. Not only had the family's arrival in
the New World predated the Griffiths', but Mary's ancestor who'd
first settled in Kentucky following the Revolutionary War had
done so on land awarded for his war service. From there, the clan's
holdings and distinction grew. Even so, Jake Griffith apparently
couldn't stop himself from adding further polish to his wife's family tree, telling his children that their mother's mother—Nancy
Carter—was a descendant of the famous Carters of Virginia, one
of the state's so-called First Families for being among its original
settlers in the 1620s. However, he had no proof for the claim.

Jake's father-in-law, Thomas Oglesby, supported the newlyweds by allowing them to stay in his home until he had a five-room
cottage built for the couple. Their firstborn, a son, died soon after
birth, but during the next decade the couple had two daughters
and two sons. (David and two more siblings would be born after

the Civil War.) Jake Griffith proved a restless spouse. Even before the marriage, he'd enlisted in a Kentucky cavalry regiment that joined General Zachary Taylor in Texas in 1846 to fight in the Mexican War. He saw some action but mostly was called on to care medically for the combat soldiers. Then, just twenty months into the marriage, he was seduced by the gold rush in California and took off in 1850 with a group of gold hunters that included two of his wife's brothers. He prospected for two years northeast of Sacramento in Nevada County, fulfilling his promise to strike gold, and managed to pile up $16,000 in earnings. But heading home he displayed the recklessness and lack of discipline that became defining traits. In Louisville, the last leg of his return, he gambled it all away in a card game. He would never see so much money again.

Jake's personality was outsize, and his blustery manner was certainly offensive to some, but even critics acknowledged his knack for storytelling—rhetorical skills that paved the way for his next adventure, election in 1854 to serve in the Kentucky state legislature. But like so many things he tried, his foray into politics was short-lived, lasting only a single term (he would return twenty-three years later for another term). Then the next year, 1856, his father-in-law died, and for the first time Jake Griffith became a veritable man of property—land, cattle, horses, and five slaves. He and his wife inherited half of the Oglesby estate, which amounted to the roughly 260 acres that became the homestead David Griffith always knew as Lofty Green. But the monotonous, staid life of a farmer did not hold much appeal to him. More than anything, Jake Griffith longed for a curriculum vitae that would crackle with the kind of gallantry and manliness he'd concocted for his forebears. It was in this regard that the Civil War became his breakout moment, providing him with a sense of purpose. Although aged forty-two, he rushed to enlist in 1861.

Twenty-odd years later young David would raptly absorb all he could about his father's service in one of the infantry units of the First Kentucky Brigade. That Jake Griffith embraced the Confederate cause only made sense, given his standing as a slaveholder in Oldham County.

The county was a hotbed of proslavery spirit, a position that was actually at odds with the larger statewide one. The majority of Kentucky families—perhaps only one in six, according to one account—did not own slaves, and the plantation model was not widely established. Moreover, Kentucky never seceded; rather, in May 1861, the legislature passed a series of neutrality resolutions, including the following: "Resolved by the General Assembly of the Commonwealth of Kentucky, that Kentucky will not sever her connection with the national Government, nor will she take up arms for either of the belligerent parties." Jake Griffith was therefore in the minority when, in October 1861, he and like-minded true believers in southern rights got involved at the very start and began recruiting. By February 1862, their Kentucky Brigade numbered more than four thousand soldiers.

Given their state's official position, Jake Griffith and his comrades aligned themselves with the army from neighboring Tennessee, and because of that eventually they were given a moniker: the Orphan Brigade. They also became known as the "wild Kentuckians" for always seeming to be in the thick of the fighting, beginning with their first battle, the Battle of Shiloh, in April 1861, where they were defeated by Major General Ulysses S. Grant. In the months that followed, the Kentuckians continued to stand out, full of bravado and swagger, a reputation fed not only by their deportment on the battlefield but also off it. They formed a debating society, and then a glee club to serenade the camps, and even staged theatricals.

No one embodied the brigade's ethos more than Roaring Jake—a saber-wielding battlefield leader who, by all accounts, fought courageously. "For whatever else he was, Jacob Griffith was a brave man, and one gathers that he was completely happy, fully alive, only when he was testing his courage," wrote one D. W. Griffith biographer. The Orphan Brigade fought mostly in the Western Theater of the Civil War—in Tennessee, Mississippi, and Alabama—which meant the Kentuckians never faced off directly against the 55th Massachusetts Volunteer Infantry, the all-Negro unit that counted William Monroe Trotter's father in its ranks. But during the war's final months, Lieutenant Colonel Griffith and

Second Lieutenant Trotter were, in fact, less than a hundred miles apart, as Union forces gained control of Savannah, Georgia, and then Columbia and Charleston, South Carolina. Trotter's 55th regiment was among the Union troops that marched into Charleston on February 21, 1865. Griffith's brigade, meanwhile, had been part of a final patchwork of Confederate soldiers trying to resist the invaders, but to no avail. The proud Kentuckians, once four thousand strong, had barely six hundred men left when Lee surrendered to Grant on April 9.

Peacetime was not Jake Griffith's time. He returned home, aged forty-five, again showing little interest or skill in managing a farm. In the years to come, the war was the biggest thing on his mind, the high point of his life, and he much preferred to replay those years, often during boozy orations. This stayed true when his third son, David Wark Griffith, was born on January 22, 1875. Of the many stories Jake retold, one included the skirmish in early May 1862 at a railroad trestle known as Hewey's Bridge, along the northern border of Alabama, where he was wounded for the first time, during a brief but bloody encounter that saw five of his Confederate comrades killed, as well as more than a dozen Union soldiers. The shoulder injury did not sideline him from action for long, but it also never healed properly and permanently nagged him to the point where, during his postwar years, he seemed crippled in the one arm. Then there was the momentous date of March 1, 1863, when he was promoted to lieutenant colonel in the third regiment of the Orphan Brigade, and fearlessly did his best as a leader of his men.

David Griffith would hear about five instances where his father was wounded in battle—a number that, as other aspects of Roaring Jake's wartime legacy, was needlessly embellished. Griffith biographers later documented only two injuries in war records. The second, also in 1863, happened during that fall's Chattanooga Campaign, when Jake Griffith, too disabled to mount a horse, was determined nonetheless to lead his troops into battle and came up with a hell-raising idea for transport. He commandeered a horse and buggy, ordered his men to help him climb aboard, and, from this perch in the buggy's seat, began waving his sword and leading the charge. More than any other, the combat episode, for which he was cited for gallantry, captured Jake Griffith's dashing, high-risk style. The story became family legend and was eventually inscribed on the lieutenant colonel's tombstone, even though no official record existed to support it. But D. W. always believed the Chattanooga anecdote to be true, just as he did most of the Civil War stories his father told him, tales embedded with the recurrent themes of Confederate virtue and manliness that had been lost in the North's victory.

The Confederate soldier and his saber always seemed to go together in D. W. Griffith's earliest images of his father—at least that's what the film pioneer told interviewers later and wrote in an unfinished memoir. The boy would watch in awe as the veteran readied himself to stage battlefield reenactments in the meadows of Lofty Green for the benefit of his offspring: the dark-eyed Jake in his sixties, a long, untamed beard covering the lower half of his face, climbing into the worn gray coat adorned with epaulets, and then buckling on his hefty sword belt. Ready for action, the lieutenant colonel "would flash his elusive weapon and thrust, parry and riposte in all the darts and flings of *carte* and *tierce*," Griffith recalled later about the blade work.

Or there was Griffith's account of his father's waving the sword as he chased one of the former slaves around the property, a story that began with a haircut. His older brother William had been to Louisville and saw that due to the influence of northern tastes, "they were doing away with the dangling locks the men were wearing," Griffith wrote later. His brother went to Uncle Zeke, a "plantation barber" before the war, who commenced to snip. The finished haircut gave the Griffith brothers pause. "I think perhaps he overdid the job a little and cut it too short," Griffith said. "It made him look like an ex-convict."

The lieutenant colonel happened along. "Father came out, stalked over to the scene, looked at brother William and pretended not to know him." This was not a good sign for the barber. Next Jake roared, "My God, who in the hell did this to you?" Once the finger was pointed at Uncle Zeke, the elder Griffith went into the house, retrieved his old cavalry saber, and chased the "erring nigger around the house."

David Griffith enjoyed telling this story with obvious relish later in life, the details of which differed slightly depending on the rendering. In one, the former slave was named Uncle Easter; in another, his younger brother Albert was the one who got the haircut. Every version ended the same, however, with his realization that his father was putting on a show and only pretending to be angry with the former slave. "Old Zeke was scared pale, and I was taking it seriously myself until with a wink and a smile from Father enlightened me." In another version Griffith added, "I always had a suspicion Father liked the old nigger better than anyone around the house."

But happy ending notwithstanding, in no version did David Griffith convey a sense that Uncle Zeke was a fellow human being who was the brunt of a cruel joke. Instead the barber was fodder—as subservient "nigger" or "darky"—for his father's charade. The tale actually oozes with subtext and symbols—the sword, the menacing display of white power, and a terrorized Negro. But the younger Griffith apparently had a lifelong tin ear for the unconscious racism that had been embedded in him as a result of his surroundings and upbringing. For him, the point of the story was not the inhumanity shown Uncle Zeke—a prop, after all—but was about his flashy father and that symbolic sword. And when it came to deciding what makes a man, the combination of soldier and sword left an indelible mark. "That flaming, flashing spirit of the sword entered my child mind, filled my imagination, and satisfied my suspicion that my father was the greatest man in the world," he said later.

David Griffith grew up steeped in the tradition of a Lost Cause that saw slavery as a gentle, paternalistic feature of the southern way of life; secession as a logical response to the North's belligerent intrusion into the South's affairs; and the North's victory as inevitable, given its larger armies and resources. His father's oral histories were reinforced by a cultural and political shift across Kentucky in the years following Lee's surrender. Having voted not to secede during the war, afterward the state, wrote one historian, "showed herself more Southern in habits of thought and sympathies, than, perhaps, any part of the former Confederacy itself" and, as a leading critic of the federal government, "posed as a champion of the states beset by the carpetbagger" (the disparaging term for a northerner who traveled south seeking to profit from Reconstruction). Kentucky's sensibilities had turned so ardently antebellum that "it was often remarked that she waited until after the war was over to secede from the Union." The medium became the message for young Griffith, at home and in school, where he studied texts in which "the Confederate tradition was nursed and nurtured." His head filled with notions of chivalry and noble warriors' taking up arms in the cause of the old South against immoral opponents. (It was a dynamic similar to how he later regarded the defense of *The Birth of a Nation* against its critics: as a noble cause in the great fight for unhampered artistic expression.)

Griffith's home in Oldham County was located just outside the small town of Beard's Station, which was later renamed Crestwood. The house stood by an orchard and was surrounded by pasture and wheat fields. "It had a very cheerful outlook from the front of the house, looking from the front windows on the left towards the main road, a sloping meadow and a field where they generally grew wheat, and on the right, at the corner line, a graveyard," he wrote later. He and his siblings ran past the graveyard and crossed a stream to attend school in a one-room county schoolhouse, although as a child he was educated as much at home as in school because his oldest sister, Mattie, became a teacher and provided "grammar, Latin declensions and catechetic instruction." He was closest to his youngest brother, Albert—a bond that lasted a lifetime—and later recalled, "Country boys as a rule haven't many friends . . . but I always had lots of pets around," a menagerie that included dogs, cats, raccoons, possums, geese, chickens, and even, he insisted, some bear cubs.

His boyhood was largely unremarkable in its start. His mother, Mary, always called him David and never let anyone call him Dave (D. W. became an adult identifier). He viewed her as quiet and stern, with a hard exterior. It was his father—and Jake's melodramatic manner—that occupied the center of his universe. But then suddenly in 1885 the center imploded. The elder Griffith was nearing sixty-six and young David was only ten, when during the night of March 30, Jake Griffith began suffering painful convulsions and a doctor was summoned. The household erupted into chaos as it awaited the arrival of medical assistance.

The cause of the emergency was never fully determined. The filmmaker always attributed the illness to inferior "catgut" a surgeon had used during the Civil War to sew up a bullet wound that had left his father's insides hanging out. Two decades later, he said, the surgical thread, without warning, had rotted and broke, leading to peritonitis, or an inflammation of the membrane lining the walls of the abdominal cavity and enclosing the intestines. D. W. Griffith's biographers uncovered evidence of another possible factor—Roaring Jake's penchant for bourbon and eating in excess whenever he felt the urge. Earlier that night he'd sat on the front porch, drinking copiously from the bourbon barrel and indulged "in no less than eight homemade pickles from another nearby barrel."

In any event, nothing could be done to reverse Jake Griffith's fast decline. David, full of fear and worry, had retreated to the rear porch to watch the commotion, and he was still there when the doctor came out of the house and reported that there was no hope. Griffith heard that his father lay dying and had only a few hours left. "I went around the house and got behind the chimney in my favorite corner when I was in trouble and, of course, I broke out into tears." In a bit, others found him and brought him to his father's bedside, where the rest of the family was assembled. "When it came my turn, I came beside the bed," Griffith wrote. Jake looked at him: "Those brave eyes now seemed so soft and tender." His father's last words to him were, "Be brave, my son."

After more family farewells, Jacob Wark Griffith was dead. David was devastated. "They took him away, that which I loved more than anything I have ever loved in my life." The hundreds of mourners who attended the funeral at the Mount Tabor Methodist Church included veterans from the First Kentucky Brigade. The service featured a rifle volley to honor the life of the Confederate veteran.

In the wake of his death, the reality of the patriarch's wayward ways hit hard. Jake Griffith had borrowed heavily against Lofty Green, taking no less than three mortgages to pay off gambling and other debts. That its financial condition was dire proved a life-altering aftershock to a family reeling from the sudden loss of a father and husband. "Nothing is so sad as poverty," the filmmaker commented later. But despite the financial free fall, he never blamed his father or accepted any other version of him than the one already impressed upon his younger self's imagination. It was as if from then on the boy's glorified portrait of the adventuresome and swashbuckling Colonel Roaring Jake was fixed, as in a child's snow globe.

"Poor Mother had to take charge of the family now," he recalled. The estate took months to probate—to round up the debts, to auction some assets and sell others. The cow named Sally, the other one named Cherry, a couple of horses, and other poultry and livestock—all were sold at auction, netting about $434. Later in the year, Mary Griffith sold what was left of Lofty Green for nearly $7,000 in cash and a mortgage. Son David cared little for the transaction, referring later to the buyer as a "villainous gentleman." In the final accounting, Mrs. Griffith had a few thousand dollars in cash but no longer owned any property. In 1886 she began receiving a monthly pension of eight dollars as the widow of a Mexican War veteran.

Griffith was turning eleven when his family headed off to neighboring Shelby County, where his oldest brother, Will, owned a small farm with his new wife. David, his mother, his other two brothers, and two sisters (his oldest sister, Mattie, moved to Louisville to work as a teacher) moved in with the couple and the crowded farmhouse became their home for the next four years. During that time Griffith retreated inward, in all likelihood a response to the tumult and hardship caused by his father's death. He later recalled being bullied in school, learning eventually to stand up and defend himself, and mostly being on his own, figuring out what it meant to be a man in the absence of a father and preoccupied older brothers.

Then, in early 1899, came another seismic jolt. Urged on by Mattie, his mother moved him and his siblings to Louisville, traveling

in two farm wagons loaded with their belongings. "Right into the
city of Louisville we trundled," Griffith recalled. "I was piled on top
of the furniture." The sight of the wagons creaking down the street
on a cold winter day drew the curious glare of "street urchins" who
were quick to mock them. "Country jakes, country jakes!" they
shouted. For the farm-raised David Griffith, the city was an alien
sight, an urban center with a population nearing 200,000 and a
worldly feel to it—a spirit generated partly by its location along the
Ohio River, where steamboats and barges guaranteed a bustling
influx of outsiders and new ideas, and also by the influential and
forward-thinking Henry Watterson, editor of the *Courier-Journal*.
Watterson was a Confederate army veteran who, after the Civil
War, staked out liberal social positions advocating civil and voting
rights for Negroes, while condemning the Ku Klux Klan. His editorials were signed "Marse Henry," and during his tenure the newspaper fostered a progressiveness—uncommon in cities in the South
and West—that for years to come continued to play a part in the
city's dynamic. Indeed, it was in Louisville that civil rights leaders
in 1915 would pursue a legal test of a new city ordinance requiring residential segregation—a ban against Negroes' living in white
neighborhoods—which had become increasingly commonplace, a
case that would go all the way to the US Supreme Court.

David Griffith, at the tender age of fourteen, landed smack in
the middle of this growing and prosperous southern city whirling
with big ideas. His compass was set when it came to such matters
as the Lost Cause and race relations, but beyond that, the world
and his place in it remained unsettled. First, though, were the Griffiths' ongoing financial worries, a paramount concern to every member of the family. His mother moved them into a boardinghouse
she'd rented in hopes of generating extra income. That experiment
foundered, and during the next several years the family bounced
around, living at seven different addresses. For his part, Griffith
decorated his room with a Confederate flag and hung a photograph
of his father on the wall. He mostly kept his head down, dutifully
attending school and earning money as a paperboy delivering the
Courier-Journal; later he even served briefly as a stringer for the
paper, providing tidbits of news and gossip from the city's racy

section known as "The District." In the evenings his sister continued to tutor him "to get some ideas through the dumb skull." By
the end of his first year as a city boy, though, he quit high school to
further help out the family by earning a full-time wage. After being
hired as a "cash boy," he became the elevator boy at the J. C. Lewis
Dry Goods Store, located on Fourth Street in the heart of downtown.

Griffith was fifteen when he began, and he worked there for
more than two years. He later said that he was in a "haze" for much
of this period—while in high school and then his time at the store.
But he was known to devour books in the elevator when things
were slow, and during off-hours he started to sample the city's theatrical life, occasionally buying one of the cheap seats to catch a
show. "Louisville at the time was quite a place," Griffith said later.
"There was Macauley's Theatre where all the best dramatic and
light opera companies played."

Then in 1893 an opportunity arose that seemed to change
everything. A cousin quit his job as clerk at one of the best-known
bookstores in Louisville—Flexner's Book Store—and encouraged
Griffith to apply. He did and was hired, and soon enough he began
emerging from that inward haze and tapping into the city's worldly
offerings—not in the fields of business or politics, but in the arts
and culture. "I moved into a brainy circle indeed," he said. His surroundings were decidedly intellectual and artistic, as poets, writers, and historians regularly gathered at the store for readings.
Griffith found excuses to linger after his shift ended. "I would dust
industriously and find something to do in order to stick around and
listen to people talk who had something to say," he said.

He was a young man now, nearing twenty, and during this great
awakening he began to imagine a future where he was a full-time
writer, possibly a singer, or even an actor. It was a bold and adventuresome way of thinking. He was just a simple farm boy, after
all, and if he had ambition for a different life, the message from
his mother was that "gentlemanly farming, ministry and the law"
were the legitimate options. The arts, on the other hand, were not,
to the point where Mary Griffith considered acting a disgrace. His
mother, Griffith wrote, "didn't even think it was right to attend the
theatre much less become an actor."

The young D. W. Griffith (back row, second from right) with his
family in the 1890s. COURTESY OF THE MUSEUM OF MODERN ART, NEW YORK.

Griffith rummaged around and recovered his father's books
from trunks, pulling out Shakespeare's plays and the novels of Sir
Walter Scott and Charles Dickens. To practice his oratory and delivery, he'd read aloud from the books at night in his bedroom. He
also took voice and singing lessons from a music teacher named
Annie H. Boustead, who once praised him in a way that must have
been satisfying—proof that he was his father's son, telling him he
had a voice of "enormous power and volume." She also worked on
softening his rural Kentucky accent and improving his elocution.

The city had a rich theatrical life, with eight playhouses, and
Griffith began working as an usher or stagehand so as to view
plays the traveling companies performed during weeklong runs
in Louisville before heading east to Lexington or north to Cincinnati. Eventually he began auditioning for small parts, and for the
first time experienced the exhilaration of being onstage, even if he
also seemed a bit insecure about his maturing looks, "tall for his

age," as one biographer noted, "loose-jointed and beak-nosed." That worry aside, momentum was building for his breakaway—for David Griffith to express his own brand of courage and bravery. There was no war at hand, and so the theater would be his field of action, where he would cut against the grain and pursue a dream with a boldness that might please the father he idolized.

Griffith's big chance came in May 1896 when, hundreds of miles away in Boston, Monroe Trotter was looking to find his footing as a young businessman—a seemingly safe path for a Harvard College graduate except for the fact he was Negro. But if Trotter seemed the pragmatist (at least for now), David Griffith was the romantic. "I saw ahead, flaring, the everlasting lights of fame and glory," the filmmaker wrote later. He had decided to leave home, having won a spot in a touring company to play the villainous Dionysius in *Damon and Pythias*. The company was traveling out of state to New Albany, Indiana, to begin performances of the popular verse drama about patriotism, loyalty, and friendship. By month's end, using the stage name Lawrence Griffith, he got notice in a review in a New York paper. It was brief but exciting nonetheless; Lawrence Griffith and a fellow actor, said the review, "were excellent."

=4=

On the Firing Line: 1895–1903

On the morning of September 18, 1895, in Atlanta, Georgia, three months after Monroe Trotter graduated from Harvard College, people began lining the parade route leading to the Cotton States and International Exposition. Special trains had been scheduled to cope with throngs of visitors arriving for opening-day exercises of the World's Fair—from the North, the West, and, for that matter, all parts of the world. Three hundred and forty-seven nation flags flew from the new buildings and displays that an army of four thousand workers had labored feverishly to complete in time. Much thought had been given to the physical layout to make the fairgrounds as natural looking as possible, with a large man-made lagoon among the most impressive features. Crowds continued to grow as the morning passed under blue skies and a blazing sun— and eventually sixty thousand spectators were assembled. Then, come noon, every steam whistle in the city blasted in unison to signal the start of an opening-day parade. Raucous cheers erupted from the packed streets.

The new World's Fair was on a smaller scale than the Columbian Exposition just three years earlier—in fact, the Cotton States expo had been conceived as a response to the Chicago event that many southerners criticized as either ignoring or misrepresenting their region. Conventional wisdom held that the post–Civil War years had been a disaster—that northern intruders and free Negroes had wreaked havoc in every way possible—politically, economically, and socially. But the "profligacy" and "dark days of Reconstruction" had passed, and now that the South's own had regained stewardship of its fate, it was time to showcase economic progress and, as far as the races were concerned, the new equilibrium. "The exposition will be essentially Southern," wrote the *New York Times*. "It is the new South, the great South." And in addition to the usual lineup of exhibitions—a Government Building, a Machinery Building, and so on—there was also something unprecedented: a Negro Building. The organizers trumpeted its inclusion as evidence of their forward thinking, although anyone entering would have noticed at once the selective perspective—the emphasis on practical advancements for Negroes rather than on the civil rights and freedoms that had been the promise of slavery's end but that had been eroding ever since. Some of the building's exhibits were devoted to farm labor, carpentry, or masonry, while others covering Negro education highlighted new schools specializing in manual and technical training. Wrote one reporter: "These schools are educating youth to be good men and good citizens." Organizers had even scheduled the principal of one such institution as an opening-day speaker—thirty-nine-year-old Booker Taliaferro Washington.

Awaiting the one o'clock arrival of dignitaries parading their way through the city toward the exhibition grounds, Washington was seated with other speakers on the small, lavishly decorated stage inside the expo's vast auditorium whose seats were filled to capacity. Asked by organizers to reflect on Negro progress and the Negro's place in the New South, he faced a rhetorical tightrope walk: The mostly white audience might be from all over, but no matter how many northerners or outsiders were present, the dominant sensibility was unmistakably southern—a sensibility he surely understood. Born in 1856 on a Virginia plantation, he was reared in slavery and, following emancipation, put himself through school. Washington graduated from Virginia's Hampton Normal and Agricultural Institute and in 1881 became head of the newly founded

Tuskegee Industrial Institute in Alabama that he then transformed into the country's leading vocational school for Negroes.

His upcoming speech represented an opportunity for Washington to grow beyond Tuskegee. Seven months earlier, on February 20, Frederick Douglass, the escaped slave who for decades had been the leading Negro voice first for emancipation and then, during Reconstruction, for equal rights, had died at the age of seventy-seven. The two men could not have been more different—Douglass fiery and passionate in his denunciation of racism; Washington humble and nonconfrontational. Now there existed a vacancy in the national position Douglass had held for so long as the leading face of the Negro race, one Washington hoped to fill in his own way.

Washington was the third to speak—following the opening address from the fair's chief organizer and remarks from a representative of the Woman's Department. Almost immediately the thousands of spectators began to realize they were witnessing something special—in both content and style—from the impeccably dressed, stocky man standing squarely at the lectern. "No race can prosper till it learns that there is as much dignity in tilling a field as in writing a poem," he began, his voice strong and his eyes piercing as he offered his take on the race question. "It is at the bottom of life that we must begin, and not at the top." Cheers erupted spontaneously here and there in the crowd as Washington continued. "The wisest among my race understand that the agitation of questions of social activity is the most extreme folly," he said. "The opportunity to earn a dollar in a factory just now is worth infinitely more than the opportunity to spend a dollar in an opera house." The random shouts spread into an uproar of approval. Men began waving handkerchiefs, raising their canes, and tossing hats into the air, and, as a reporter for the *New York World* wrote, "The fairest women of Georgia stood up and cheered. It was as if the orator had bewitched them." Washington brought down the house when he raised one hand over his head, spread his fingers wide apart, and displayed it to all parts of the auditorium. "In all things purely social we can be separate as the fingers," he declared, "yet one as the hand in all things essential to material progress." The crowd, reported the *World*, was now beside itself, "the whole audience on its feet in a delirium of applause."

Washington was a huge hit. Fair officials swarmed him at the finish, shaking his hand and slapping his back. The next day, so many admirers accosted him on the street to offer their kudos that he had to retreat to where he was staying. His speech came to be called the "Atlanta Compromise"—for its conciliatory tone, accommodating approach to race relations, and emphasis on vocational training rather than civil, political, and economic rights. Its wording was such that people could read into it what they wanted. Racists heard a speech conceding Negro inferiority and submission, while those considering themselves progressive heard what seemed to be a nonthreatening and realistic strategy for Negro progress. "What he said was so moderate, so sensible and so instinct with true patriotism," the *Washington Post* editorialized, calling the speech "the most interesting and significant utterance" made during the opening-day ceremony. Young academic W. E. B. Du Bois joined the chorus. "Let me heartily congratulate you on your phenomenal success at Atlanta—it was a word fitly spoken," he wrote to Washington the very next week from Wilberforce University, a Negro college in Ohio where he was now a professor teaching Greek and Latin.

In an instant Washington had rocketed onto the big stage, moving out of the shadows as a regional, relatively unknown head of a vocational school and into the national limelight as a commanding Negro leader who preached a gospel of quiet self-reliance and was himself the ultimate example of the self-made man. In short order, his foothold became established nationally, as he gained financial support from northern philanthropists and opened branches of his Negro Business League in key cities, including in Boston. Soon Negro mothers—by the hundreds each year—began naming newborn sons "Booker T."

Others were less enthused. Washington's speech was criticized as a sellout and surrender in a few corners of the Negro press. Not only did critics find its appeasing tone offensive, they questioned a self-help doctrine rooted exclusively in agricultural and blue-collar employment. It seemed off the mark, as the industrial revolution was entering a period of enormous expansion, where demand was growing for new managers and white-collar personnel to supervise the legions of assembly-line workers. Why couldn't blacks aspire to fill those positions? Moreover, Washington's self-help doctrine— however catchy and laudable in theory—only worked if the game was played fair. Reality screamed otherwise. Terrorism against the Negro was rapidly on the rise. Lynchings topped a hundred a year, and the robust spread of Jim Crow—the term for antiblack codes and laws—had created systemic discrimination in voting, politics, housing, public facilities, and virtually all walks of southern life. Even the US Supreme Court weighed in later that fall, agreeing to hear the appeal of Homer Plessy of New Orleans, who'd been convicted of boarding a "whites only" railroad car in violation of the state's newly adopted Separate Car Act. Plessy said the law violated his civil rights. But eight months after Booker T. Washington's speech, on May 18, 1896, the justices, in a 7–1 ruling, rejected that argument and upheld the constitutionality of "separate but equal." It was a historic decision that added the powerful imprimatur of the nation's highest court to Jim Crow. Washington was not blind to any of this, but he claimed that a strategy of accommodation was the only way for Negroes to find their way forward in a starkly worsening society. He chose words that served as comfort food for racists and progressives alike—and, as such, paved the way for his voice to rise above all others.

If Monroe Trotter was paying any attention to these developments, he didn't indicate so in any of the correspondence and documents that have survived from the fall of 1895. Instead, the college graduate was preoccupied with finding the right first step in business that would lead to realizing a fortune. The same month Washington was making history in Atlanta, Trotter was holding down a temporary job in Boston while hunting for something better. Employed as a clerk at the Huntington Avenue offices of an organization that counted Paul Revere as one of its cofounders in the 1790s, his job was to help the Massachusetts Charitable Mechanics Association

get ready for one of its triannual exhibitions showcasing innovations in mechanical trades. He now lived with his mother and sisters in a house owned by family friend William Dupree on West
Cottage Street in the city's Roxbury neighborhood. Mrs. Trotter
had moved there from Hyde Park after her husband's death, and
her son told his friend Fairlie he'd furnished his bedroom with pictures, books, and decorations so that it looked "somewhat like my
college room." He joked that whenever a young woman came by
for a visit, she was "supposed to make some decoration for it." He
further teased that he had "secured only three decorations thus
far," although everybody in their circle of friends knew that he and
Deenie Pindell were becoming inseparable.

Trotter had had a lead on a teaching job in Washington, DC,
with a starting annual salary of $1,000, but teaching did not inter-
est him, plus he didn't want to move: "I desired a business career,"
he wrote Fairlie, "and besides the place is too far South and the
school a separate one." He also turned down a local business opportunity, when the editor of the *Hyde Park Times* said he could
have the paper for the price of $2,500. Even though he had funds
from his father's inheritance, Trotter decided buying a newspaper
was too much when he was just starting out—especially in a field
he knew nothing about. "I did not want to carry that load on my
back yet, especially as I should be a 'green back' at the business."
He was still after what he'd told everyone in college—a career in
banking and finance—and was initially optimistic about his prospects in the months following graduation. "I am working all my
influential friends," he told Fairlie, bragging as if he knew all the
angles, "In business nowadays, especially in getting a start, 'pull' is
everything." Hardly sitting on his duff at his temporary clerkship,
Trotter pulled at every string he could think of among his downtown connections, ranging from high-ranking executives—such as
the president of the National Bank of Commerce and a vice president at the Bell Telephone Company—to lower-tiered employees,
such as the cashier he knew at the National Bank of the Republic.
"I secured their efforts," he said, "on my behalf."

But even with these advantages, it wasn't as if the prestigious
houses of finance were throwing open their doors and putting out

a welcome mat for Monroe Trotter. "I have not yet received any notice of a place from them," he reported back to Fairlie. In fact, mixed with his eagerness, Trotter shared with his friend other key lessons learned about the Boston business world. "Business is a hard field in which to work," he said. "The prizes go to a comparatively few, and only the pickings are left for the great majority." Trotter was beginning to glean that the "comparatively few" often did not include *You People*, a commonly used identifier for the Negro race that rolled off the lips of friend and foe alike. It was a label his father had always hated, feeling offended when someone addressed him that way, especially when the speaker was an alleged friend. James Trotter had thought supporters of equal rights, of all people, should know better and realize such a reference to his race reinforced separateness and segregation. Even were the slight unintentional, the senior Trotter had strongly resented the "Jim-Crowing implied in the use of *You People*." For Monroe Trotter, his Harvard degree and Phi Beta Kappa key were terrific assets. Yet he was different—*You People*—and that, he told Fairlie, was a problem, "one large impediment that other men do not have to hinder them."

Trotter began to look at things differently, wondering whether going to Europe might be a better option, where working as an agent for a European company he would be "recognized as a man." He even confided to Fairlie he had begun to consider an alternative to the world of high finance, which suggests he was scaling back his ambition. His father had been good at real estate, although mainly as a sideline, never his principal interest. The younger Trotter now weighed this field as possibly his most realistic option. "My present plans are to go into the real estate business for myself, but I want to get into an office first, in order to learn the 'ins' and 'outs,'" he wrote Fairlie. Once again he indicated that he had "pull": "I have several well-known men using their influence." Most intriguing was one of the largest firms in New England—H. W. Savage & Company—which "has promised me a place as soon as there is an opening for another man."

But at the same time Trotter was describing his latest idea and reveling in his ability to tap connections, he confessed he actually had nothing to show for it all—no job, no word of any opening, and no idea when there might be one in the future. In fact, in a fourteen-page letter to Fairlie, he careered between cockiness and undisguised disappointment about his start in life after college, with one line capturing most candidly where he stood at the end of a year that saw Booker T. Washington assume the mantle as national spokesman for the Negro. "[I am] floundering around," Trotter wrote, "in my attempts to decide as to my future plans."

Four years later, an estimated two thousand spectators yelled in approval as a mob in Georgia began stringing up a farm laborer named Sam Hose. Before his capture just outside Newnan, thirty miles south from where Washington had delivered his famous speech, Hose was on the run for crimes the *Atlanta Constitution* called so horrific they "dethroned the reason of the people of Western Georgia." The facts, the newspaper said, were this: Hose snuck into the home of a white farmer on April 13 at suppertime and buried an ax into "the brain of the unsuspecting victim." He grabbed a baby boy and "flung it into the pool of blood oozing from its father's wound." Still not done, Hose set his predatory eyes on the farmer's wife. "The wife was seized, choked, thrown upon the floor, where her clothing lay in the blood of her husband, and ravished." The *Constitution*'s account, which ran in papers around the country, urged readers who might question the resulting lynching frenzy to "Remember the facts!"—especially the "shocking degradation that was inflicted by the black beast, his victim swimming in her husband's warm blood, as the brute held her to the floor!"

On Sunday, April 23, 1899, and without any trial in a court of law, Sam Hose was hanged before the excited crowd, doused in kerosene, and set afire. His charred corpse was mutilated—ears, fingers, and other body parts dismembered by souvenir seekers. During this stretch of days W. E. B. Du Bois, who had moved to Atlanta in 1897 and was teaching economics at Atlanta University, set out one morning to hand-deliver a letter he'd drafted about the Hose case to the *Constitution*'s editor. Until this moment his life had tilted overwhelmingly toward academia, but current events increasingly challenged the notion of his remaining in an ivory tower. The Sam Hose case, he said later, "startled me to my feet." But Du Bois never made it to the newspaper that day; on his way, "the news met me: Sam Hose had been lynched, and they said that his knuckles were on exhibition at a grocery store farther down on Mitchell Street, along which I was walking." The experience marked a shift for the educator, now thirty-one. "I began to turn aside from my work," he said. "One could not be a calm, cool and detached scientist while Negroes were lynched, murdered and starved."

The evolution for Du Bois from scholar to civil rights activist was a work in progress. But another prominent Negro, former journalist Ida B. Wells, was already there—as the antilynching activist. Wells was angered by the hanging of Sam Hose. She and several other Chicagoans sent a private detective to Georgia, who in June reported back his findings: Hose had killed the farmer in self-defense after the latter had drawn a gun during a dispute over a debt. The detective also said there was no evidence Hose had entered the house after the killing to rape the wife in front of her infant son. Wells included the detective's report in a pamphlet she published that same month, *Lynch Law in Georgia*, in which she recounted a dozen lynchings, including Hose's, during the two months of March and April 1899.

Wells was also shocked at Booker T. Washington's reaction—or lack thereof. The purported spokesman for the Negro race was quoted in one instance as blaming Negroes for racial tension in the South. "Is there any reason why the Negroes in the South should continue to oppose the Southern white man and his politics?" he asked. "Is this not the source of nearly all our troubles?" Then, arriving in Philadelphia two days after Hose's lynching, he had ducked reporters' questions, saying he did not want to "engage in any controversy" that would take away from what mattered most to him—his Tuskegee Institute and Negro education. He did oppose mob violence, he said, but added—without naming Hose—that men guilty of "these outrages are ignorant individuals who should be surely, swiftly and terribly punished, but by legal methods." He then made sure to score a point for Tuskegee, citing an "encouraging fact"—that "of the hundreds of colored men" educated at Tuskegee and other schools in the South "not one has been guilty of the crime of assaulting a woman."

Wells had been harboring doubts about Washington's approach—as too soft and accommodating—but still saw him as an ally in the fight against Jim Crow. Just a few months earlier she had spoken favorably about him at a rally, and as founding secretary of a new national civil rights organization—called the Afro-American Council—she tried to collaborate with his minions even as they took control of the group and sought to mute her aggressiveness. But by June 1899 she could not abide Washington's failure to denounce the lynching of Sam Hose and others—while instead relentlessly marketing Tuskegee. By the end of the year 106 lynchings were recorded; the next year, 115; and the year after that, 130. "Mr. Washington's theory had been that we ought not to spend our time agitating for our rights," she said. "That we had better give attention to trying to be first-class people in a Jim Crow car rather than insisting the Jim Crow car be abolished." Although Wells was vocalizing her disaffection for Washington, for the time being her criticisms remained within Negro circles, where his supporters labeled her a troublemaker, "a bull in a China shop," as one said. Most of mainstream America still knew little about anyone other than Washington when it came to Negro leadership, a position he worked hard to solidify as a frequent speaker and by writing his high-impact autobiography, *Up from Slavery*.

Meanwhile, Monroe Trotter was also in transition—in any number of ways. Two months after Sam Hose was lynched in Georgia, he and Deenie Pindell were married in Boston on June 27, 1899. The newlyweds moved immediately to 97 Sawyer Avenue, on Jones Hill in Dorchester, a mostly white neighborhood. Purchased from a shoe store owner and his wife, the property's assessed value was $3,600, and the Trotters took out a mortgage for $2,900. The two-story, farmhouse-style clapboard house had three bedrooms and featured pine wood floors; bay windows; and, in the living room, such decorative touches as a mirrored mantel and tiled hearth. The best part, though, was that it sat atop a hill and was designed to catch cooling breezes during hot summer days through the front and back doors

Geraldine "Deenie" Trotter.

as well as the bay windows in the bedrooms upstairs. Its elevated position provided commanding views of Dorchester Harbor in one direction and the Blue Hills in nearby Milton in another. Trotter appreciated his house on a hill, noting with pleasure that from his second-floor sitting room window he could see all of the city and the countryside beyond.

He began commuting from his new home to the downtown business district aboard one of the newer electric trolleys—electric propulsion was fast bringing an end to the horsecar era. In fact, along the way and all around him, the look of the city was changing rapidly: Track lines were sprawling everywhere like a spider's web—at the street level, elevated, and even underground. The Tremont Street Subway—the first subway in the country—had opened in 1898, and aboveground, electric trolleys would replace every horse-drawn streetcar by 1900. Electricity now jumped off

overhead wires, trolley bells rang, and iron wheels screeched—the
new noises of a congested downtown reflecting a country that, at
the start of a new century, "was a nation of steam shovels, loco-
motives, airships, combustion engines, telephones and twenty-five-
story buildings."

Amid the buzz of the city, Trotter was awakening to the fact he
could never be fully a part of it. His prospects at the H. W. Savage & Company never panned out. Starting with his first, temporary job after college in 1895, he held one clerk's job after another:
during the Christmas season of 1895, as a shipping clerk for a Boston bookseller; the next year, indexing clerk for a Boston book publisher, then statistical clerk for a genealogist in Boston (hardly an
impressive job, but one he nonetheless had to use a connection to
get; the genealogist who hired him was a white officer in the 55th
regiment who had served with his father). Trotter finally caught
a break in late 1896, when he was hired by the respected mortgage firm Holbrook & Co. But, again, it only came about because of
pull—an insider at the company who was a yet another veteran of
his father's regiment. Trotter trained at Holbrook as a "mortgage
negotiator," his first authentic position in business, and he worked
at the company's downtown offices at 12 Post Office Square for
nearly two years. That was when he decided he'd learned enough
to go out on his own—as he'd told Fairlie was his goal. Upon marrying Deenie, he began renting a small office in the heart of the business district not far from Holbrook—Room 1 at 35 Court Street.

Trotter was finding his way, and between his income and inheritance he did well enough to acquire some properties. In September 1899, for example, he bought a two-family house—assessed at
$5,200, and for which he took out a $4,400 mortgage—at 67–69
Sawyer Avenue, just down the street from his own house. He began
collecting monthly rents from the chef, salesman, "draughtsman,"
clerk, and others who came and went as the property's tenants.
But he was hardly on a fast track—never mind the fact that he
had long abandoned his initial dream of becoming an international
banker. However, Trotter now began to signal the broadening of
his perspective. The evidence came in small ways, such as a comment made to Fairlie on the nature of friendship. "I enjoyed your

visit immensely," he wrote while still an underling at Holbrook, "for there is a great difference between friends you make in college and friends you make out of college." He came to view college life as far closer to a meritocracy than the real world. "I had been out of college and in real life but four years," he wrote later, "when I realized that the Democracy which I had enjoyed at dear old Harvard was not secure for Americans of Color, just because of their pigmentation." Throughout 1899 new ideas were taking shape that would propel a life-altering pivot for Trotter toward a more public life. For the city's observance of Lincoln's birthday in February he presented a paper, "Higher Education for the Negro." The notion that vocational training was the path for Negro progress was not enough, he argued; college-educated Negroes were essential as a force for equality on all fronts.

Trotter didn't take aim at Booker T. Washington at that particular moment, but over the next two years he forged relationships with other Negro intellectuals and religious leaders who were fed up with the Tuskegee educator. The argument was that Washington's accommodating approach had only helped Jim Crow spread by enabling racists to spin his message as confirming Negro inferiority. When a minister from Woburn, William H. Scott, created the Massachusetts Racial Protective Association to oppose Washington, Trotter joined it, and by 1901 he was an officer in the organization. In the same year, Trotter became a cofounder of the Boston Literary and Historical Association—described as a "forum for militant race opinion"—whose December 2 meeting featured as guest speaker William Lloyd Garrison Jr. Trotter was also becoming fast friends with a man named George W. Forbes, an assistant librarian at the Boston Public Library's branch in the West End, who had written for a now defunct Negro newspaper. Although Trotter was eight years younger, he and Forbes were acquainted from when Trotter was starting out at Harvard College and Forbes was a senior graduating from Amherst College. A longtime admirer of Trotter's father's Civil War service and activism, Forbes eventually researched and wrote an appreciation of James Trotter's life that ran twelve single-spaced, typed pages. Forbes had plenty to say to Monroe Trotter against Washington. Into this mix was added Archibald Grimké, who had been the Trotters' neighbor in Hyde Park and who, like the senior Trotter, was a man of racial accomplishment—a lawyer and author of biographies of William Lloyd Garrison and Charles Sumner. Grimké and others talked to Monroe Trotter and Forbes about the need for a newspaper to challenge Washington's dominance as the country headed into a new century—and what better place for that paper than Boston, the cradle of abolition.

In the fullest sense, Trotter was on the cusp of becoming his father's son, as he took to the idea—radical at the time, especially in contrast to Washington's views—that agitation was required, and that rather than lower his head when addressing a white man, the Negro needed to glare into the white man's face. "Trotter's turn to radicalism," one historian later wrote, "reflected the collision of his optimistic expectations for his future with the realities of his racial position in the nation." He had seen his father fight for the rights of Negro soldiers in the Civil War and then watched him make his mark in government service—however briefly—in terms of Negro accomplishment. The race war had seemingly been won, and Monroe then took a giant step his father could not: He'd gained entrance into one of the nation's most prestigious colleges, where he joined one of its more elite academic fraternities and studied hard to prepare for success in a booming economy. He believed that upon graduation the world was waiting for him—only to discover that, in practice, it was not. The things he had done that ought to lead to prosperity—and would have brought prosperity if he had been white—did not work for him, and he realized that the war his father had won had not produced enduring benefits that extended to him.

Indeed, in 1901 Trotter's transformation was completed, as he concluded "that pursuit of business, money, civil or literary position was like building a house upon the sands, if race prejudice and persecution and public discrimination for mere color was to spread up from the South and result in a fixed caste system. So I plunged in to contend for full equality in all things governmental, civil and judicial, as far as race, creed and color were concerned."

The plunge became real during the autumn as Trotter and Forbes were finalizing the launch of the new and alternative newspaper Grimké and others had been advocating for. In mid-October Booker T. Washington did something to give them plenty to write about; he accepted an invitation from President Theodore Roosevelt to dine at the White House—a first for a Negro. When news of the shared supper spread, southerners exploded in outrage. "White men of the South, how do you like it?" asked the *New Orleans Times Democrat*. "White women of the South, how do you like it? When Mr. Roosevelt sits down to dinner with a negro, he declares that negro is the social equal to the white man." Georgia governor Allen D. Candler told reporters in Atlanta, "No self-respecting Southern man can ally himself with the President after what has occurred." Editorial writers at the *New York Times* sought to quell southern fury, but in doing so simply revealed their own prejudice, in their claim that a meeting with the Negro leader was the president's "plain duty" and did not at all signify the president saw Washington as an equal. "The notion," the paper said, "he was endorsing the idea of social equality between all whites and all colored men is absurd."

Much of the mainstream news coverage assumed that Negroes were delighted Booker T. Washington had dined with the president of the United States. But not all were. One week later, Trotter, Forbes, and others in Boston criticized Roosevelt for not having invited other "negro politicians and prominent colored men," saying Washington was not their spokesman. "He is controlled by the whites, and therefore must do as the whites wish," Trotter said. The remarks, made at a meeting of the Massachusetts Racial Protective Association on October 24, drew mention in such local papers as the *Boston Globe*, but not beyond. Boston supporters of Washington, however, certainly took notice. "Guess you have seen by the Boston papers some of the cheap talk of Wm. M. Trotter," Dr. Samuel E. Courtney wrote to Washington. Courtney, one of the Negro leader's biggest backers, hoped few would pay attention to "that set of idiots," and that their criticisms would go unnoticed elsewhere.

But rather than ending there, Trotter's first public comments against Booker T. Washington signaled a beginning. Two weeks later, on November 9, 1901, the first issue of the *Guardian* hit the newsstands. It sold for a nickel, ran eight pages, and was to be published every Saturday. The masthead listed "Wm. Monroe Trotter" as managing editor. The paper's office was in Room 18 at 3 Tremont Row, where atop his rolltop desk Trotter placed a bust of William Lloyd Garrison. The editorial page featured the motto "For Every Right, with All Thy Might," coined by Trotter. Among the stories in the *Guardian*'s inaugural issue was the fullest account anywhere of the White House dinner controversy, including Trotter's pointed censure of Booker T. Washington.

For Trotter, the public comments and debut of the *Guardian* marked his bold entry into the civil rights movement. "I am henceforth on the firing line," he wrote excitedly to Fairlie in June 1902, two months after his thirtieth birthday and six months into his new career as crusading newspaper editor. "It has cost me considerable money but I could not keep out of it." He poured out to his friend the details of how he'd come to start the paper with "a friend named Forbes" after becoming alarmed at the viral spread of Jim Crow and "so angered at Booker Washington's betrayal of the Colored people." He was fed up with the Tuskegee Wizard's dominance in the national conversation about race and the media's role in it—for either attacking anyone who criticized him or ignoring criticism altogether. "In the columns of *The Guardian* we have at least the relief of expressing our views on colorphobias in all its forms," he said. "I can now feel that I am doing my duty."

Trotter and Forbes certainly did not mince words. They called Washington "the traitor within" and the "great compromiser," denouncing the "aristocratic press of the north" for giving "praise and space to the compromiser while shutting out the honest and manly Negroes from its columns." Diatribes against Washington, however, were not the only matters the weekly addressed. The *Guardian* also included social notes, church news, sports, and fashion, in addition to its primary focus: reports about Jim Crow, race politics, and civil rights. Upon publication in late 1902 of the debut novel by a southern writer named Thomas Dixon Jr., for example, Trotter had a fit. Titled *The Leopard's Spots*, the book was intended as the first in a trilogy dramatizing the ways Reconstruction had ravaged the South and its antebellum values. In his newspaper Trotter ranted against Dixon, calling him an "unasylumed maniac." But the paper's main order of business was going after Washington in a bid to both wake up the country to the fact Washington did not own a monopoly on the civil rights movement and to steer race advocacy in a more militant direction. One editorial cartoon showed Washington tap-dancing to a group of pleased, well-dressed southern gentlemen who were singing a parody of a slave song: "We take the bread and give the crust; We fry the meat and give you the skin; We give you hell and rub it in!" The *Guardian* got personal and downright nasty when it ran a "news" story in October 1902 about Washington's daughter, Portia, flunking out of prestigious Wellesley College. Two months later the paper's coverage of a meeting of the Boston chapter of the Negro Business League—which was founded in 1900 by Courtney—oozed with sarcasm as it reported Washington was a special guest but that "this meeting was notable for the small attendance."

But even after two years of relentless invective, and even as Washington eventually decided the upstart Boston weekly could not be ignored and began a counterattack, Trotter, Forbes, and their newspaper still had not attained sustained national exposure as a necessary and urgently activist voice. Their emerging Negro radicalism was, in effect, hiding in plain sight, unknown to white America and to many southern Negroes. This all changed, however—spectacularly and virtually overnight—when Washington traveled to Boston on July 30, 1903, to give a talk to a capacity crowd at the African Methodist Episcopal Zion Church.

The talk had been arranged by the Boston branch of the business league, and early in the evening of the stifling hot July day, hundreds of spectators packed into the redbrick church in the city's South End. Infiltrating the crowd as it shuffled into the expansive front gallery was Trotter, his sister Maude, Forbes, and a man named Granville Martin who worked as a butler. Deenie Trotter was not there; she had stayed home hosting W. E. B. Du Bois's wife and daughter, who had just arrived for a stay with the Trotters in their Sawyer Avenue home. Du Bois, meanwhile, had completed teaching a summer session at Tuskegee at the invitation of Washington and was en route by coastal steamer. He was completely unaware of what was in the works for the Tuskegee Wizard.

Trotter and his companions moved into the sanctuary and took seats in a pew toward the front. Up to three dozen more Trotter supporters were scattered throughout the main floor and balcony, including Bernard Charles from Everett, a town north of Boston. People just kept coming; the church had a seating capacity of two thousand and before long there was standing room only. The altar had been turned into a stage, and seated on the platform was the guest of honor, Booker T. Washington, dressed in a black suit and bow tie; his wife; the church's minister; and such local Bookerites as Courtney. Presiding over the event was William H. Lewis, the attorney and former Harvard football star. Trotter had once considered Lewis a friend but now regarded him as a Washington toady and a spineless status-climber. Earlier in the year Theodore Roosevelt had had Boston's US attorney name Lewis an assistant US attorney—a Negro first—an appointment Trotter and others saw as a payoff for Lewis's publicly throwing his support to the president's token Negro dinner companion.

Since learning about the talk Trotter had been busy making plans, fueled by fresh anger toward Washington and his iron grip on race politics. He and Forbes had traveled to Louisville on July 1 for the annual meeting of the Afro-American Council, the national organization its founders had intended as a more aggressive option in the civil rights movement. In the past couple of years, however, Bookerites had managed to win key offices in the council—for example, replacing the likes of Ida B. Wells, its national organizer, with one of their own. Trotter had worked alongside Wells in pushing back, but with little success. Now at the Louisville convention, Trotter and Forbes wanted get the council to adopt the use of agitation as official policy. "Resolved: that we remain unshakable in the belief that agitation is the best means to secure our civil and political rights." Trotter also objected vociferously when the council wanted to offer President Roosevelt its unqualified support. He insisted any such resolution be amended to include the group's "regret the President has made no recommendation to Congress to pass legislation to secure our civil rights or political rights, or to protect our lives from lynching." But Trotter failed utterly on both counts; he was prevented from even introducing his resolutions for discussion. Defeated, he returned to Boston fully aware that Booker T. Washington's minions had assumed complete control of the one national organ allegedly pushing for civil rights. Trotter was so incensed about its impotency that, after his return, a *Guardian* editorial seemed to go a step further than agitation to endorse violence in the battle for equality—saying, "Beyond a certain point the Negro will not show his back to his pursuers. He will turn and fight."

Trotter's dissension in Louisville was covered extensively in the Negro press, but mainstream newspapers, while mentioning a "stormy debate" and some hostility toward Washington, minimized the opposition as comprising a few outliers from a Boston delegation whose names were not even mentioned. To Trotter and Forbes, Washington's decision to travel to Boston so soon after the convention was to rub his national prominence in their faces, and they decided that his visit could not go uncontested. They drew up a series of nine questions they intended to put to the speaker to challenge his positions on voting rights and higher education, concluding with a deliberately provocative interrogatory: "Is the rope and torch all the race is to get under your leadership?" In addition, one in their group smuggled a bundle of cayenne pepper into the church to scatter across the pulpit.

The event organizers had picked up word earlier in the day that Trotter might be up to something, and he realized as much when he and his cohorts noticed the two Boston police officers that William H. Lewis had summoned taking up their position at the church's main entrance. Lewis finally called the meeting to order at about eight p.m. At the mere mention of the keynote speaker's name, hissing and catcalls started from all corners of the church. Granville Martin, seated next to Trotter, stood and began yelling at the stage, louder than anyone. Lewis ordered the audience to sit down and be quiet. The heckling only grew louder. The two patrolmen moved quickly down the aisle and seized Martin by his collar.

Trotter jumped to his feet, yelling, "Put me out, arrest me!" and then rushed from his seat to follow the officers as they dragged Martin away. Outside he and others circled the policemen, shouting they had no cause to remove Martin and demanding his release. From here on, as the melee unfolded, accounts of the action varied. Police later told reporters the two patrolmen were "jumped upon by a maddened throng, struck and beaten with umbrellas and walking sticks and, in an instant, before they had time to protect themselves, the prisoner was torn from their grasp."

Martin returned with Trotter to their seats—an apparent triumph for the protesters—while the two patrolmen hurried to the nearby Station 5 for reinforcements. Onstage, Lewis and church leaders sought to quell the noise, but their actions only seemed to inflame Trotter and his group. Lewis again demanded quiet, threatening further police action, while others denounced the disruption and instructed that only light applause and the waving of handkerchiefs would be tolerated. Trotter would have none of it, and he and his supporters loudly demanded their free speech rights. The two sides—one on the floor, the other up onstage—hurled insults. One local Bookerite, a Negro attorney named Edward Everett Brown, admonished the crowd for its disgraceful conduct and sniggered that the source of the trouble were malcontents who "have read a little, swallowed a few words of Latin." Another Bookerite mocked Trotter and Forbes for their futile appearance at the Louisville convention, saying the pair "ought to be spanked for their attitude." When this speaker suddenly began coughing at the pulpit— so uncontrollably he could not continue—the Trotter group howled, knowing the source. Cayenne pepper.

Throughout, Washington had sat passively with his wife, and Lewis plowed forward and finally began an introduction when it appeared the dissidents had exhausted their taunts and would settle in for the talk. But once the keynote speaker rose and stepped to the pulpit, the protesters stood and began yelling as never before. Martin, in a booming voice, declared Washington was "leading the colored race to hell." Trotter, standing up on a bench in the pew, shouted, "Booker Washington, we want to ask you some questions. We know what you're going to say, and we don't want to hear it." Lewis and the church's minister waved at deacons to move in against the two, and as they did, a dozen or more Boston police officers burst through the door. "The rush of the body of uniformed men into the church created wild excitement," according to the *Boston Post* account the next day. "Children were trampled upon, women fainted, benches were overturned and general disorder prevailed." The police circled Trotter and Martin as Courtney yelled from the stage, "Get Trotter out of here." If necessary, he bellowed, "throw him out of the window."

The police did not throw Trotter out the window. They hauled him up the aisle while a riot—or near riot—erupted, depending on the account. Supporters, including his sister Maude, rushed to Trotter's aid. There was plenty of shoving and pushing. Fistfights broke out. Some drew razors—exactly how many was later in dispute. Not in dispute was that Trotter supporter Bernard Charles, while pulling at the officers' arms to free Trotter, was stabbed in the thigh—likely by an ally by mistake. Charles stumbled away, calling he'd been cut, and eventually he was hospitalized for his wound. In the scrum, another officer shouted he'd been stuck in his left ribs by a hatpin, and Maude Trotter was later targeted by police and charged as the assailant. Trotter, while not resisting arrest, was roughed up as he was taken into custody. It took about twenty minutes for police to restore order, and Washington was then able to commence a talk that lasted nearly two hours.

Police transported Trotter and Martin to the East Dedham Street station less than a mile away, where they were booked on charges of disturbing a public meeting. They were followed by supporters, who cheered on their behalf, and Trotter's mother, Virginia, soon arrived at the station to post bail for both men. Her son hurried back to the Zion Church but was too late. Booker T. Washington was gone. The *Guardian* editor had missed the talk (regardless, his newspaper's extensive coverage three days later portrayed the Tuskegee Wizard as "reeling off his usual rot"). The speech had included a line that might have given Trotter pause had he heard it, insofar as it echoed the reality of his own experience. "You will find it easier to enter a college in Boston than to enter a shoe factory or counting room," Washington had told the audience that

SCENE DURING THE HEIGHT OF THE RIOT AT THE COLORED METHO-
DIST CHURCH LAST EVENING.

Illustration of the attack on Booker T. Washington
during a Boston riot, printed on the cover page
of the *Boston Post* on July 31, 1903.

remained following the melee. "In other words, it is easier to secure
an education in the north than to find opportunity to use it after
it is secured." But common ground notwithstanding, Trotter was
fiercely at odds over how to confront Jim Crow and the erosion in
Negro voting rights, and he saw Washington as the problem.

Outside the church, Trotter faced reporters and issued a statement blaming the disturbance on the "absurd ruling" by Lewis,
"when he said that any one who hissed or manifested objection
to the speaker of the evening, or who demanded the right to ask
him to explain some of his previous statements favoring disenfranchisement and discriminating in 'jim crow' cars, would be subject to arrest." Trotter and his supporters then distributed in the
church vestry the list of nine questions that they never got to ask
during the event—unhappy that after he had delivered his speech

as planned, Washington had brushed off Trotter by saying he and his cohorts had upset a great meeting "just as a few flies are able to spoil the purity of a large jar of cream."

Reporters had a field day covering "the Boston Riot," the arrests, and the finger-pointing. It was page one news everywhere, the kind of story that a century later would have gone viral and drawn non-stop reports on television and online. The front-page story in the *Boston Globe* was headlined "Negroes Make Riotous Scene." The *Boston Post*, meanwhile, ran an illustration showing Booker T. Washington seated in a church surrounded by knife-wielding Negroes and, farther back, Boston police attempting a rescue. The more southern, the more outrageous—and inaccurate—was the coverage. "Boston Blacks with Razors Rush at Booker Washington," screamed the front-page story the next day in the *Atlanta Constitution*, a story that went on to describe the "bloody riot" that erupted as "razor wielders tried to reach Washington."

The direct action proved to be a breakout moment—Trotter's name was not only splashed across the front pages of the mainstream press in Boston but also around the country—appearing for the first time ever in such prominent newspapers as the *New York Times*, the *Washington Post*, and the *Los Angeles Times*. News of deepening anti-Washington sentiment—something Washington had worked strenuously to keep under wraps—had crossed the color line into white America. He, in fact, did have forceful opposition—that was the big story out of Boston—and at the forefront was William Monroe Trotter, a civil rights roughrider with a weekly newspaper as his bully pulpit for a new brand of activism.

=5=

Character Work:
1896–1907

D. W. Griffith spent eleven long years trying to make it to the big time as a stage actor. He fell short but not for want of effort. He applied himself tirelessly, establishing a work ethic that characterized his career, as he auditioned regularly for parts and, if not cast, took such odd jobs as a hop picker in California or ditch-digger in rural New York as he scouted other possible roles, all the while reading voraciously and attending plays to study fellow actors' craft. He was an autodidact who acquired a sophisticated knowledge of the dramatic arts rivaling that of any student formally educated at, say, Harvard College.

He was nothing if not ambitious, although during this period in his life, the 1890s, the fledgling film industry had no foothold in his thinking—a career option as motion picture director did not even exist. Griffith aspired, therefore, to succeed in the theatrical world, as a stage actor. He performed in all manner of roles—as Abe Lincoln, a detective in a comedy, an American Indian, even the prophet John the Baptist. He managed to land a few leading roles, although some he got by default. For example, as an understudy he stepped in to play one of the key male parts in Henrik Ibsen's *Hedda Gabler* when the marquee actor who had the role was too drunk to handle it. Despite his persistence, though, Griffith just was not that good, and most of the time the best he could hope for was secondary and minor roles. "He was an ineffectual actor," one critic concluded, "a man of deplorably finite acting prowess." He was tall, gangly, and prone to overacting, "with a prominent nose that made him look hawk-like."

But Griffith stayed the course for more than a decade. He had found encouragement during that first outing on the road in May 1896, when he played the villain Dionysius for what one critic wrote was a "small but well-pleased audience." The run was brief, although Griffith was lucky to hook up soon after with another Kentucky company, playing a villain again, in the well-known English drama *East Lynne*, based on a best-selling Victorian novel. The play was reliable fare—usually an easy sell—for traveling companies, and the production made it through small towns for four months before negative reviews caught up with it and attendance dwindled. The experience captured the recurring cycle of Griffith's acting career—promising and then not so. He often worked alongside actors who, like himself, had little experience but plenty of dreams. They joined troupes that traveled into the neighboring states of Indiana and Ohio to perform for up to a week and often less. The pay was meager; the food, lousy; and sleeping quarters, often flophouses. More than once Griffith limped back to Louisville—broke, riding the rails, and sharing a campfire with hoboes—after a company he was part of went belly-up. Back home he found work on several occasions in 1897 and 1898 with the Meffert Stock Company, and although performing with Meffert meant he was earning his way, he was not appearing under the lights of the city's biggest stages. The company usually performed at the Temple, one of Louisville's least-known stages, a gaslit theater located above a store in a former Masonic hall. During this rocky period Griffith also was unsettled about his identity; in addition to using the name Lawrence Griffith, he tried Alfred Lawrence, then Thomas Griffith, and once even used Lawrence Brayington to avoid any confusion with a more senior cast member also named Griffith.

By 1900 he settled on the pseudonym Lawrence Griffith and also began reaching beyond the local circuit of small midwestern cities, heading first to Chicago and then to New York City, where the roller-coaster ride of his acting career continued. In New York City, for example, he managed to sign on in February 1900 with a company going on the road with a new play called *How London Lives*. The gig proved a high point of sorts. Griffith won a key role, portraying a man falsely accused of murder, and it marked the first time he appeared in a play on its first run. The troupe then toured in thirteen states on the longest road trip he had ever experienced. But, as was so often the case, the upward flight ended abruptly when, in Minnesota, the company's finances fell apart and the show closed.

Griffith found himself out of work and penniless. Desperate that autumn, he began working in what any serious actor would not consider to be legitimate theater—vaudeville. He appeared in the so-called variety theaters, where short sketches, lasting about twenty minutes, were part of a program that might also include a comedy act, jugglers, trick cyclists, a comedic pianist, and an acrobatic team. Later in life Griffith avoided mention of the nearly three years he spent making a living this way. He certainly had reason to. Besides its low status, he likely wanted to sidestep the fact he entered vaudeville as a strikebreaker. In 1900 vaudeville actors had organized their own labor union and walked off the job. There was suddenly plenty of work to be had for the willing. Griffith answered the casting call and found ample employment as a scab actor throughout the East Coast and Midwest. He also responded to an urgent need for new material. His scenario *In Washington's Time*, a one-act melodrama about an American soldier trying to hide important letters for General Washington from the British, played for six months, starting in February 1901, and Griffith acted in one of the lead roles during its tour to vaudeville houses in Washington, DC, New York City, Boston, Philadelphia, and Chicago. Entering vaudeville as he did may have meant he had exploited the heartbreak of others, but it enabled him to catch a career break with collateral benefits unforeseen to him at the time: to experience firsthand—as an actor and as a scenarist—how classical works and historical dramas were compressed from their original length into the compact playlets that were the staple of vaudeville. It was the kind of training that would prove invaluable to him in a few short years.

Vaudeville gave Griffith reason to believe in his writing, and the work generally helped him regain his footing, so that his next burst of energy was directed westward to California, a swing that completed his coast-to-coast education as a journeyman actor who, over the course of a decade, traveled all over the country. He had come a long way from his farm boy days in Kentucky, and in San Francisco in 1904 he resumed his quest for a place in legitimate theater as an actor and, now more than ever before, as a writer. It was in San Francisco that he began writing a full-length play in the chunks of time during what had become frequent gaps in his acting work. His life was about to change on another front as well—soon after his arrival he met his future wife, young actress Linda Arvidson. Both had been cast in a play at the Grand Opera House on Mission Street, where Griffith portrayed a police inspector and Linda, a striking brunette from the Bay Area, had a one-line part as a boy servant. The couple was at the start of their romance in early 1905 when Griffith, having bounced around between small parts and day-labor work, managed to land a major role as an American Indian called Alessandro. The play was *Ramona*, named for the title role, a Mexican woman involved in a scandalous romance with Griffith's character. The company toured California for two months, including Los Angeles, the first time Griffith ever worked in the city that would one day become his base of operation.

The play featured early evidence of Griffith's lifelong knack for a self-aggrandizement, a trait he shared with his father. In publicity materials he hyped his acting credentials and, worse than that, falsely claimed credit for having coauthored the stage adaptation of the romance novel on which *Ramona* had been based. Griffith got some decent reviews as Alessandro ("He looks the part to perfection," wrote the *Los Angeles Times*) but the play was panned by the time it fizzled in San Francisco ("No one in the company knows how to act," complained the *San Francisco Argonaut*). Griffith again faced piecing together an income—and his budding romance now added pressure. The remainder of 1905 included a role as a cigar-smoking detective in a farce that toured the Northwest and also a foray back into vaudeville, when, returning to San Francisco, he and Linda restaged his sketch *In Washington's Time*.

D. W. Griffith in a production of *Miss Petticoats*,
which toured New England briefly in 1903.
COURTESY OF THE MUSEUM OF MODERN ART, NEW YORK.

Griffith's next gig not only represented the approaching summa-
tion to his decade-long quest for stardom on the stage, it captured the
best and worst of a period taking him through his twenties and into
his early thirties. He had the good fortune by early 1906 of winning
a spot with a repertory company run by and starring an actress of
national acclaim, the statuesque Nance O'Neil. Her San Francisco–
based troupe headed out on a cross-country tour, intending to perform a mix of new plays and classics by Shakespeare, Dumas, Ibsen,
and others in ten states and four Canadian provinces. But after the
tour was well under way, events not only forced Griffith's hand personally but also cast a shadow on the company's fortunes. In the
spring of 1906, he and his fellow actors were performing in Minne-
apolis. Before dawn on Tuesday, April 18, an earthquake hit San
Francisco. Much of the city was suddenly in ruins after the historic
quake and fires. Nearly three thousand people died.

Linda Arvidson, who had stayed behind, reached Griffith by telegram to report that she was shaken but unharmed. The news for

Nance O'Neil, meanwhile, was not good; her theatrical materials and property were destroyed, causing huge financial losses. Instead of heading home, though, the company decided to keep going, and after several frantic days Griffith urged Linda to join him where the players were heading to complete their four-month tour—Boston, Massachusetts. Linda did not hesitate; she traveled across country in what was called a "refugee train," clothed and fed by the Red Cross. She arrived the second week of May just as O'Neil's troupe was completing its first week there. Delighted to see her, Griffith did not hesitate, either. On a cool, clear Monday, May 14, 1906, he led Linda into the city's North End to a church with historic firepower—the Old North Church, site of the two lanterns in the steeple used to warn patriots in April 1775 as to whether the British Army was coming by land or by sea. In choosing this church, it was as if Griffith was showing off his flair for the dramatic. Significantly, he filled out their marriage certificate with the following response to the question asking for the groom's occupation: "writing."

On his wedding night, Griffith took to the stage in the city's theater district a mile or so south from the church. The company was presenting a single performance of *Magda*, a four-act drama by the German playwright Hermann Sudermann that at the time was one of the most popular plays in Europe and the United States. Its eponymous strong, assertive heroine was an ideal vehicle for Nance O'Neil. In fact, O'Neil had starred as Magda in the work's successful London debut in 1902 and then during a US tour that had included a previous stop in Boston. Griffith played the supporting role of Pastor Heffterdingk, a young clergyman who tries to mediate a conflict-filled relationship between the rebellious Magda and her strong-willed father that is at the center of the story.

The company appeared at the Hollis Street Theatre, a spacious showplace regarded as Boston's most fashionable playhouse—built in 1885 just off Washington Street, it seated 1,600 and was lushly decorated in gold, blue, and white. Newspaper editor Monroe Trotter likely passed it daily on his way to his office near "Newspaper Row" farther up Washington Street. Not that Trotter would have had much interest in the productions, which mostly attracted white audiences—just as Griffith, during this swing through Boston, would not have had much interest in either Trotter or the nasty power struggle in Negro circles involving the challenge the editor was spearheading against Booker T. Washington. Indeed, during the year Washington had stepped up his covert actions against Trotter, hiring a Boston detective to conduct surveillance of him and his wife, Deenie, to determine whether she worked. "Don't say for whom the information is wanted," Washington wrote the detective, James R. Woods Jr., by telegram. Woods tailed Trotter, talked to workers in adjacent offices, chose not to "excite suspicion" by talking to his neighbors at home, and ultimately established for Washington that Deenie Trotter worked side by side with her husband. "There is no doubt," the detective reported, "Mrs. Trotter is at *The Guardian* office every day."

Even had Negro politics been of interest to him, Griffith had no time to spare. For its two-week run in Boston, the O'Neil troupe was working at a breakneck pace of evening performances along with matinee shows, presenting a rotating schedule of such popular plays as Ibsen's *Rosmersholm* and *Hedda Gabler*; Sudermann's *Fires of St. John*; an adaptation of Alexandre Dumas's love story *Camille*; American playwright Augustin Daly's *The Jewess*, also known as *Leah, the Forsaken*, an adaptation of a German play, Salomon Hermann von Mosenthal's *Deborah*; and, lastly, Charles Dickens's *Oliver Twist*. The run was a warm welcome back for Nance O'Neil. "Bostonians have taken this gifted actress to their hearts as they have taken no other actress within the memory of the present generation of theatre goers," wrote one critic. Boston was the ideal place for her theatrical company to finish its tour, especially after the disaster affecting the troupe's home base. Before the run ended, an extra performance was even added to honor O'Neil, whose "great financial loss sustained by the earthquake and fire in San Francisco has deeply touched her Boston friends."

O'Neil played to rave reviews. Griffith, meanwhile, generally went unnoticed, whether playing the lover Armand Duval in Dumas's romance, the thief Toby Crackit in *Oliver Twist*, or a clergyman in *Magda*. He did get a positive mention in a review of Ibsen's *Rosmersholm*, in which the critic noted that "as the unkempt, hard-up dreamer socialist Brendel, Mr. Griffith gave a delightfully amusing bit of character work." But ultimately, as far as Griffith's acting career was concerned, that brief mention, no matter how complimentary, captured his usual state: "character work." He had had a good run with Nance O'Neil but was never going to make it big. The tour, one biographer has observed, "confirmed that Griffith's future as an actor had limits." He would earn his keep, perhaps, but little more, "doomed to the exhausting routine of road shows and one-night stands."

Sensing this, and with his finances in decent shape at the tour's completion, Griffith hunkered down in New York City during the summer of 1906 to work further on the four-act social comedy that became titled *A Fool and a Girl*. The plot followed a young, wealthy southerner as he leaves his sheltered country life, travels west to gain experience in the world, and meets a wily ingenue who tries to cheat him out of his fortune. By fall, however, Griffith was facing the same-old—want of an income. He auditioned and won a key role in a traveling show. Fortunately, Linda also got a part so that they could be together, starting with the play's opening in Virginia.

In another way, too, the experience proved fortuitous, although unrecognized at the moment. The play's author was none other than Thomas Dixon Jr., Griffith's future collaborator, who had become one of the country's most successful writers. A fellow southerner and, at forty-two, a decade older than Griffith, Dixon was an intense, steely-eyed man of enormous energy who, in short order, had burned through vocations—actor, lawyer, North Carolina legislator, and preacher—before hitting it big as a writer in 1902 with his first novel, *The Leopard's Spots*. He was never going be a literary lion, but the book showed he knew how to construct a page-turning melodrama about the anguish of Reconstruction from the South's perspective. As evidenced in its text, Dixon was energetic in another way—his racism. Virulent contempt for the Negro resonated through this work and in his third novel, *The Clansman* (part 2 of the trilogy begun with *The Leopard's Spots*), which in 1905 was a best seller and also glorified the Klan.

To top everything, Dixon was a relentless self-promoting schemer always ready to launch stunts to further his works or tap his connections. To sell his first novel, for example, he had turned to an old friend from North Carolina—Walter Hines Page, a principal in the eventual New York publishing powerhouse of Doubleday, Page and Company. To promote *The Clansman*, Dixon decided to taunt Booker T. Washington. He paid a messenger to approach Washington as he entered a fund-raising event for the Tuskegee Institute that was about to take place at Carnegie Hall, attended by such luminaries as Mark Twain and Mrs. John D. Rockefeller. Dixon's envoy handed Washington a note challenging him to debate "The Future of the Negro in America." The stunt got what Dixon was after—newspaper headlines—and he stoked the fire of publicity by continuing to press Washington. In one letter Dixon said he would donate $10,000 from the profits of *The Clansman* if Washington would assert publicly that the goal for his doctrine of Negro self-improvement was not to achieve "Social Equality for the Negro" and that his Tuskegee Institute was "opposed to the Amalgamation of the races." Washington refused the bait, as he and his aides privately condemned the novelist's appealing to prejudice as a marketing tactic. "Dixon's challenge to you to discuss the social equality question," wrote one of Washington's supporters from Ohio, "was but a scheme to advertise his book." But Dixon's move showed he was light-years ahead of his time, his era's version of the author who in the twenty-first century is expected to hustle constantly to increase sales through Twitter and other social media. Griffith would eventually adopt Dixon's viewpoint: any publicity was good publicity.

Oblivious to Dixon's campaign against Washington, Griffith was then juggling his writing ambition, his new marriage, and a foundering acting career. He and Linda appeared that fall in the adaptation of Dixon's second novel, *The One Woman*, presented throughout the South in small venues. But before it moved on to New York City, Griffith suffered a further setback: he was dropped from the play. The reasons for his firing have never been clear, despite all of the interviews, records, and writings about Griffith and Dixon. Clearly, though, given their future work together in film, the dismissal did no lasting harm to their relationship.

But it did mean Griffith—at thirty-something—was desperate professionally. Then came the kind of surprise turn that he had every reason to think signaled a break in the logjam of his career. He sold his play *A Fool and a Girl*, and so, on their first Christmas Eve together, he presented Linda with the $700 advance the producer had paid him. The sum was eye-popping, more money than either he or his wife had ever seen.

Griffith began riding a writer's high—imagining leaving acting behind for a different kind of audience cheer, that of, "Author, author!" The start of 1907 saw publication of one of his poems in the January 10 issue of a well-regarded literary and news magazine called *Leslie's Weekly*. He was only paid six dollars for the six-stanza verse, but with publication came prestige and further validation that he was transforming himself from a struggling actor into a successful writer. Emboldened, he'd feverishly gone to work on a second play, taking on nothing short of a colossal subject, America's fight for independence. He decided to call it simply *War*, and he set the three-act melodrama in the American colonies during the revolutionary years 1775 and 1781.

Splitting his time in New York City between writing in his railroad flat on the Upper West Side and going to the New York Library to do research, Griffith either ignored or was too busy to notice the rumblings of another type of revolution. A new medium—short "story films"—was exploding in popularity, particularly among immigrant workers filling US cities, audiences that could enjoy the moving pictures' silent slapstick comedies and adventures unhindered by language barriers. To satisfy the fast-growing market, a different kind of space was called for, and so storefront theaters were popping up everywhere; by the end of 1906, about 2,500 of them were already operating around the country.

If Griffith paid heed to this seismic filmic development he gave no indication, focused instead on his writing. These were heady days for him. One mild morning in late September 1907 he boarded a train bound for Washington, DC. By his side was his adoring wife, the two en route to the nation's capital for the grand opening of his first play at the Columbia Theatre, one of the city's leading playhouses located a few blocks from the White House. The season had become one filled with hope—a time, finally, for him to make it, and for the first time he'd attached his true name to his work in the theater. No longer Lawrence Griffith but the real deal, he was David Wark Griffith. The stakes, of course, were huge—he hoped a successful debut would be the game changer, propelling him out of a seemingly lost decade as a struggling journeyman actor and into a limitless future as a playwright of national renown.

The reception of *A Fool and a Girl*, therefore, proved devastating. It suffered mixed to negative reviews after its premiere, at which a good number of attendees stood up and walked out of the theater. "First class audiences will not accept it in its present form," wrote the *New York Dramatic Mirror*. "Business at the Columbia theatre with a new production was far below par." After only five performances in Washington, DC, and then a week in Baltimore, the show was closed, "an artistic and financial failure," as one film historian described it. Griffith and his wife returned to New York City, where their survival in the months to come depended partly on money sent by one of his brothers, along with Linda's personal savings. His first play had flopped. No one was showing an interest in his second, *War*, so that instead of celebrating a new career, a defeated D. W. Griffith ended the year 1907 facing the existential "What now?"

PART II

Finding Their Voices

Courtesy of the Museum of Modern Art, New York

Courtesy of the Boston Public Library

D. W. Griffith

Monroe Trotter

— 6 —

Trotterism:
1903–1908

In the predawn hours of July 31, 1903, after he was done giving interviews to Boston reporters about the rowdy night of protest at the Zion Church, Monroe Trotter finally headed home. He was only able to stay a few hours, however; he had to return downtown for his arraignment in court later in the morning.

Reaction to his militancy against Booker T. Washington was quick. Seemingly overnight Trotter had become a lightning rod for anti-Washington sentiment—and therefore a target of Washington devotees. The same morning he was in a Boston courtroom, a convention of Negro Baptists meeting in Tuskegee, Alabama, passed a special resolution attacking him and his supporters for trying to "insult and humiliate Dr. Booker T. Washington of the Tuskegee Institute," while reiterating high praise for Washington as "a conservative, worthy and safe leader." Washington's underlings quickly wrote up the resolution into a press release, spiced it with anti-Trotter taunts ("Trotter's stay in the public jail will give him an opportunity to review his foolish life"), and distributed it through the Associated Press and to such southern papers as the *Atlanta Constitution*. But the hurried effort at public relations was hardly needed. Without prodding, most white-owned newspapers voiced shock and horror at Trotter's conduct—"an atavism suggestive of the Congo forests," complained the *Buffalo Courier*, while the *New York Times*, eschewing inflammatory language, called the protest "a most disgraceful and lamentable episode." Many white progressives—supportive of civil rights generally—were likewise appalled. One of the most notable was Oswald Garrison Villard, a grandson of William Lloyd Garrison and publisher of the family-owned *New York Evening Post*. Villard would eventually change his views on civil rights policy but for now was a big backer of Booker T. Washington. He said, "I consider young Trotter a very dangerous, almost irresponsible young man whose conduct at the Boston riot should make it impossible for anyone to consider his opinions upon any subject related to his race." Then there was the Negro press. Much of it also rushed to Washington's defense. "What is the matter with those Boston Negroes?" asked the *Freeman* of Indianapolis. "Has much learning made them mad?"

Even so, Trotter had clearly tapped into a gathering, albeit unorganized, call for change in the civil rights movement. "Editor Trotter of the *Boston Guardian* has the congratulations of the country," said the *Washington Bee*, a newspaper that was now strongly anti–Booker T. Washington, while the *Chicago Broad Ax* came out in support of the protest leader for pressing the Tuskegee Wizard in public. "Booker T. Washington has become such an autocrat lately that he absolutely refused to answer these questions which are of vital importance to the Negro."

It was almost noon when the criminal case against William Monroe Trotter was finally called in Boston Municipal Court. The delay was due to an unusual number of defendants charged with drunkenness who were on the docket ahead of him. The corridor outside was crowded with Negroes, many there to support Trotter, while others belonged to Washington's camp. During the morning wait, arguments broke out. "The little groups," noted one newspaper, "with much eloquence and many gestures fought the battles of last night all over again."

The arraignment resembled a mini Harvard reunion: Trotter—class of 1895; one of his defense attorneys, Clement G. Morgan—class of 1890 (W. E. B. Du Bois's classmate and good friend); William H. Lewis—law school class of 1895 and presiding officer at the prior night's event. Lewis was in court, as was the Zion Church pastor, should the prosecutor need them to testify about the disturbance. But no witnesses were necessary. Trotter and the other two men being arraigned with him—Granville Martin and the injured Bernard Charles—all entered pleas of not guilty to charges of disturbing a public meeting and committing "lewd and indecent noises and tumults." The judge continued the cases until the next week, and then released the men on $100 bail each. As for Maude Trotter, the charge she had stuck a Boston police officer with a hatpin was eventually dropped.

Trotter went home to his house on the hill in Dorchester, where W. E. B. Du Bois had arrived to join his wife and daughter as the Trotters' houseguests. News of the melee floored the scholar, who explained to his host how upset he was. "I thought that he had been needlessly violent, and had compromised me as his guest."

Du Bois was indeed in a fix—fresh from teaching a semester at Tuskegee for which he was beholden to Booker T. Washington, yet now staying with Trotter. The awkward circumstance symbolized the middle ground Du Bois had been trying to straddle for too long between the two antagonists. But in truth, the middle no longer held. Ever since the Sam Hose lynching in 1899, and more recently under Trotter's influence, Du Bois was convinced the pursuit of civil rights was in crisis, at a time "when every energy is being used to put black men back into slavery and when Mr. Washington is leading the way backward." He had become an avid reader of the *Guardian* since its inception in 1901. He found the newspaper bitter and satirical, and at times, too personal, "but it was well edited, it was earnest, and it published facts." He watched the paper's—and through it, Trotter's—prominence grow, as it circulated around the country and Negroes everywhere followed its crusade against Booker T. Washington and its forceful demand for a new radicalism in the civil rights movement.

Du Bois saw in Trotter a leader taking up the fight because he, and a very few others, realized that there was still a fight. Trotter understood that Washington's "compromise"' was not a compromise based on equality at all; it was one that enshrined the inequity of the age, that choked off the prospect that Negroes could be equal to whites and was the worst kind of political cowardice, because while ostensibly representing the concerns of black Americans, Washington's position preserved the differences between the races—separate and unequal.

Du Bois might not agree with *every* position the paper took, and thought few Negroes did, but he also saw "nearly all read it and were influenced by it." Including him. The previous year he'd written an article for the *Atlantic Monthly* titled "Of the Training of Black Men," which endorsed higher education for Negroes—one of Trotter's major talking points. Then in the spring, his own book, *The Souls of Black Folk*, came out, and it included a groundbreaking chapter, "Of Mr. Booker T. Washington and others," questioning the educator's effectiveness. Du Bois's conclusion: "Mr. Washington represents in Negro thought the old attitude of adjustment and submission."

The public and in-depth criticism of the nation's most celebrated Negro leader quickly became all the rage and had a huge impact on releasing Washington's grip on the national conversation about civil rights. In Chicago, Ida B. Wells raved about the book to political activist Jane Addams, the founder of Hull House in Chicago, the country's first settlement house, and wrote Du Bois a fan letter on May 30, pleased by the commotion *Souls* was causing among Chicago Bookerites. William James, the Harvard psychology professor who had taught both Du Bois and Trotter, mailed a copy of *Souls* to his brother, writer Henry James, then in England, saying it was "the only 'Southern' book of any distinction published for many a year." In Boston, Trotter took it upon himself to promote the scholarly author. "Do me one favor," he wrote his friend Fairlie in a quick note. "Buy and read *Souls of Black Folk* by W. E. B. Du Bois, specifically chapter on B.T. Washington." Eager for everyone to see where Du Bois now stood, Trotter began running free ads for the book in the *Guardian* and offering it for sale at the paper's offices.

But Du Bois still had further to go—looking back years later, he said it was the Boston Riot's aftermath that "quite changed my life." During the extended stay in Boston that summer and in subsequent months, he witnessed firsthand Bookerites' waging war against Trotter. In public, Washington might act as if Trotter were a minor nuisance who garnered little support, but furtively he sought to destroy him, backing libel actions against the *Guardian* to exert financial pressure on its editor as well as its cofounder George Forbes, and with William H. Lewis's help, hiring a spy to infiltrate Trotter's political meetings. In one instance, the spy reported Trotter and his supporters were planning to shoot Washington during his next talk in the area—in Cambridge in September. Lewis found the claim unbelievable, advising Washington that their spy was not always credible and prone to "overdraw," but that they should keep the intelligence for possible future use "as a club over their heads" to further disparage Trotter. Ever cautious, Lewis arranged for plainclothes policemen to be stationed in the Mt. Olive Baptist Church for Washington's talk, which, despite the presence of some of the troublemakers from the previous event, went off without a hitch. Given their remarks, some speakers used the opportunity to address the Trotter problem. The Cambridge mayor welcomed Washington as a leader "whose name is on the tongue of every right-thinking man and woman in this country," and Washington himself opened by saying, "We need at this time in the history of my race prudent leaders and wise counselors."

In other moves, Bookerites lobbied Boston city officials to fire Forbes from his job as librarian at the West End Public Library, citing his role in the Zion Church melee. Although unsuccessful, the effort rattled Forbes. Du Bois saw how Washington's influential press and public relations apparatus, what became known as the "Tuskegee Machine," was asserting its power in Massachusetts and around the country, such as by funneling funds to Bookerites in Boston in late 1903 to launch a newspaper, the *Colored Citizen*, to oppose Trotter. Du Bois learned that, in what he termed the "bribery" of the Negro press, the Negro leader was also giving hundreds of dollars to other editors whose papers "follow the same editorial policy, print the same syndicated news, praise the same persons and attack the same persons." Washington's underlings regularly provided these editors with material, stories, and even editorials to publish. To his dismay and disillusionment, Du Bois concluded that Washington, rather than welcoming a healthy debate about the future course of the civil rights movement, had a "policy for wholesale crushing of all criticism and the crushing out of the men who dared to criticize in any way."

The remainder of 1903 wasn't all dirty tricks and Negro politics, however. With her husband out on bail, Deenie Trotter hosted a late summer evening of music, a large social gathering that included the Du Boises; Archibald Grimké and his daughter Angelina; Grimké's brother Rev. Francis J. Grimké and his wife, who were visiting from Washington, DC; Trotter's attorney Morgan and his wife; Forbes and his wife; Trotter's mother-in-law, mother, and sisters; and other friends. They listened to Deenie's cousin on the piano, playing Ballade in A Minor by the young and popular British-born Negro composer Samuel Coleridge-Taylor, and then two violin solos by another guest. Late in the evening, following "light refreshments," things got a bit raucous, as Trotter and his fellow Harvard alums huddled together and then announced everyone had been "voted to be a Harvard man." They ushered everyone around the piano where, according to a social note, they boisterously sang the school anthem "Fair Harvard," and then led "the Harvard yell for Prof. Du Bois, the old Harvard graduate; for Morgan, the first Colored class day orator; and for Trotter."

But on a more profound note, this was a period that proved a tipping point for Du Bois, the future civil rights icon. By year's end, as he monitored the escalating pressure the Tuskegee Machine and Bookerites applied against the *Guardian*, Du Bois had broken publicly and formally with Washington. The pressure, however, proved too much for *Guardian* cofounder Forbes. He soon quit the newspaper, preferring the bookish comfort of a civil service career as a librarian to the rough and tumble of advocacy journalism. But Trotter did not bend—the stubborn, uncompromising, and true believer in agitation seemed to get an adrenaline rush from challenging the establishment. Du Bois might never approve of Trotter's ambush at the Zion Church, and he always told him so, but he'd grown to admire Trotter and chose to side with him, even in the face of Washington's formidable reach—his access to political power in the nation's capital, his acceptance in the mainstream press and by white philanthropists, and his widespread popular support across the country, both white and Negro. "Brought into close contact with Mr. Trotter for the first time, my admiration for his unselfishness, pureness of heart and indomitable energy even when misguided grew," Du Bois wrote in December 1903.

Keenly observed by Du Bois, the criminal case against Trotter and his codefendants played out over the rest of the summer and into the early fall. In a bench trial lasting two days before a municipal court judge in August, William H. Lewis was the first in a parade of government witnesses who testified that Trotter, Granville Martin, and Bernard Charles had triggered a riot and then resisted arrest. Three Boston police officers testified that upon their arrival they witnessed "acts of disorder" by the defendants. The proceedings drew front-page coverage in Boston newspapers, and each day the courtroom was packed, mostly with Trotter supporters. In fact, during the midday recess, a pail of coffee and a hamper of sandwiches were available, courtesy of the *Guardian*. Trotter's defense attorney called a number of witnesses who attested to his good character and rebutted the charge that the *Guardian* editor had been the provocateur, but the editor did not take the stand. Cutting short the defense's bid for more time to show the disturbance had been instigated by those on the platform while Trotter was merely trying to address the speaker, the judge declared he'd heard enough, saying, "I find the evidence is overwhelming that these three defendants are guilty of disturbing the meeting." Trotter and Martin received the maximum sentence: thirty days in jail. Charles was fined $25.

The three men appealed their convictions to Suffolk Superior Court, resulting in a virtual replay of the whole matter at a second trial before a jury that began October 1, 1903. Trotter's position throughout was that his conduct at the Zion Church was constitutionally protected. "I was unlawfully ejected while maintaining my rights of free speech," he wrote to a friend. The First Amendment was his shield, he argued, to speak out in the manner that he did. To be sure, the argument was handy, and hardly surprising, coming from a newspaper editor whose free press rights were likewise protected by the same amendment. But over the course of his career, Trotter left scant indication of his overall take on the First Amendment—how he viewed its scope, especially when forms of expression other than the media were involved. That a free press was seen as the bedrock of democracy was firmly established by the early twentieth century, so a newspaperman like Trotter was able to do his work in a manner, as one social historian noted later, "exceptionally uninhibited and free of government control." But other forms of expression were another matter, and the early 1900s was a time of widespread government regulation of what later became known as civil liberties. In fact, limits on expression—in literature, the performing arts, and in speech—were seen as more extreme in the United States than in England, the home of Victorianism.

Seven years after the Boston Riot case, Trotter would again wave the First Amendment banner energetically against government censorship, this time of a prizefight film showing heavyweight boxing champion Jack Johnson crushing Jim Jeffries. Following a July 4, 1910, bout in Reno, Nevada, hyped as "the fight of the century," cities and states across the country, including Boston, moved quickly to stop a film taken of the slugfest, citing its violence. Trotter and many others cried foul, saying the bans were only pursued because the bout showcased black supremacy—a Negro champion defeating a fighter who'd been dubbed "the Great White Hope." What if the white boxer Jeffries had won, Trotter asked rhetorically in a series of questions he issued publicly to the leaders of the suppression movement, continuing: "Have you ever made a nation-wide attempt to prevent the exhibition of pictures shown of lynchings of colored men by white mobs? Are not the lynching pictures more brutalizing and objectionable than the prizefight pictures?"

The bans, Trotter argued, unconstitutionally infringed on free expression. But did these two displays mean he was a First Amendment absolutist? Or did he believe there were circumstances that warranted restrictions on expression—such as the showing of lynching pictures? Or was his approach less about any sort of doctrinal consideration and more about pragmatism and tactical strategy? Within days of protesting the ban of the prizefight film as unconstitutional, Trotter and a group of Negroes went to see the mayor of

Boston to complain about a play that had just opened at the American Music Hall. The southern writer Thomas Dixon, the one whom Trotter had called an "unasylumed maniac," had adapted his popular novel *The Clansman* into a stage play. Trotter and his delegation explained to Mayor John F. "Honey Fitz" Fitzgerald and the theater's manager that the play was, like Dixon's other works about Reconstruction, racist and "intended to foster race prejudice," and that "it was a blunder to bring a play to Boston that did violence to its traditions." The manager came away from the session saying he had not realized the play was so objectionable and that, at the mayor's urging, he did not want to continue a show that was offensive to "the colored people of the city." He announced he was going to close down *The Clansman* and replace it with a new comedy, *Bingo of Bingville*, by popular comic strip writer Newton Newkirk. The outcome was a complete victory for Trotter. It was voluntary, nonconfrontational, and without any kind of First Amendment rumble that could have broken out so easily in the clash of the two competing factors: his civil rights agenda and the constitutional right to freely express ideas, even ideas that were racist. This would not be the case a few years later—far from it—once *The Clansman* was adapted to the new medium of film and, retitled, became America's first blockbuster movie.

In defending himself in 1903, though, Trotter surely sounded like a hard-core civil libertarian in arguing his arrest at the Zion Church was in violation of his free speech rights. The Superior Court jury decided otherwise: it found Trotter and Martin guilty on October 8, 1903, after a weeklong trial. Bernard Charles was acquitted. In sentencing Trotter, the judge told him he was flat-out wrong about his claimed right to disrupt the meeting. He said Trotter and Martin "should have pleaded guilty in the lower court and said that they made a mistake." Instead, Trotter was unapologetic, and the judge, citing his lack of remorse, reinstituted the maximum sentence of thirty days behind bars. He ordered court officers to take Trotter immediately to the Charles Street Jail a few blocks away.

Although "Forbes is badly scared in this and wants me to join him in an abject apology," Trotter wrote to a friend after serving three weeks of his sentence, the idea was anathema—"which I should almost rather die than agree to." Instead, emboldened, he wrote, "This jail has brought many Colored people and some white people around to our side and generally cemented and strengthened our forces."

He was also not the only public figure and Charles Street "jail bird" garnering headlines at the time. While Trotter had been busy getting ready for his second trial, twenty-nine-year-old James Michael Curley—a local state representative and future Boston mayor—stood trial in US District Court in late September on charges he had defrauded the government, after he had been caught taking a civil service examination for a campaign worker. The federal jury found him guilty and he was sentenced to sixty days at the Charles Street Jail. Curley's two-month stay there the next year was cushy. The sheriff, a fellow Democrat, put Curley in a cell twice as big as most of the others. Despite rules permitting only one visitor a week, Curley's friends freely came and went. The rising political powerbroker was permitted to take a saltwater bath every morning, and guests joined him for a Thanksgiving Day feast. When he was released, Curley was met with cheers back at his political hall.

Trotter did not get such royal treatment; he was assigned to the typical eight-by-ten-foot granite cell in what he called "the stone prison." But, like Curley, Trotter did conduct his affairs from jail. He met with Deenie to instruct her on the continued operations of the *Guardian*, and he wrote letters and columns for the newspaper. He was unrepentant, even energized: "I have not bit my tongue since here but have been sending stuff right from behind the bars," he told one friend. Like Curley, Trotter was cheered upon his release November 7, treating a gathering of about two hundred supporters to a rousing speech he had written in his cell that stressed Negro voting rights and political power. Perhaps most of all, though, Trotter was over the moon about W. E. B. Du Bois's coming over to his side with the public rejection of Booker T. Washington. If Du Bois "keeps on," Trotter wrote in the *Guardian*, "he will even outfoot us in true and manly statement." He added with satisfaction, "The iron seems to have entered his soul."

Mostly in sync—at least for the time being—Trotter and Du Bois
began building organizations to compete with the Tuskegee Wizard. The idea was to supplement the *Guardian*'s coverage and editorials with organized activism. During a series of meetings at his
home that fall of 1903, Trotter created the Boston Suffrage League
(later renamed the New England Suffrage League), which began
with about fifty Negroes from the area and neighboring states. The
group's first resolution read: "We call upon President Roosevelt to
dispense with Booker T. Washington as our political spokesman."
It was a call that fell, of course, on deaf ears. The president's White
House dinner with Washington two years earlier had cemented his
view that the Negro leader was "the most useful, as well as the
most distinguished, member of his race in the world." In other de-
mands, the group wanted the halt of Jim Crow in public facilities,
a federal antilynching bill, and enforcement of the voting rights
guaranteed by the Fifteenth Amendment, one of three so-called Reconstruction Amendments to the US Constitution that had been
ratified following the Civil War. "Colored men should work and ag-
itate for the possession of the ballot," Trotter insisted. He was developing a keener sense of politics, and the potential power of the
Negroes voting as a bloc. "We mean to throw the Negro vote to the
side which will give us the most for it," said another in his group.

The local league would remain Trotter's, but in the summer of
1905 he and Du Bois created a national organization they called
the Niagara Movement. Unable to find a hotel in Buffalo, New
York, to accommodate the initial gathering in mid-July, Du Bois
crossed into Canada and lined up rooms in Fort Erie, Ontario.
In confidential mailings they had invited fifty-nine Negroes from
eighteen states to attend a conference to form "a permanent national forward movement." Trotter had insisted the new group be
exclusively Negro—no white members, and "no white man . . . can
pay expenses." He believed firmly Booker T. Washington was un-
dermined and beholden to a fault to his white financial backers. He
did not want to risk the new movement's independence by relying
on support from whites, however well intended that support might
be. Trotter might advocate fiercely for integration and equality in
all areas of civic life and in access to public institutions, but he

considered it unwise and, to use a favored term, "unmanly" not
to have Negroes in charge when it came to advancing their civil
rights.

Twenty-nine of the invitees managed to make the inaugural
meeting. Traveling from disparate regions of the country, they
were unified in their calls for a more radical, activist approach to
civil rights, revealing that anti-Washington sentiment had spread
beyond Boston and Trotter. Delegates came from Rhode Island,
Pennsylvania, Ohio, New York, Kansas, Illinois, Iowa, Minnesota,
Washington, DC, and also from the southern states of Virginia,
Maryland, Tennessee, and Georgia. Joining Trotter from Massachusetts were five other delegates, including Clement G. Morgan,
his attorney in the Boston Riot case. The group selected Du Bois as
its leader, naming him general secretary. Trotter was made chairman of the powerful Press Committee. Trotter and Du Bois wrote
up a "Declaration of Principles," a radical document that reads as
if it were written (or rewritten) a half-century later during the civil
rights protests of the 1960s. They declared that "any discrimination based simply on race or color is barbarous," and then asserted
a succinct prescription to end that oppression. "Persistent manly
agitation is the way to liberty." They went on to demand equality with the white man in education, suffrage, economic opportunity, and civil rights—and were not done until taking direct aim at
Washington. "We refuse to allow the impression to remain that the
Negro-American assents to inferiority, is submissive under oppression and apologetic before insults." Looking over the declaration,
Trotter was satisfied with a statement that challenged the status
quo (Washington) but also aimed higher and served as a blueprint
for taking on white society at large.

The first year the Niagara Movement grew to 170 members in
thirty-four states, as its founders pursued a strategy of top-down
growth establishing local chapters. They pushed for new recruits
and distributed materials broadcasting the organization's goals
and civil rights ideology. Their work fostered public awareness but
also further alarmed Washington and his supporters. Washington
regularly sent spies to infiltrate and monitor the Niagara Movement and Trotter's Suffrage League, additionally hiring a Boston

detective agency to tail the editor and report back the daily movements of him and Deenie between their home and the *Guardian*'s downtown office at 3 Tremont Row. Washington had the Negro newspapers under his control step up the war of words with "Trotter's gang." Trotter was called "a crazy jail bird" in one such paper; "this toad," in another; and a third editorialized that he "take something for his mental malady lest it become chronic—perhaps fatal." In his private correspondence, Washington unleashed his own enmity about the *"Guardian*'s evil work" and the man behind it. Trotter "is so utterly wanting in truth or honor," he wrote in a long rant sent to one of his loyal Boston supporters, Francis J. Garrison— the same "Franky" Garrison, youngest son of the abolitionist, who during the Civil War had corresponded with James Trotter. Monroe Trotter might have revered William Lloyd Garrison, but the son grew up to prefer Washington's civil rights philosophy. Francis Garrison even shared with the Negro leader a copy of one of James Trotter's Civil War letters that included comments about unequal treatment in pay and promotions. Washington thanked Garrison for sending it to him, saying the senior Trotter's letter "throws a good deal of light upon the queer make-up of his son."

Washington did not limit his remarks to discussing Trotter. Writing to the editor of the *New York Age* a few months after the Niagara Movement's first meeting, he had choice words about W. E. B. Du Bois, whom he said, "in his new role of an agitator is fast making a fool of himself," was "following in the wake of a crazy man like Trotter." Washington had his press office secretly prepare a lengthy brief for the *Age* to use as the basis of an editorial denouncing Trotter and the new movement. It was an extended smear of what they called "Trotterism." Washington wanted the newspaper to warn against Trotter's brand of activism and his "criminal and riotous record and disposition," and to put readers on notice that "in the future we shall hold to a strict account those who have respect for Trotter and Trotterism." But the truth was Trotter's radicalism—such as it was—only applied in the context of his time. He was no anarchist, subversive, or revolutionary— whereas plenty in early 1900s America were seeking to upend the political and social order. Trotter was actually a patriot; he wanted black citizens to have the same political, economic, and social rights as whites. Nothing more. He was asserting, demanding, and agitating for civil rights now, not later—all of which seemed radical only in contrast to Washington's philosophy of accommodation. That was Trotterism.

—7—

The Moviemaker:
1908–1913

On the evening of Thursday, April 23, 1896, New Yorkers filled one of the largest vaudeville theaters in the city, Koster and Bial's Music Hall on Broadway and 34th Street. They were there to witness cinematic history, the debut of a machine that could project a motion picture onto a giant screen. And what they saw was mesmerizing—a series of shorts that included two blondes dancing with umbrellas; a roaring surf breaking on the coastline; a comic boxing match between a tall, skinny fighter and a short, fat one; and, lastly, the enchanting dancer Annabelle Whitford Moore, moving about in a serpentine fashion in a flowing white gown. The films, according to the *New York Times*, "were all wonderfully real and singularly exhilarating."

The audience, cheering frequently, found itself rubbernecking between the action on the screen and the alien-looking contraption sitting in the center of the balcony—a box with two turrets sticking out and two oblong holes in the front. The machine was covered in blue velvet brocade and made a loud buzzing sound as it threw bright light onto a white screen. Edison's Vitascope, as it was called, after its inventor Thomas A. Edison, was not the first mechanism of its kind. Others in America and Europe were creating similar devices to replace the Kinetoscope that, though popular, could only be used by one person at a time to watch a film through a peephole. But Edison's was the first public use of a large-screen projector to its fullest effect—inside a spacious and darkened theater before paying audiences swept away by all the emotion and sensory overload from the oversize moving pictures.

The new projector opened the floodgates in the film industry. Vaudeville stages, retrofitted quickly with big screens, offered a way for movies to be shown far and wide without delay. Technology continued to advance rapidly, with new and better projectors appearing seemingly overnight, the way computer and cell phone technology was constantly enhanced a century later. Edison, for example, developed a new model within just a couple of years of the Vitascope's debut. Then, in June 1905, while D. W. Griffith was casting about for theater work in San Francisco, a businessman in Pittsburgh converted a storefront into a movie house. To brand it, he combined the price of admission—a nickel—with the Greek word for theater—*odeon*—and came up with the term *nickelodeon*. It marked the beginning of an entirely new venue, independent of theatrical stages, to showcase the collection of shorts that made up the moving picture programs. By the end of 1907 nearly five thousand nickelodeons were in business—filled on a weekly basis by more than sixteen million patrons.

The nickelodeon phenomenon occurred at a pace mirroring the speed at which so much else was stirring at the turn of the century. New technologies, rapid industrialization, waves of immigration, and swelling urban ghettos combined to create a remarkable social upheaval, peopled by revolutionaries, anarchists, labor activists, and captains of industry. The old mentality of frugality, practicality, and Puritanism was fast being replaced by the pursuit of pleasure, fueled by the new abundance of goods that a first generation of advertising copywriters hustled relentlessly to consumers. Breakthroughs in the film industry came at just the opportune time. "The motion-picture shows fit the new high-volume, low-price entertainment calculus perfectly," one social historian noted later.

The new medium also played into a timeless human reaction to the new and unknown—fear. Although most films produced in the 1890s seemed safe—about a news event, sports, or travel destination—the occasional sex and violence on-screen quickly became flashpoints in the public conversation. Suddenly the cinema was a new front line for the nation's moral police already busy monitoring the evils of vaudeville and any other staged dramas, dime novels, and published materials sent through the mails. And the spread of nickelodeons simply accelerated that concern, as the demand for new product steered filmmakers away from news and nonfiction "actualities" and into the increasingly popular realm of comedies and melodramas. These entertainments were seen as hotbeds of "urban vice," worlds of visual illusion that tempted children into a life of delinquency and crime. The long list of putative cinematic vulgarity included a scene shown the same month Edison's Vitascope was unveiled at a Broadway theater: the first-ever screen kiss—the lip engagement of a middle-aged couple at the climax of a short film. While some critics marveled at the realism only a motion picture could attain, many condemned the kiss as crude and disgusting. People were simply afraid of a motion picture's sway over captive and vulnerable viewers seated in a darkened theater, as if a spell might result from the intense connection between the audience and actors moving electronically about the big screen. It was the kind of hyperworry that would accompany every new media technology during the century to come—television, computers, videocassette recorders, cell phones, and the myriad handheld media devices of the twenty-first century.

No public figure during this time embodied vice-busting fever more than did a Civil War veteran, originally from Connecticut, named Anthony Comstock. By the time the film industry began expanding, he had already been monitoring morality for a long time. In 1873, as head of the New York Society for the Suppression of Vice, Comstock lobbied Congress to grant him federal authority to inspect the mail as part of his war against moral depravity. The federal law became known as the Comstock Act, and it criminalized just about anything people like Comstock judged obscene, providing penalties of up to ten years in prison for using the US mails to send "any article or thing intended or adapted for any indecent or immoral use."

Large-bodied and sporting groomed muttonchops, as a public figure Comstock commanded attention for himself and his crusade.

He staged raids and released annual reports documenting his successes stamping out evil—877,412 pieces of alleged "obscene" material by 1900, for example. In 1905 the writer George Bernard Shaw, told one of his plays had been removed from the New York Public Library, coined the term "Comstockery" as a synonym for *censorship*. The deck was certainly stacked in Comstock's favor. His powers flourished at a time when the First Amendment provided far weaker protection for free speech and expression than it did decades later. At the time, constitutional coverage was limited generally to mainstream political activity, not extending to the arts, culture, or virtually anything to do with human anatomy. For example, Comstock would target Margaret Sanger for years, considering her birth control materials criminally obscene.

If Comstock was the individual embodiment of censoring power at its most muscular, the city of Boston was its geographic center. In the nineteenth century, the city's Watch and Ward Society, dedicated to "the protection of the family life in New England," was a WASP bastion governed by the Peabodys, Cabots, and Lowells. In its first year, 1878, the group succeeded in having the poet Walt Whitman's *Leaves of Grass* banned. In the early 1900s, the words "bitch" and "bastard" in one stage play were replaced with "dame" and "buzzard"; and in another show, Isadora Duncan's interpretive Grecian dances caused a scandal because her legs were bare. The phrase "banned in Boston" entered the vernacular during the mayoral tenure of James Michael Curley, the self-styled protector of civic virtue. Elected to a first term in 1913, Curley became far more of a civil authoritarian than civil libertarian. Stage plays that had runs in New York City or Chicago were often not allowed within his city's limits. When it came to books, during his four nonconsecutive terms as mayor Curley would ban the works of Ernest Hemingway, John Dos Passos, and H. G. Wells. Nor did he limit his broad powers of censorship to morality; he curbed political expression as well. In his first term, 1914–1918, amid mounting concerns about national security, he sent a monitor to a meeting of local socialists, warning that if anyone spoke ill of the "country, the President or the flag" he would block the group's future meetings.

The legal muscle Curley flexed as culture czar was drawn from a state law that had been codified on May 5, 1908, when the Massachusetts Legislature adopted Chapter 494 of the Revised Laws. The statute gave Boston's mayors broad powers to license the city's theaters, "upon such terms and conditions as he deems reasonable." Key to the censoring power was the law's second section, which allowed the Boston mayor to suspend a theater's license if he and the police commissioner found "any part of the show obscene or immoral or tends to injure the morals of the community and is not eliminated at the request of the mayor."

The film industry got rolling during this apex of morals regulation, and laws like the one in Boston, originally adopted with stage shows in mind, began to be interpreted expansively to include the new medium of moving pictures. In 1911, Pennsylvania became the first state to create a state film censorship board to handle motion pictures exclusively, and to prohibit "films that were deemed to be indecent, incite crime or otherwise corrupt public morals." Massachusetts did not follow suit at the state level, relying instead on local regulation; it was the Boston law of 1908 that would come to have special relevance to the likes of William Monroe Trotter and David Wark Griffith as it applied to one film in particular.

The evidence is sketchy for when D. W. Griffith first viewed a movie. Some have reported it happened in the late 1890s while he was in Chicago with a touring theatrical company. Griffith himself claimed it wasn't until 1907, the year he was preoccupied with writing plays—although he added he couldn't be sure. Either way, he did recall that that first movie was "some boreful affair . . . silly, tiresome, inexcusable. It was in no way worth while." Beyond his own revulsion, though, he made two key observations. The first was how many viewers the movie had attracted. "The great interest the audience evinced impressed me," he said. The second went to his talents, as he perceived them. "My thinking was that I could write far better scenarios than were being shown, and that the acting of the pictures could be improved."

After his play *A Fool and a Girl* bombed in the fall of 1907, Griffith and his wife, Linda, returned to New York City. He was broke and despondent. One or more friends suggested he try finding work at one of the new studios that were working frantically to meet the exploding demand for nickelodeon movies. In the Bronx, for example, Thomas Edison had built a studio that resembled an airplane hangar, constructed solely for the making of one-reelers. Meanwhile, on the Lower East Side, another growing film company had rented a rundown mansion at 11 East Fourteenth Street to house its offices, wardrobe, property room, cutting room, and a studio made from the former ballroom. This firm was known as Biograph, short for the American Mutoscope and Biograph Company. Despite the popularity of the new medium, Griffith preened as a stuck-up stage actor who saw moving pictures as crude and pedestrian, and thought that to appear in one would be shameful and damaging professionally. Even after he rose to prominence as a director, he continued to display snobbishness about filmmaking in its earliest days. He hated when interviewers called what he produced "movies," as if the word—in use since at least 1902—was an epithet. In 1916, when a reporter recapped his career and began asking about his transition into "the movies," Griffith quickly interrupted: "And then came the *photoplay*." Eventually, of course, he lost this contest over terminology—the movies were the movies. Even so, for the longest time he insisted on using "photoplay" as the proper term to distinguish the technically and aesthetically accomplished works he created from earlier "movies" of lesser quality.

The failed playwright was desperate for work at a time when, providentially, the nature of movie employment provided cover of sorts, making it easier to give it a try without word's necessarily getting around. In these early silent short films, names of actors and screenwriters were not credited at the end, nor were they included in publicity material used to promote the movie. Snootiness aside, he could get started anonymously. So, beginning in December 1907, D. W. Griffith crossed over into the world of motion pictures, taking acting jobs at both the Edison and Biograph film companies, for which he earned between three and five dollars per day. "Reduced to a state of hardupshipness," he said, "I gladly accepted work as an extra with the Biograph Company." By midwinter he was working mostly for Biograph, and by June had appeared in more than a dozen films. At this time, the company was churning out one-reelers as fast as possible.

During his first months at Biograph, Griffith forged a friendship with a cameraman from Boston named G. W. "Billy" Bitzer, who was just a year his junior. It was a relationship that would prove to have career-long consequences for both. At Biograph, Bitzer had an up-close perspective on Griffith the actor, and right away he saw that the camera did not lie and, in fact, only magnified what Griffith's middling track record in the theater had shown—his ungainly height and a stiffness that projected awkwardness rather than physical naturalness. Griffith "seemed to have three or four arms instead of the usual two," Bitzer recalled. "He acted with so many gestures because . . . that has been his stage style in costume dramas with Nance O'Neil and other stars of the theatre." While filming Griffith's second film for Biograph, Bitzer was aghast by the extra's overacting in the role of a bartender: "I asked him if he was trying to get me fired, or wasn't he aware his mugging was taking the action away from the lead. He confided that a friend had told him that was the way to act in pictures." Griffith promised not to do it again.

Griffith also confided in Bitzer that he wasn't as interested in acting, except for the money, as he was in writing for the movies. Plus, curious now about filmmaking itself, he wanted some insight about the director's work. "He asked my advice about directing," Bitzer wrote later, and so the cameraman bluntly told Griffith to not even think about it. "I couldn't see how a man who wasn't a passable actor could direct a flock of geese." But the ever-ambitious Griffith was indeed thinking about both screenwriting and directing. He began submitting scripts—called scenarios—for which Biograph paid him up to $15. The first one he sold was about a Jewish pawnbroker who comes to the rescue of a girl and her sick mother on the verge of eviction from their slum apartment. The ten-minute story, titled *Old Isaacs the Pawnbroker*, was filmed in March 1908. Griffith played two parts in it, as a charity worker and a doctor. Bitzer was the cinematographer, and the director was the only director working for Biograph at the time, Wallace McCutcheon. In short order, McCutcheon bought six more of Griffith's scripts.

Then, in June, Griffith stepped behind the camera and got his directorial start—at thirty-three and just over a year removed from his disastrous stab at playwriting. The first movie he made was about a girl taken from her parents by gypsies and then rescued by some boys. He filmed it in Connecticut in two days at a cost of $65. His wife played the distraught mother, and the silent drama, titled *The Adventures of Dollie*, opened in July at a nickelodeon in Union Square, a few blocks away from the Biograph studio on East Fourteenth Street. It quickly became the company's top box office earner. By that time, Griffith had already directed a handful of other one-reelers, and when Wallace McCutcheon fell ill, the company offered him a full-time directing slot. The contract provided Griffith with financial security, paying him $50 a week. He began working at a breakneck pace, filming on average two one-reelers weekly.

Griffith was on his way. His timing for making a career change was fortuitous—amid surging demand for product—and, even better, he discovered he was pretty good at making movies. It turned out his occasional work in vaudeville a few years prior now helped him. Vaudeville variety shows featured playlets that were usually compressed, stripped-down versions of either full-length classical plays or hefty literary works. By acting in vaudeville and writing playlets, Griffith had obtained experience in seeing and shaping a mini-drama out of a much longer story. The Biograph one-reeler scenarios required the same elements, whether the story was original or an adaptation—the ability to establish character, plot, climax, and an ending in a silent film that had a running time of only fifteen minutes or less. Moreover, the year 1908, when Griffith began directing movies, was still the dawn of the film age, meaning filmmaking was a virtual blank slate. His goal to be an artist and not a hack—an ambition long frustrated on the stage—could be redirected to the new medium. Nothing stood in the way—no hidebound traditions or suffocating formalities. He could elevate the form and take moviemaking to new heights. The sky was the limit.

Displaying, like his father, a lifelong tendency toward hype, Griffith would later habitually overstate his contributions to cinema. "I think that I was the first person to use the close-up," Griffith once told a reporter, speaking of the camera technique used to bring inescapable focus and intimacy to a particular object or character. "I'm not sure of this, because it might have been used in foreign pictures without my knowledge. But I do remember that when I suggested it to the cameraman, he refused to take it. He claimed that you couldn't take pictures of people's faces and leave their bodies out. My answer was a trip to the art gallery. I saw plenty of paintings without bodies attached. I won the argument." Griffith's statement was untrue. The close-up had been used in a number of one-reelers by the time he had begun directing at Biograph, most notably in the 1903 one-reeler *The Great Train Robbery*, directed by another giant in early American cinema, Edwin S. Porter. The twelve-minute cowboy drama featured a close-up of the outlaw leader shooting a gun at the camera (and thus at the audience). But for Griffith, taking credit not only added to notches on his innovator's gun belt, it burnished his image as an aesthete. He was the film director attuned to the fine arts, the one who visited art galleries to discover new ideas for his work.

Griffith would also muse with reporters about how rich he might be if, less the artist and more the businessman, he'd had the savvy to patent techniques he vainly (and erroneously) laid claim to. "Suppose I had patented the fade-out," he posed to another reporter, referring to the method to conclude a scene, also known as a dissolve. "I would be drawing at least a million a year in royalties." The technique has actually been credited to Georges Méliès, a French filmmaker, but that fact did not get in Griffith's way. Indeed, he rambled on to the reporters as if he were an expert in US patent law, describing various other cinematic techniques—some of which might have been subject to patent protection, while others were not—with the implication being D. W. Griffith had invented every one of them.

"You can patent anything derived from a mechanical device," Griffith explained during his tutorial. He said, for example, "I might have patented the shooting of scenes through gauze. Sometimes it is called soft focus. They used to call it 'mist photography.'" He said that technique would have qualified as a "mechanical device," one he should have had the acumen to protect. "The revenue from the gauze appliance would have been good for another million easily each year." Not that every filmic device could be patented. "It wouldn't have been possible to patent the flashback or the close-up," he said. They were different—*"ideas* of technique"— and the federal patent law, which provided the holder sole control over use, did not cover ideas. Even so, boasted Griffith, "with the other two devices under patent, I wouldn't have needed them. I would have my millions, anyway."

The bluster was certainly unnecessary. Griffith's lasting impact on cinema, beginning with his apprenticeship at Biograph, proved considerable and historic in every possible way, from on-the-ground filmmaking methodology to high-minded foresight of the expanding possibilities for moving pictures. Griffith may not have invented the close-up, but he brought a new sophistication to its use. Early movie directors had used the technique simply as a way to vary images; Edwin S. Porter, for instance, paid little heed to a scene's composition and was seemingly unaware of the images' emotional value. But Griffith, according to film historians, was all about composition and discovered that beyond its functional purpose, the close-up "brought the audience closer to his characters, increasing their involvement with them, and, most importantly, signaled for that audience that it was in those emotions that a great deal of the substance of his films reside."

In terms of the potential impact of film, Griffith was visionary. "The future of the picture is a topic that usually makes me go into ecstasies," he would tell reporters. His remarks about film made him sound like a technology geek on the cusp of the Digital Age. "Just think of what it would mean as an educational force," he told one journalist. To another he prophesized, "Imagine a public library of the near future. There will be long rows of boxes of pillars, properly classified and indexed, of course. At each box a push button and before each box a seat. Suppose you wish to 'read up' on a certain episode in Napoleon's life. Instead of consulting all the authorities, wading laboriously through a host of books . . . you will merely seat yourself at a properly adjusted window, in a scientifically prepared room, press the button, and actually see what happened."

D. W. Griffith on the set, directing.
COURTESY OF THE MUSEUM OF MODERN ART, NEW YORK.

The five years Griffith worked for Biograph saw him evolve from apprentice to skilled filmmaker, a training period during which he developed a narrative language that took a simplistic entertainment form and lifted it artistically. He became a master of editing to drive a storyline and to build suspense, especially by using quick cuts during the chase or rescue scenes for which he became known. He began composing final shots in ways that deepened a film's impact, depending on whether the ending was happy or sad. Happy endings tended to consist of close-ups of the lovers or family members; sad endings involved longer shots showing barren surroundings that emphasized the defeat the characters had suffered. The attentively framed final shots came to be called "lyrical postscripts."

In terms of structure, Griffith often organized a film around a central image, coming back to that image—and altering the look of it slightly—as a way to reveal the passage of time and emotion. By the end of his first year, 1908, he discovered the power of a circular structure, where he used the same location and composition for the opening and closing shots of a film. Griffith relied on this strategy to great effect in a 1909 one-reel adaptation of a Frank Norris novel. Titled *A Corner of Wheat*, the movie featured a greedy stockbroker who corners the market on wheat to drive up the price of bread so that it is unaffordable to the starving masses. In the climax to the twelve-minute drama, the stockbroker comes to a shocking end—he gets stuck in a pit that suddenly fills with wheat and he suffocates. Griffith used expansive shots of the same harvesting wheat fields in Kansas to open and conclude the film—a device that, as one critic later noted, embodied "the endless cycle of nature which overrides the individual destinies in the film."

In short order, Griffith drew on his repertory experience in theater to assemble a quasi company for his film work. He recruited actresses, actors, and other talent to work regularly with him. The former stage actor Henry B. Walthall joined Griffith in 1909; he played an associate of the greedy "Wheat King" in *A Corner of Wheat*. Unsurprisingly, early on at Biograph Griffith often cast his wife, Linda, but their marriage faltered and the couple would split in 1911. He was impressed instantly with a young Canadian actress named Gladys Smith who, using the professional name Mary Pickford, became one of his regulars beginning in 1909. Within a couple of years, Pickford's friends, sisters Dorothy and Lillian Gish, had joined Griffith's stable, along with Mae Marsh and Blanche Sweet—all of whom became stars under his direction. With his own acting experience to draw on, he was adept at demonstrating for his players what he was after in a particular scene. Beyond the actors, Griffith developed an affinity with one of the company's scenarists, a former newspaper reporter from Pennsylvania named Frank E. Woods. Griffith came to rely on Woods for many of the scenarios he filmed.

Then there was the cameraman Billy Bitzer. During the Biograph years, Griffith certainly had a sense he was part of something
big and new—a media revolution—as he waxed poetic about the
power of film and invented groundbreaking filmic devices, all the
while embracing his role as artist and innovator. But for Bitzer,
the grueling Biograph pace of making several one-reelers a week
constituted an assembly line full of logistical challenges that needed
solutions. He did not see what they were doing as high art. "I did
not pay much attention, as to what the Trades, etc., were lauding
as marvelous achievements, both Directorial, or Photographic,"
Bitzer said later. "What I'm trying to say is this. It was just in a
day's work. If Mr. Griffith yearned for some effect, whether a Fade
Out or what not, without reference as to whether it had been done
eons ago by Méliès, I tried one way or another to produce what he
would like."

Starting in 1910 Griffith headed to California to escape the East
Coast winters for a climate more suitable for continuous filming,
and it was in California the next winter that, for a Civil War story
titled *The Battle*, he filmed the first-ever large-scale battle sequence. For Biograph he would go on to make a dozen movies set
during the Civil War and Reconstruction—all infused with his own
romantic view of the Lost Cause and rural Kentucky values.

In other films for that company Griffith revealed a social con-
science. The struggle between the hungry masses and the vulgar
"Wheat King" he had dramatized in *A Corner of Wheat*, for example, was cited as the modern equivalent of a "sermon in stone,"
with one critic calling it a "film editorial with a punch." In response
to the praise, Griffith said he preferred films with impact. "I like
to work on those pictures, and some day I hope to get back to them
and do some really big things, for I think that some of the greatest
work of the motion picture is to be done along those lines." That
comment showed Griffith to be serious-minded and wanting to be
taken seriously. He was not a mere entertainer but an auteur who
cared about history and science.

In addition to the Civil War stories, in which he had a special
interest, Griffith directed westerns, comedies, gangster, suspense,

and Indian and maritime one-reelers, along with the mini-adaptations of literary classics. He was nothing short of a work-aholic, sometimes making five films in six days. In five years he made some 490 films, singularly responsible for Biograph's finan-cial success and for the company's decision to abandon the studio in a converted mansion in lower Manhattan for a new state-of-the-art studio it had built in the Bronx on 175th Street. Griffith shared in the prosperity. His 1911 contract included provisions that earned him an estimated $3,000 a month (or about $73,000 in 2014 dol-lars), enabling him to buy up land in California for investment pur-poses and, on a smaller symbolic scale, pay $1,250 in cash the next year for a new Packard touring car.

He had grown in skill and confidence. But tensions—artistic and financial—mounted in his relationship with the company's owners. Griffith was emerging as a master of his craft—finally fulfilling an ambition to be somebody—but few knew, save for industry insid-ers. Not only did the names of the director and cast go unmen-tioned in one-reelers, but Biograph's contracts imposed a virtual gag order on its star director, barring him from discussing his work in public. "The party," read the contracts, referring to him, "further agrees not to furnish information to other parties or to grant inter-views to representatives of newspapers or other publications." The clause ensured he'd not get the public notice he felt he deserved.

His bosses made half-hearted attempts to appease him. When Griffith headed to California for the 1913 season of moviemaking, they finally gave permission for him and his main actors to appear in a picture's publicity and promotion. But they did not budge on the custom of having no names or credit in the actual films. Grif-fith, who turned thirty-eight in January, also failed in his effort to use his stature inside the company as leverage to win a contract provision he'd long sought—a 10 percent cut of Biograph's profits. Continuing to work under the terms of his 1911 deal, he felt un-derappreciated, a nameless cog in a film factory producing formula films.

Griffith wanted more, for himself and his movies. The standard short format of one-reelers had become increasingly like a straight-jacket, undermining his ability to tell a story. Getting his bosses to approve the making of his first two-reel film in 1910 had felt like the proverbial fight against City Hall. And he was fully aware that others, especially foreign directors, were spreading their wings, producing longer and more innovative films for which a new name had to be created—the *feature* film. The Biograph bosses were stubbornly shortsighted, stuck in their success with shorts and unable to appreciate what Griffith envisioned for narrative filmmaking. Then in April 1913 Griffith became aware of the New York premiere on Broadway of *Quo Vadis?*, an eight-reel Italian film with a running time of two hours. The historical drama, set in Rome during the rule of the emperor Nero and featuring elaborate sets with hundreds of actors, was a box office hit. In its review, the *New York Times* hailed *Quo Vadis?* as "the most ambitious photo drama that has yet been seen here."

It was as if a gauntlet had been issued. Insatiably ambitious, Griffith was determined to make his mark in American motion picture production. Lillian Gish, for one, seemed to detect this during filming that very same month of *The Mothering Heart*, a story about a pregnant woman whose husband abandons her. Griffith insisted he needed two reels—almost 30 minutes—to fully convey the drama. "With two reels to work with," Gish said later, "Mr. Griffith could concentrate more on the effects that he wanted and exercise more subtlety in his direction." Griffith was demanding more and more leverage as a filmmaker, a course that was soon incompatible with his station in the Biograph system.

8

Fame Rising, Fame Falling, Circa 1913

The Niagara Movement that Monroe Trotter and W. E. B. Du Bois had founded in 1905 continued to meet for the next several years and chip away at Booker T. Washington, helping to initiate a gradual decline in his influence and signal an eventual changing of the guard in the civil rights movement. But by 1908 the organization had, for all practical purposes, failed. One big reason was financial; the founders had trouble collecting basic dues from members (even Trotter was in arrears at one point) and, as a matter of policy, would not pursue donations from liberal whites sympathetic to their cause. The other big reason was Trotter who, despite his roles as founder and national committee chairman, was not a particularly adept organization man. He had difficulty working within structures where he was not in charge—a trait that seemed to become more pronounced as his stature grew. "He is a good locomotive, but not a wise engineer," a Niagara member said of Trotter, "a good fighter, but a poor general." "He acted as though only he had all the answers," one biographer observed. "He admitted no mistakes or weaknesses." The Niagara Movement, Du Bois said, "began to suffer internal strain from the dynamic personality of Trotter and my inexperience with organizations." Although Du Bois tried repeatedly to reconcile the two, Trotter feuded with Clement G. Morgan, secretary of the local Massachusetts chapter, and the breach in their relationship never repaired. Relations between even Trotter and Du Bois grew frosty to the point of mistrust, as the latter ended up siding with his close friend Morgan. In the growing divide, critics complained Trotter's "bumptiousness and egotism, and eagerness for notoriety" sabotaged their efforts, while Trotter and his supporters rejected the carping as evidence of the critics' lack of "boldness, daring, and risk-all-to-win courage." Either way, Trotter alienated many who were natural allies. He did not attend the Niagara Movement's winter meeting held in Cleveland in 1908, after members had rebuffed his demand beforehand that Du Bois not serve as presiding officer.

By the decade's end Trotter was faltering in what had been his gutsy and determined role as prime mover in the reshaping of the civil rights movement, to the degree that when the next and most lasting race organization first began to coalesce, he was, in effect, shunned. On May 31, 1909, about three hundred men and women concerned about the "status of the Negro" gathered in New York City. The conference followed a call to action issued three months earlier—on Lincoln's birthday, February 12—reflecting outrage and horror at a bloody two-day riot that had taken place in Lincoln's hometown of Springfield, Illinois, the previous summer. Federal troops—nearly four thousand—had been required to end the confrontation that had seen eight Negroes killed, dozens of others injured, and Negroes fleeing the northern city en masse. The progressive journalist Oswald Garrison Villard—no fan of Trotter's—wrote the manifesto that became known as "The Call" and published it in his *New York Evening Post* and weekly magazine the *Nation*. It was signed by sixty notable figures. Most were white—among them educator John Dewey, social reformer Jane Addams, journalists Lincoln Steffens and Ray Stannard Baker, and best-selling writer William Dean Howells. Seven were black—and they included Du Bois and Ida B. Wells.

Trotter was not asked to sign the document. Nor was he invited to attend the conference. He showed up anyway, and over the course of the next two days was outspoken, offering proposals and delivering a talk at least one listener liked. "Excitement bubbled over," wrote Wells, "and warm speeches were made by William Monroe Trotter." But Villard, the conference's main organizer and sponsor, was not impressed. He found Trotter unbearable and ensured the defeat of the uninvited guest's resolutions, while insisting that Trotter not be named to the select "Committee of Forty" charged with creating the structure and mission for what became christened the National Association for the Advancement of Colored People (NAACP).

Du Bois and other radicals from the floundering, cash-poor Niagara Movement cast their lot with the new entity that, while biracial, was dominated by white liberals. But Monroe Trotter was persona non grata; he never became a player in what was in part an outgrowth of his decade-long agitation and advocacy journalism— the most important and powerful civil rights organization of the twentieth century.

Back in California in the winter of 1913, D. W. Griffith began a new season of cranking out films for Biograph at his characteristic breakneck pace—nine in January and February alone. But now, in his sixth year with the company, he was also determined to follow his storytelling instincts and began mixing into his output films that ran longer than one reel and were ever more sophisticated. A benefit of working three thousand miles away from Biograph's executives in New York City was that he had the independence to go off in ways he might not have been able to were he under the close scrutiny of studio bosses.

By spring he dispatched his crew to the nearby San Fernando Valley to construct his most ambitious and costly set yet—one that did not consist simply of flat storefronts to create an illusion, but was tantamount to a genuine western frontier town. Griffith wanted a three-dimensional set so that he could position cameras to film different angles, and then, when editing, be able to cut back and forth from the various perspectives to ramp up the action. The movie he shot there, *The Battle of Elderbush Gulch*, showed off his maturing technical skills and his ability to interweave several story

lines. The narrative threads included two sisters (one portrayed by
Mae Marsh); their uncle and his family; a young couple and their
missing baby (the wife played by Lillian Gish); and a local Indian
tribe and the killing of the chief's son. The story climaxes with an
Indian attack on the town, an action-packed assault that appears
fatal for the sisters and other town folk until the US Cavalry, sabers
drawn and pistols firing, come riding on horseback to the rescue.
Griffith used high-angle shots to capture the chaos and terror of the
siege—as Indians storm the town, women and children run in all
directions, some men fire wildly at the attackers—and do so to such
great effect that when the film opened one viewer exclaimed, "The
audience went into a frenzy of delight. 'Come on, come on, come on!'
they called. That troop of cavalry hit those Indians with the impact
of a huge sea swell bursting over a rock."

Griffith was well on his way transitioning permanently to long-
form narrative, making films of greater length that allowed for
deeper storytelling and continued experimentation with filmmaking technique. "Often we got a picture completed in two days," he
would say about his early work at Biograph. "Now we take that
much time to decide on the costumes we will use." By year's end,
a corner suite at the luxurious Alexandria Hotel in downtown Los
Angeles became his home as he began his most ambitious period
of filmmaking yet. The daily routines he followed while making
shorts were adapted to the new and longer filmmaking timetables:
waking by 7:30 a.m. and starting the day with a quick workout—
maybe a swim but frequently boxing. In California he often boxed
with Charles "Kid" McCoy, a slightly built light heavyweight known
for his toughness and corkscrew punch. McCoy also appeared in
films and had become friends not only with Griffith but many other
Hollywood figures, including Charlie Chaplin. After taking his
morning exercise Griffith headed over to his studio, where he met
with assistants to go over the day's work and only then had break-
fast. By midmorning he was on the set for rehearsals with actors
and the actual filming. "He is always busy," said a reporter who
followed him around one day at work. "Work is his recreation."

While filming *The Battle of Elderbush Gulch*, his crews began work nearby constructing an even larger and costlier set—a

walled-in Biblical city supposedly situated in the hill country of Judea—for use in what became a four-reel, hour-long feature film titled *Judith of Bethulia*. The movie was an adaptation of a stage drama about a widow named Judith who devises a scheme to save her city of Bethulia from a conquering king. Griffith had first learned about the play while a member of Nance O'Neil's company in 1905. In addition to building his new set, the director rented the grounds of a sprawling estate south of Los Angeles. He planned to use both locations to shoot exterior action and then return to New York City to film the interiors at the new studio Biograph had built in the Bronx. The movie would be his response to all the commotion that spring in New York City created by the groundbreaking Italian epic *Quo Vadis?* Going into production, his actors and crew fed off Griffith's obvious thrill at being able to put art on the screen.

But by the time the sets were completed and Griffith was ready to start filming early that summer, he had already busted the film's $18,000 budget. Biograph executives were alarmed at the rate at which he was spending money. They urged Griffith to turn off the spigot, and even sent an accountant to Los Angeles to monitor expenses. He was allowed to make the movie, but tensions between the director and his bosses continued to escalate. When he returned to New York to finish *Judith*, he likely sensed this picture might be his last for Biograph—the working conditions had become suffocating and his bosses' attitudes about film were so shortsighted. The extent of his troubles came as a surprise, though. Unbeknownst to him, the company's executives had actually come around on the issue of a movie's length. They had recognized, finally, the trend toward longer films, and had decided to steer the company's future more fully in that direction. The news should have delighted Griffith and would have, were it not for the surprising part: Biograph's new course did not revolve around him or properly acknowledge his talents.

For Monroe Trotter, staking out the role as freelance agitator—begun in his early challenge to Booker T. Washington and by 1910 evident in his distancing from the NAACP—came with a price. "I am still running *The Guardian*," he updated a college friend at one point, and then included this cold truth: "though hardly for a livelihood." The editor's financial struggles began right after his cofounding of the newspaper in 1901, when he had tapped into his inheritance to launch the paper. When George Forbes quit in late 1903, Trotter needed to raise $200 to pay a debt to the paper's printer. Then, to keep the paper afloat, he continued to draw on his family's assets. He and Deenie moved out of their marital homestead at 97 Sawyer Avenue in Dorchester in 1904, and for the next decade collected rental income from their tenant, a city official. The couple moved in with Trotter's widowed mother, Virginia, and lived with her at various addresses around Boston. To raise money in 1908, Trotter sold the two-family house at 67–69 Sawyer Avenue—valued at $5,200—he had bought soon after marrying, and Boston city records reflect the refinancing and sale of other Trotter properties year after year.

Trotter spent a fair amount of his time soliciting donations from the same small circle of supporters and friends. "Will you help to the extent of your ability?" he asked more than once of George A. Towns, an educator and civil rights activist from Atlanta. "*The Guardian* is really a philanthropic enterprise," he said in the pitch letter he signed, "Yours for freedom and a free press." Once, he asked a dentist friend to expedite payment of a $2 bill owed the paper for an advertisement of the man's dental practice: "I am desperate in my effort to make *The Guardian* meet its expenses this week," Trotter said. The editor occasionally sought to explain to his readers why he regularly required their financial aid. The *Guardian*, in his view, was not a business bent on earning profits, but "a public work for equal rights and freedom." Trotter's devotion to maintaining the paper's purity, however, seemed to ensure ongoing money troubles. Not only was he determined never to be beholden to white money men or nonsympathizers who voiced a racial ideology contrary to his, he adopted a policy of refusing paid advertisements from retailers for hair straighteners, skin lighteners, and alcohol (his abhorrence of drinking dating back to his Harvard days).

His business practices hurt him, a state of affairs his enemy Booker T. Washington certainly gloated about. While funneling funds to newspapers opposed to Boston's radical editor, Washington seemed giddy as he told a friend how Trotter "has to go about on Saturdays with his hat in his hand to collect money in order to get his paper out of the printing office. In the meantime, he has lost every cent of property he owned, and is in a miserable condition financially." Meanwhile, Trotter's friends were steadfast in their concern. Some worried that if the *Guardian* ever failed, white opponents would seize upon its demise as proof "of the unfitness of the Negro race for twentieth century civilization." Others suggested Trotter soften his hard-line positions or, as some would have it, his zealotry—both ideologically and in his business practices—as a way to open new avenues of financial support. But he would have none of it. "I had rather have people criticize my poverty than get money against my principles." He also took comfort in citing the editor of the *Liberator*, his personal hero William Lloyd Garrison. "Garrison's paper never paid, never supported his family," he pointed out. The "pass-the-hat" system of running the *Guardian* was simply following in Garrison's footsteps. "The pass-the-hat method was Garrison's and by it brought about the abolition of slavery." If it worked for Garrison, Trotter said, it would work for him as a means to stay fiercely independent in the fight against Jim Crow and racism in the twentieth century. "I feel as Garrison felt that I must promote oral agitation and organization in order to do the cause and the race any good."

While scraping by, Trotter took the time to sponsor dances or sell tickets to weekend "*Guardian* Picnics" as one way to supplement the paper's coffers. He also kept moving the paper's office, always in search of a better deal, and to cut costs once even sublet half of his space: "I have let half my office to a younger lawyer, of Hebrew extraction, being more liberal than my landlord who would not let an office to a Jew," he told a friend. In 1910 he managed to move into an office at 21 Cornhill Street—a congested little street only two blocks long that connected bustling Scollay Square to Washington Street. It was the very address Garrison, decades earlier, had used for a time as editor of the *Liberator*—and almost immediately Trotter proudly streamed his new and distinguished address across the top of each issue of the *Guardian*: "21 Cornhill, Garrison's Old Stand."

Helping him in every way was his wife, Geraldine Pindell Trotter. The affluent life she may have envisioned when she married him in 1899—back when Trotter had aspired to a career in international finance—had become a kind of genteel poverty once Trotter founded the *Guardian* and became a civil rights crusader, yet Deenie stepped up during her husband's brief incarceration in late 1903 to run the office's daily operations, and from then on served, in effect, as equal partner. She brought order to the chaos of the *Guardian*'s business operations, working "mostly on obtaining advertising and circulation," said one employee. Deenie, said a coworker, had a "very deep interest in his public career," and, on occasion, spoke publicly about her own special interests, whether women's suffrage or fund-raising for St. Monica's Home for elderly Negro women. The couple never had children, and she would tell people they did not want any, that they were too busy.

Although Trotter started the *Guardian* to go after Booker T. Washington, the newspaper was always much more than that, whether listing social notes to running feature stories showcasing the achievements of local Negroes. Most important, he documented the backsliding in civil rights and pointedly reported the spread of Jim Crow, lynchings, and racial violence to the North. In the summer of 1908, for example, he ran a front-page story about the shooting of a young Negro man in New York City. The piece quoted the shooter, a white man from New Jersey, on why he did it: "I didn't like the nasty, decisive way the fellow looked at me." In another issue, Trotter published an article about the attempted lynching of a Negro in Long Island, New York. His crusading came in smaller ways, too, what one writer called "the quiet work": taking up individual causes as pet projects, "when anyone complained of discrimination in restaurants, employment or the civil service. Many a boy or girl in Boston obtained a first job through his efforts."

The grind of newspaper publishing was the couple's life. Because of the many nighttime meetings they either ran or attended, the Trotters' workday often began late in the morning. They would commute to the newspaper's office on Cornhill Street around the corner from the city's famed Newspaper Row, a bustling stretch of Washington Street where the seven major dailies were headquartered and where, in addition to selling morning and afternoon papers, news blackboards and bulletin boards on the street were kept updated with the latest breaking news. The mustachioed Trotter was a regular fixture downtown, hustling about from interview to meeting, always carrying a bundle of *Guardians* under one arm and never wearing an overcoat, even in the dead of winter. He favored dark suits, often well worn and wrinkled, and a black derby hat; and as he entered his late thirties, he filled out into a stocky build. He often ate lunch at the U-shaped counter at Waldorf Lunch on Washington Street, a new kind of inexpensive lunchroom appearing in cities around the country to meet the quick-service needs of businessmen. When work got especially hectic, he—and Deenie— sometimes bunked at the office. The week's typical pace was such that it built daily into a manic peak Friday nights, when they were on deadline to close the weekly paper for publication the next day, and then came Saturday and a big exhale of relief, when the couple gathered with employees for "get-togethers in *The Guardian* office in a relaxed atmosphere with the paper having come out." Generally solemn in his everyday demeanor, Trotter revealed a playful side at the dances he sponsored as fund-raisers. "More dancing than any one else," one friend said, recalling the sight of Trotter on the floor, coattails flying, his legs slightly bowed, and "pretty well liked by the ladies." The Trotters were known to their co-workers and friends as virtually inseparable and devoted to each other.

The other firm commitment was to his alma mater, Harvard. Over the years Trotter stayed in touch with a handful of friends, notably the political scientist John Fairlie; attended class of 1895 reunions; and regularly contributed to alumni reports. For his fifteenth reunion in 1910, he made sure to update fellow alums about his newspaper career and raison d'être: "The paper is published in the same building and on the same floor where Garrison published the *Liberator* before the Rebellion, and where the first edition of 'Uncle Tom's Cabin' was published, whence comes inspiration to battle against the undoing of the results of their effort."

When D. W. Griffith returned to New York City in July 1913 to complete *Judith of Bethulia*, he learned some surprising news:

Biograph had a new deal with two prominent Broadway producers, Klaw and Erlanger, to turn nine of their most successful stage
dramas into movies running up to five reels in length. The insult
to Griffith was not just that he was kept in the dark about the contract, which was signed during the spring, but that he was not in
line to direct any of the films. In a bid to soften the blow, he was
told he could supervise new directors that were hired.

Things were getting worse. For his part, Griffith was convinced
he deserved far better—for starters, a new deal for himself to replace the outdated 1911 contract still in play, a new contract giving him a piece of the profits, more control, and independence. But
instead of his receiving more, he was told he could expect less. No
longer would he be in charge of budgets and expenses for his projects, for example. Then came a final affront: while incoming junior
directors would be taking the helm of the feature films that he felt
most skilled to make, Biograph wanted him to resume pumping
out one-reelers. In just about every way, Griffith now saw himself
treated as a replaceable part in an assembly line rather than the
principal source of the company's box office success. "Once Griffith
declined this humiliating proposition," one writer noted, "his career with Biograph came abruptly to an end."

Over the course of several weeks that fall, he talked to other
production companies, created his own business entity called the
David W. Griffith Corporation, and began working with his attorney to make sure the public at large knew what the film world
knew already—that he was somebody. He cut ties officially with
Biograph on October 1 and, about ten weeks later, his attorney
arranged for a full-page advertisement to run in the *New York Dramatic Mirror*, a must-read entertainment publication. The ad announced that Griffith was not just any director, but a giant in the
burgeoning film industry, responsible for "revolutionizing motion
picture drama and founding the modern technique of the art." For
two years starting in 1908, it said, he had "personally directed all
Biograph motion pictures," and thereafter supervised all Biograph
productions while directing "the more important features until Oct.
1, 1913." The print equivalent of a paid infomercial then listed 151
films he had directed, and credited Griffith as being responsible for

inventing a whole host of filmmaking techniques, from the close-up to the long panoramic shot to the fade-out. Many of the claims were exaggerations or outright falsehoods, and making them in such a grand, splashy way seemed unnecessary, given Griffith's true contributions to the craft, but it was as if the spurned director could not help himself, wanting to be certain the public understood his stature, even if Biograph did not, and channeling his father's knack for hyperbole and self-promotion to make sure he accomplished that.

On the heels of the ad anointing him a film master, Griffith followed up with greater press availability, and soon stories appeared cementing his fame. In the January 3, 1914, issue of *Moving Picture World*, a fawning reporter described Griffith as "the man who in whole truth may be said to have done more than any other to advance and bring us now to the day of the universal recognition of the greatness of the screen." The next week, a reporter for *Dramatic World* seemed determined to top that, writing, "Were film progress to be measures in miles, the steps of advancement contributed by David W. Griffith placed end to end would gird the earth."

Puffery aside, there was no question that Griffith now had marquee status as a movie director. He also had a new and promising deal with Harry Aitken, a film entrepreneur originally from Wisconsin whose company, Reliance-Majestic, had studios in Los Angeles and Yonkers, New York. Griffith's deal called for a relatively modest weekly salary of $300, but he could live with that because the contract included two provisions of utmost importance to him: stock in the company and a mandate to make at least two longer films a year as part of his output. In his five years at Biograph he had directed, acted, or written scenarios for about 490 films. Starting out at Reliance-Majestic, he went to work quickly producing a handful of short, minor films to make the company some fast money in early 1914.

He was free now to think big, however, and so even before shooting the short "potboilers," as he called them, he had begun casting about for ideas for the grand epic he was aching to make. He asked his friend Frank E. Woods, the writer at Biograph whose scenarios he had always favored, whether he knew of anything suitable. Woods replied he did have something Griffith should take a look at,

D. W. Griffith with Dorothy and Lillian Gish. The Gish sisters began
acting in D. W.'s productions at the Biograph Studios in 1912.
COURTESY OF WIKIMEDIA COMMONS.

a project on which Woods had worked on and off for the past couple of years but that had become stalled, ending up in what later
became called the film industry's "development hell." The idea was
a film adaptation of Dixon's *The Clansman*, the best-selling 1905
novel that, in its stage version, had proven a huge financial success. "It hit me big," Griffith said. "I hoped at once that it could be
done, for the story of the South had been absorbed into my very
being." Right away Griffith became obsessed, imagining the panoramic outdoor action, ranging from Civil War battle scenes to the
Ku Klux Klan riding to the rescue. "I could just see these Klansmen in a movie with their white robes flying," he said later. Early
in January 1914 when talking to a reporter, the director already
seemed to know what he was going to do, aware he was onto something big, a story matching his ambition to create a film of unprecedented impact. "I'll wager that in a year from now," Griffith said,

"even you with some knowledge of the film business and rosy expectation of what is likely to happen, will come to me and admit that you are absolutely surprised, that you had not the faintest expectation of the things that will have happened during the coming year." He did not give the journalist any specifics, any hint of his plan to adapt Dixon's novel about the Civil War and Reconstruction. It was all a big tease from a confident, eager D. W. Griffith, and so the interview piece concluded with this line to readers: "Let's watch 1914 and see."

From about 1910 on, Trotter was overshadowed by the new NAACP and by W. E. B. Du Bois, its highest-ranking Negro and, as director of publications and research, editor of its influential quarterly journal, the *Crisis*. Trotter's attitude toward the NAACP ran hot and cold. He acknowledged its growing popular support and access to money from white progressives who, in the wake of the Springfield Riot of 1908, had begun shunning Booker T. Washington in the belief that civil and political rights trumped economic self-improvement. But for a variety of reasons, Trotter would remain deeply ambivalent—in sync often with the NAACP's goals, but at odds over the nature of its activism and who was in charge. For its first few years the NAACP was more of a think tank than an organization engaged in active and pointed protests for racial equality. In addition, the association, especially its founder and treasurer Oswald Garrison Villard, initially coddled Washington in the hopes of bringing the power of his brand to bear. Villard eventually broke with Washington and got behind Du Bois as the rising Negro star, but that did not change Trotter's view that the NAACP was too conciliatory and never radical enough. Then there was internal politics; the Boston branch, the first to be established, was, from its start in 1911, run by men with whom Trotter continually tangled, whether Clement G. Morgan or Francis J. Garrison, a former Bookerite.

Finally, there was that matter of white control of the NAACP. Du Bois might appreciate the possibilities of the new group's interracial makeup, seeing the potential in the merger of Negroes' civil rights concerns with white reformers' broader social causes in education, housing, and economic opportunity, but Trotter always wanted Negroes to be in charge. The first president of the NAACP was white—the distinguished lawyer Moorfield Storey from Boston, someone with whom Trotter mostly got along. The two men worked hand in hand to defeat a bill before the state legislature in 1911 that would have outlawed interracial marriage in Massachusetts. But the comity ultimately did not matter; Trotter believed having whites leading the way implied Negroes were inferior and incapable.

Trotter was indeed correct in detecting paternalism—as well as racism, however latent—in the NAACP's leadership ranks. No better proof was an astonishingly candid letter written in 1913 by one of the founders of the Boston branch, a white attorney named Albert E. Pillsbury to Archibald Grimké, who by then had become head of the NAACP branch in Washington, DC. In the letter Pillsbury disclosed his racism, something he "feels in my bones," something embedded in him despite his commitment to civil rights. It was a bias, he said, that "cannot be stopped." Further, he said, it infected "the best of us" and made hypocrites of any white who claimed to be progressive. Pillsbury then cited none other than Villard as Exhibit A in his argument. "Would Villard himself invite Negroes, though gentlemen and scholars, to his house or his clubs, or invoke general association with them exactly as though they were white men? No, he would not. He could not. I am obliged to confess that the same is true of myself. If we attempted any such thing we should be in trouble with our friends, our wives and even our cooks, and it would not be long before we too would be socially ostracized."

The private admission powerfully captured a social and political reality between Negro activists and their white progressive friends during this period—a dynamic that kept Monroe Trotter always wary. It was a condition the poet Langston Hughes later addressed in his poem "To Certain Intellectuals." He wrote:

> *You are no friend of mine.*
> *For I am poor,*
> *Black,*

Ignorant and slow,—
You yourself
Have told me, so—
No friend of mine.

Instead, Trotter stayed at arm's length, creating his own political action organizations to rival and often run parallel to the NAACP—organizations, he noted proudly, "of colored people, and for the colored people and led by the colored people." But he had lost momentum in terms of national stature, even if he always managed to maintain a base of ardent supporters scattered around the country—including Ida B. Wells in Chicago, another rugged individualist who had rubbed Villard and other NAACP leaders the wrong way. He was determined to make his mark, crusading in the *Guardian* and pushing his way into national affairs. For example, he threw himself in a big way behind the rising political fortunes of the president of Princeton University, Woodrow Wilson. It began in 1910 when Wilson, a Democrat, ran for governor of New Jersey. Trotter, showing the same independent streak in politics as his father in eschewing blind loyalty to the Republican Party, steered his organization into backing Wilson's gubernatorial run. "We realize all democrats are not our enemies nor are all republicans friends," one of Trotter's associates wrote Wilson during his campaign, adding in another letter that the Trotter faction saw the candidate as a friend of "our people." Despite his southern Virginia roots, Wilson impressed Trotter with his erudition, forward-looking ideas, and general sense of fairness; when he won, Trotter was thrilled. "I congratulate you on your election with such a magnificent majority," he wrote on November 10, 1910. But with praise came a subtle warning of concern, likely reflecting the fact that Wilson had thus far avoided being pinned down on the Negro question. "We trust that no word or action of yours on the great question of equal rights will ever cause us to regret our stand," Trotter told the new governor of New Jersey.

That inkling of apprehension notwithstanding, the *Guardian* editor immediately appraised Wilson as having the right stuff for a presidential run. Trotter's political action league promised the new governor that it would "continue organizing for the campaign of 1912." But unknown to Trotter, he and every Negro backing Wilson had an unlikely ally in wanting to see the southerner elected the nation's twenty-eighth president. The ally was an old friend of Wilson's, dating back to their days as graduate students at Johns Hopkins University, a friend who had become a best-selling novelist and playwright. "I've been rooting for you on my recent tour of the South launching my new play," cheered Thomas Dixon in a letter written a few weeks after Wilson's victory in New Jersey. "Let me know if I can help you to the White House. I'd like to see you there."

That Trotter and Dixon—polar extremes on race matters—both began working for Wilson's presidential bid reflected the almost desperate wish Trotter had for Wilson to be something he was not. Wilson remained carefully evasive on the Negro question; he curried favor with Negro voters but promised nothing. In fact, throughout his gubernatorial run he never gave explicit support for racial equality, instead uttering bland assurances he would be a leader to all of his constituents. It was wordplay Trotter and others chose to interpret hopefully, if not naively. To Trotter, Wilson was the lesser of evils in presidential options: Theodore Roosevelt, William Howard Taft, Eugene Debs—all unpalatable. Republicans Roosevelt and Taft had been endlessly disappointing, whether in their ties to Booker T. Washington or their failure to act forcefully against lynching and the spread of Jim Crow. Debs's socialism was too radical compared to the classical belief in economics Trotter had learned at Harvard. New to electoral politics, Wilson represented a fresh start. Trotter and Trotterites were hoping the gubernatorial candidate's campaign pledge to be fair to all Americans was his way of promising presidential advocacy for civil rights and racial equality.

They were dead wrong. Dixon, the rabid racist, had it right about his fellow southerner and classmate. Wilson might prove an activist in exercising executive power to rein in the excesses of big business and the barons of industry, but not so in matters of race. "Woodrow Wilson was in essence a white supremacist," a Wilson biographer wrote, "holding a romantic view of the courtesy and graciousness of the ante-bellum southern plantation owners, as well as uncritically the post-Reconstruction South that arranged to keep black Americans in their place." Following his decisive win in November 1912, which made him the first Democratic president in the twentieth century, Wilson watched passively as southern Democrats in Congress began filing a series of discriminatory bills, such as to outlaw interracial marriage, allow residential segregation in Washington, DC, and block Negroes from serving in the army or navy. Wilson also permitted his cabinet appointees, many of whom were southerners, to step up segregation in federal workplaces.

Trotter grew alarmed, as did Du Bois, Villard, and other leaders of the NAACP. In one instance, the *Guardian* editor wrote to the new president to question his appointment of a Texan, "a man of the far South where color prejudice is so lamentably strong" as postmaster general. The post office, Trotter reminded Wilson, was the federal department in which "most of the Colored government employees work." Nine months into Wilson's first term, Trotter managed to secure an appointment with the president to convey mounting concerns about Jim Crow in the national government. Joining him that mild November 1913 day at the White House were Wells and four other Trotterites from his National Independent Political League. They brought an antisegregation petition, containing twenty thousand signatures of concerned citizens from thirty-six states, as well as a flow chart Deenie had drawn by hand, showing the spread of Jim Crow in various federal departments. Trotter read the president a prepared statement. The meeting lasted thirty-five minutes. It was the same day Wilson's staff was scrambling to ensure delivery to dignitaries throughout the city of about four hundred invitations to the White House wedding of the president's daughter that was less than three weeks away. If the president was distracted, he did not show it, and Trotter left the cordial encounter encouraged. He voiced confidence the president will "seek a solution to the problem."

But instead of improving, Jim Crow in federal government continued to worsen as Wilson began his second year in office. Trotter followed up, sending letters and a telegram to the president. They went unanswered. He began to fume—had he been played for a chump? Wilson, meanwhile, was always quick to reply to notes received from well-wisher Tom Dixon. In one he reassured the meddlesome author, who was concerned that segregation in the federal workplace might be slowed, "I do not think you know what is going on down here." Wilson described "a plan of concentration" to put Negroes "all together" in the workplace so as not to "mix the two races."

Other exchanges were obsequious. Dixon reported, for example, he was going to dedicate his next novel to Woodrow Wilson, "our first Southern-born president since Lincoln," and Wilson replied that the news "went straight to my heart." When 1914 dawned, the president offered only a cold shoulder to Trotter's urgent insistence on being heard, but happily accepted New Year's greetings from his racist writer friend. "My best wishes for a great year for your administration in 1914!" Dixon began in his January 1 note, sent from his office in New York City. He reiterated his devotion, telling Wilson, "I have watched with loving pride your brilliant conduct."

Dixon penned his note on personalized stationery. The letterhead listed titles of three of his works—two novels and a play, all starring the Ku Klux Klan and dramatizing the suffering of whites during Reconstruction. One was *The Clansman*. When he wrote the president, he had some good news he could have shared: he was in talks exploring an adaptation of *The Clansman* into the new medium of film. The talks were going well, and might mean working with a leading Hollywood filmmaker by the name of David Wark Griffith. But Dixon saved the information for another day, instead staying on task of buttering up Wilson. "I have an abiding faith that you will write your name with Washington and Jefferson as one of the great creative forces in the development of our Republic." The president was flattered. Your "generous letter," he told Dixon, "warmed the cockles of my heart."

PART III

A Birth of a Nation

Film still of Ben Cameron (Henry Walthall)
leading a Civil War charge on foot

— 9 —

1914

Walking across the set one spring afternoon, D. W. Griffith leaned in to Lillian Gish and whispered that he had some news he wanted to share with her at the end of the day. He and his company were in the middle of making a film at the Sunset Boulevard studio of Reliance-Majestic. Based on the life of John Howard Payne, a nineteenth-century American actor who wrote the lyrics for the 1823 "Home! Sweet Home!," and titled after the famous song, the drama was a five-reeler, nearly an hour long. But Griffith was bubbling with excitement about a new project, bigger than *Home Sweet Home*, bigger than anything they'd ever attempted. That evening he told Gish and other principal actors—Mae Marsh, Miriam Cooper, Walter Long, and Henry Walthall, to name a few—that he and Harry Aitken had acquired the rights to Dixon's *The Clansman*. The negotiations had been touch and go: Dixon first had demanded $25,000 (or nearly $600,000 in 2014 dollars), then lowered his price to $10,000, which was still too costly, given that Griffith had informed Aitken he expected to need up to twelve reels and a budget of about $40,000 to do the story justice. Fortunately, Dixon ended up coming down further and agreed to take a payment of $2,500 along with a 25 percent stake in the movie's profits. The director excitedly explained to his actors that he aimed to use the novel as a vehicle "to tell the truth about the War between the States." He said, "It hasn't been told accurately in history books. Only the winning side in the war ever gets to tell its story." Rehearsals and set construction would begin on his fresh acquisition, Griffith told the company, as soon as they finished up *Home Sweet Home* and made one more film.

The story for the new movie was indeed big—the Civil War and Reconstruction—and would be largely built around two families: the Stonemans from the North, and the Camerons from the South. The epic would track their intersecting lives during and after the war, dramatizing their suffering and losses and, through the families' experiences, convey the suffering of a nation. It would re-create history on a grand scale—with Civil War battles, the assassination of President Lincoln, and the rise of the Ku Klux Klan as saviors of the southern tradition. Interestingly, the home state chosen for the Camerons was South Carolina: where, forty-nine years earlier, Griffith's father had been stationed as the invading Union army— an occupying force that included James T. Trotter of the 55th Massachusetts Infantry—closed in to help end the Civil War.

The actors and crew could certainly detect that Griffith was inspired. Cinematographer Billy Bitzer noticed as much in his talks and brainstorming sessions. The new project, Bitzer would recall, changed Griffith's "Director Personality entirely." In the past, Bitzer said, Griffith called the start of a new picture "as grinding out another sausage." In contrast, "This one was all eagerness; he acted like here we have something worthwhile." Griffith talked constantly about the project, conducting his own research about the Civil War and its battles, making plans for large-scale action sequences and for the chase scenes he had become so good at staging. He would bring to bear all these skills, finally, on a story with gravitas. "We had had all sorts of runs-to-the-rescue in pictures and horse operas—East one week; West the next," Griffith said. "Now I could see a chance to do this ride-to-the-rescue on a grand scale. Instead of saving one poor little Nell of the plains, this ride would be to save a nation."

The theme of the film would be that Negro freedom and voting rights during Reconstruction had been an awful mistake carrying tragic consequences, a view that by 1914 was actually de rigueur, validated by Professor William A. Dunning of Columbia University, whose revisionist history favored white southerners and portrayed Negroes as inferior, ignorant, and incapable of the honest exercise of political rights and power. Dunning influenced slews of budding historians in what became known as the "Tragic Era" and the "Dunningite" analysis of Reconstruction. At about the same time, anatomical studies—purporting to show Negro brain inferiority—were conducted by the likes of Dr. Robert Bennett Bean of the University of Michigan. For someone like Griffith, the academic brand was mighty impressive. No matter that the Dunning historiography and the Bean brain study would later be debunked—their findings bolstered conventional wisdom at that time, a trend of anti-Negro thought accepted widely in history, law, science, and politics that had gained traction after Reconstruction and became entrenched during the early twentieth century. To Griffith, such studies confirmed what he already knew about Negro inferiority—knowledge gained not from a laboratory, but from growing up in Kentucky and listening to his father, the raconteur of the Old South, carry on.

Griffith also had his own acute sense of history (and his place in it). Looking ahead to a 1915 release, he knew the year itself practically guaranteed buzz for his tour de force—the fiftieth anniversary of the end of the Civil War. He needed to get going, and so starting in May, while finishing other films, he began rehearsing his actors and casting the new movie's many roles. He ordered sets built on an empty lot he leased adjacent to his studio on Sunset Boulevard, near where Hollywood Boulevard began, while more sets were constructed on the grounds of his studio. They included an entire southern street, a house for the Camerons, and the interior of Ford's Theatre. Griffith scouted for locations in Los Angeles and the valleys beyond for his battle scenes.

While Griffith was fully engaged in preproduction to make his movie about an old war, escalating tensions in Europe were about to erupt into a major new one. On Sunday, June 28, 1914, a Serbian nationalist assassinated Archduke Franz Ferdinand, the heir to the Austro-Hungarian empire, and his wife. Exactly one month later Austria-Hungary declared war on Serbia. Nations began picking sides—Germany, Britain, France, and Russia entering the conflict. The Great War had begun. Initially in the United States

it was called the European War, President Woodrow Wilson telling
the American people on August 19, "The United States must be
neutral in fact as well as in name during these days that are to
try men's souls." As the international crisis unfolded, Griffith commenced shooting in California, choosing a start date that revealed
again his sense of history and knack for timing: July 4.

While Griffith and Harry Aitken were negotiating to buy the film
rights to Dixon's *The Clansman*, a senator from Georgia named
Hoke Smith introduced a bill in Congress to create a federal motion picture commission. Filed in March, the legislation would
grant commissioners the power to license all films, the goal being
to replace the hodge-podge of state and local entities with a single,
national system.

The bill eventually failed, but it reflected a surge in censorship
fever rooted in widespread worry about the growing film industry
and advances in film technology. Being so relatively new, this medium was the new front in culture wars that pitted tastemakers
and the nation's morality police against those seeking the protection and expansion of civil liberties. Indeed, 1914 saw no letup in
Anthony Comstock's crusade against indecency. He became apo-
plectic when, the same month as Smith's bill was filed, Margaret
Sanger debuted a journal called *The Woman Rebel*, which advo-
cated for sex education and a woman's right to family planning and
abortion. Comstock moved instantly to ban the material as "obscene, lewd, lascivious," in violation of his namesake law of 1873,
and then saw to it that Sanger was indicted in federal court on
nine criminal charges. Following her initial court appearances in
The People v. Margaret Sanger, the feminist editor fled to England
under the name Bertha Watson.

The controversy that would arise around film involved a different context and different facts but shared a common conflict—that
is, the tension between the government's police powers regarding
public safety (and morality) and the right to free speech and expression. Where, in a democracy, does the line get drawn? Until
the filing of Smith's bill, the burgeoning film industry had been
able to ward off control of its products by Congress. Industry

leaders had backed a form of self-regulation by private citizens, resulting in the founding of the National Board of Censorship in 1909. Based in New York City, the board comprised representatives from the motion picture industry as well as from education, church, and women's groups. Upon viewing a film, the organization could recommend cuts or outright censorship. It was essentially a volunteer group with no legal authority. Most filmmakers and movie exhibitors bought into the idea, agreeing to the board's pre-release "review" as a lesser evil than an official government agency legally empowered to rule what motion pictures got shown.

Even so, local censorship boards, created decades earlier in response to moral panic that "dirty" novels, magazines, and stage plays led to criminal and immoral conduct, had turned to passing judgment on films. Three states formed new film boards. Pennsylvania was the first, with passage of 1911 legislation; followed by Ohio and Kansas, both in 1913. In the face of these censorship trends, and now with the filing of federal legislation in March 1914, one leading film company began plotting a legal challenge. The Mutual Film Corporation, which made, coproduced, and distributed movies and newsreels nationwide, decided to pick a fight in Ohio for what would be the first constitutional challenge to a film censorship law.

D. W. Griffith and Harry Aitken had more than a passing interest in these developments. They were in business with Mutual Film; the company had helped to finance and coproduce a number of Reliance-Majestic's films, including *Home Sweet Home*. Moreover, given his aspiration for film as art, Griffith was all for a constitutional showdown that embraced the civil liberties argument Mutual Film's lawyers were planning to use as the core of its lawsuit. "There should be no censorship," he asserted. "The movies should have the same freedom of speech as the press." The company's lawyers had, in fact, made the tactical decision to focus on its newsreels—and not film dramas—as the basis for its challenge, a legal strategy banking on the reality that the nation's press, more than any other form of expression, historically had won the strongest constitutional protection. To get under way, Mutual Film flouted the Ohio censorship law by refusing to submit its newsreels to the state board for review. It then filed its legal challenge in federal court in the northern district of Ohio, a first step that by early 1915 would see the case for free speech go all the way up the legal ladder to the highest court in the land, the United States Supreme Court.

In his approach to casting, D. W. Griffith once said, "I would rather spend a week coaching a young, inexperienced girl who knows nothing of picture acting but who looks the part, than spend ten minutes reading 'business' to an experienced stage actress." The comment captured Griffith's belief that performing onstage was of little help when it came to acting in a movie—that the kind of exaggerated gestures and movement necessary for a stage actor to project to a large theatrical audience would come across as overacting to the point of comic if done on camera. "How many of them," he said, referring to stage actors, "make you believe they are real human beings? No, they 'act,' that is, they use a lot of gestures and make a lot of sounds such as are never seen or heard anywhere else."

During his years making films for Biograph, the director had discovered and made stars of many young actresses—including Lillian Gish, Mae Marsh, and Margaret Cooper. Of the three, only Gish had previously acted on the stage as a child actress before going to work in film for Griffith, and all were still so very young when he hired them in 1914 to play leading roles in his new project. Marsh and Cooper were teenagers, aged eighteen and nineteen, respectively, while Gish was only twenty when Griffith began shooting in July. Gish played Elsie Stoneman, of the northern Stonemans; her character has two brothers in the movie, and her father, Austin, is an abolitionist and Radical Republican. Marsh and Cooper played the southern Cameron sisters—Flora (the younger) and Margaret (the older)—who have three brothers. Their father, Dr. Cameron, and mother preside over the family's cotton plantation.

During production, Griffith, as was his custom, never worked from a script or finished scenario, even as this production was unprecedented in length and complexity. "I carry the whole scheme and the smallest detail of production in my mind," he once said. His scheme for the epic was to break it into two parts. The first part, set in the Camerons' South Carolina, was to establish the friendship between the two families amid the grandeur of the Old South. Love stories get going, with more than one romance blossoming between the Cameron and Stoneman offspring. Then comes the Civil War. The families are torn apart. The five boys, enlisting for their respective sides, battle one another; some die. The war ends and Lincoln is assassinated. The movie's second part then dramatizes the putative horrors of the Reconstruction era. Austin Stoneman, the Radical Republican congressman from the North, is charged with overseeing implementation of Negro equality in South Carolina. It was a process in which, in real life, James T. Trotter had played a brief role before returning to Massachusetts. In Griffith's retelling, Stoneman and the Radical Republicans are bent on punishing the fallen South, and Negroes take over the South Carolina legislature by stuffing ballot boxes. Additionally, several main Negro characters are treated as villains: one, a northern mulatto named Silas Lynch, a protégé of Austin Stoneman; the other, a former slave simply called Gus. Both are portrayed as hypersexed, predatory men who lust after white women. Silas Lynch eyes his boss's daughter, Elsie, while Gus is determined to marry Flora Cameron. The Ku Klux Klan then enters the story in time for a climactic rescue. The hooded heroes restore order to the chaos of Reconstruction, cleansing South Carolina of the corrupt alliance between northern carpetbaggers and free Negroes. The families are reconciled, and so, too, is a nation. "The birth of a nation began," Griffith said in one interview at the time, "with the Ku Klux Klans, and we have shown that." In another he said, "The Klan at that time was needed. It served a purpose."

Over the summer months and into the fall, Griffith pushed his cast and crew. The reenactment of General Ulysses S. Grant and the Union army's assault on Petersburg, Virginia, in 1865, which led to the South's surrender, was the largest-scaled and most sophisticated war scene ever filmed. It took three days. For the battlefield, the filmmaker leased acres of open, rolling countryside not far from his studio. Using different angles and camera placements, he and cinematographer Bitzer magically made their several hundred extras appear on-screen as two armies numbering

A film still from *The Birth of a Nation*.
COURTESY OF THE MUSEUM OF MODERN ART, NEW YORK.

several thousand soldiers. A commanding presence at over six feet tall, the director stood atop a tower with a megaphone, shouting instructions to his massive cast (Griffith devised a system of flags and mirrors to communicate when to start and stop the action to actors too far away to hear him). "The battle of Petersburg, with the armies in the trenches, yes, that is the biggest," said Griffith when asked which scene posed the greatest challenge. He listed in second place his staging of the November 1864 burning of Atlanta. But throughout the filming, in every scene, especially action ones, he always wanted multiple camera angles so that he had plenty of shots to edit with quick cuts that built tension. There were times when Bitzer stood behind the camera as Griffith had soldiers shooting their rifles in the cinematographer's direction. Smoke bombs the special effects crew had made to simulate cannonballs were detonated right next to Bitzer. To film robed Klansmen galloping on their horses, Griffith and Bitzer raced alongside in a car with a camera mounted on it; at other times, Bitzer climbed down into a trench to film the horses' leaping overhead. Griffith brought the same meticulousness to the smallest moments as well. "The littlest thing," he said, "is the sigh of General Lee as the papers of surrender were signed."

The filmmaker was legendary in working with actors for "his gift of getting quickly in touch with folks," as one observer noted. He was patient and methodical, making sure the camera was positioned just right and then taking a seat in his high-legged director's chair, megaphone by his side and surrounded by his actors, to discuss the scene. He usually solicited the players' interpretations and then had them rehearse over and over again before signaling Bitzer to roll the camera. The scene of John Wilkes Booth's jumping to the stage of Ford's Theatre after shooting President Lincoln was filmed more than fifteen times until the director was satisfied. A reporter once said watching Griffith direct his actors and crew was like watching "a sculptor molding a beautiful statue."

Not surprisingly, given the movie's size and scope, Griffith told Harry Aitken late in the summer, several months before filming was completed, that he had no more money, having already used up the $40,000 budget. Aitken was not happy but came up with another $19,000. Griffith said he needed more. On his own he pieced together a financing plan that included the leading actors' going without paychecks as well as his selling stock in the film. He persuaded the costume and uniform supplier to take a $6,000 stake in the movie: the supplier paid $3,000 in cash and received another $3,000 worth of stock for voiding an outstanding bill. Griffith got Billy Bitzer to invest $7,000 of his own money; then the director set his sights on William Clune, "my big game." Clune, a wealthy impresario, had leased a theater in Los Angeles the previous year and converted it into the West's largest movie palace, Clune's Auditorium. Griffith lobbied Clune aggressively, showing him some early rushes, and walked away with a $15,000 check. In all, the movie would cost $110,000 ($2.6 million in 2014 dollars), the costliest film of its time.

By the time he ended his punishing pace of dawn-to-dusk filming in November 1914, Griffith had more than thirty hours of film—having shot 140,000 feet. Then he began juggling the monumental task of paring down the more than twenty-six miles of film into a cohesive, three-hour drama of twelve reels; writing text for the intertitles used to convey information to the audience, which had to be printed in a shop, filmed, and spliced into the movie; and overseeing the musical score as it was composed to make sure the music matched the image. One of Griffith's many directorial strengths was his attention to the musical score, and for this film he had hired Joseph Carl Breil, a renowned composer of music for stage plays. With Griffith looking over his shoulder, Breil combined classical pieces with original ones to create what one Boston critic would later hail as "wonderful art, this—the marriage of music and spectacle." For some of the major action the composer drew upon such "big music" as Tchaikovsky's 1812 Overture and Wagner's "The Ride of the Valkyries," whereas for other scenes set in the South's plantation era he tapped the obvious choices, such as "Dixie" and "Marching Through Georgia." Breil also created new sounds; there was, for example, the "disturbing, barbaric-sounding tom-tom motif" used for some scenes involving groups of Negroes, and another that became known as the "Klan call." When filming the Klan sequences, Griffith had often let out a whoop to set the action in motion, and Breil later arranged the call for the orchestra to use at key Klan moments in the movie. Together, the director and composer also decided on specific sounds to amplify specific actions—drums, for example, to signal cannon fire or the sound of horses' hooves.

Watching him work, Harry C. Carr, entertainment writer for the *Los Angeles Times*, said, "In these terrible days, at the end of a picture, he will shoot close-ups all morning, arrange music with a professional conductor all afternoon, have financial conferences all the early part of the evening, and write sub-titles all the rest of the night." Throughout, Griffith somehow managed to continue stoking press interest in his new, big thing, as he gave interviews and pontificated on the greatness of film.

"The motion picture, although a growth of only a few years, is boundless in its scope, and endless in its possibilities," he said that fall. "The whole world is a stage."

On the evening of Thursday, May 28, 1914, while D. W. Griffith was planning his adaptation of *The Clansman*, Monroe Trotter settled into a seat in the crowded Grand Army room of the town hall of Brookline, a community bordering Boston. He was there to cover an address a noted doctor was giving to the Brookline Historical Society. The speaker, Dr. Burt G. Wilder, was, in effect, a local boy of accomplishment. Wilder had grown up in Brookline and Newton, had served in the Civil War, and was now a distinguished professor of neurology at Cornell University.

Trotter's interest in reporting on the event for the *Guardian* was a mix of personal and professional. Like Trotter, Wilder attended the First National Negro Conference in June 1909 in New York City, the conference from which grew the NAACP. Although Trotter had showed up uninvited, Wilder had appeared as a scheduled speaker. In his talk, titled "The Negro Brain," Wilder had rebutted the notion, still popular in certain scientific circles, that Negro brains were smaller and thus inferior to Caucasian brains. He had recapped the flawed science used to back up the claim, taking particular aim at the 1906 study by Dr. Robert Bennett Bean of the University of Michigan that had gotten so much public attention, and which Trotter had denounced at the time in both the *Guardian* and private letters, writing to friend at Michigan to condemn the research as junk and even call it "un-American."

To Trotter and other civil rights leaders, such as W. E. B. Du Bois, this was false science with pernicious results, providing so-called proof of Negro inferiority for racists of all stripes—from extreme haters (e.g., Thomas Dixon) to those less so (e.g., D. W. Griffith). Wilder had also reported to the conventioneers the news that earlier in 1909, the Bean study had been discredited and practically ridiculed by Bean's former teacher and mentor, Dr. Franklin P. Mall of Johns Hopkins University, who, first off, revealed Bean had not used a blind sample of brains in his study—a basic, inexcusable mistake—and, second, that when Mall conducted his own blind study of the frontal lobes from Negro and Caucasian brains, he found no discernable differences in their weight, size, or brain power. Mall forcefully concluded that such studies as Bean's were governed less by science than by "a strong personal prejudice." To all of this Wilder, in his address at the New York conference, had said, "Respecting the brains of American Negroes there are known to me no facts, deductions, or arguments that, in my opinion, justify withholding from men of African descent, as such, any civil or political rights or any educational or industrial opportunities that are enjoyed by whites."

The other reason Trotter wanted to cover the Brookline event was closer to the heart. Burt Wilder had known his father, having served as regimental surgeon in the 55th Massachusetts Volunteer Infantry. The doctor's topic for the evening was the 55th, about which he would be sharing his Civil War experiences, and once he began he did not disappoint. For more than an hour Trotter listened as Wilder described the harshness of the regiment's daily life, mostly spent in South Carolina, and the soldiers' valor in combat, specifically mentioning the bravery he had witnessed and the losses suffered in the defeat at Honey Hill. Wilder also discussed the bias Negro soldiers had to put up with, citing the inequities in pay and saying how much he had admired the stand James M. Trotter and his comrades had taken against the Union army's discrimination. "The enlisted men were offered the pay of laborers, they refused to accept it," Wilder said, and then, with emphasis, added, "and served more than a year without a dollar." In this regard, Wilder's lecture likely served as a poignant reminder to Monroe Trotter of his father's strong and uncompromising commitment to civil rights—a refresher beneficial to the editor, given his struggle to keep his newspaper going and stay active in the movement.

"Most of all I need money," Trotter wrote to one of his agents in Washington, DC, in January, urging the collection of monies owed for subscriptions and ads. "There is a real question whether I can survive another week or 2 weeks." To help, his mother took out two loans totaling $460 from the Hub Loan Co. She used several Dorchester properties as collateral and, as a sign of their financial desperation, accepted the usurious interest rate of 18 percent. During Harvard's commencement in June, Trotter ran into a friend from New York to whom he described the *Guardian*'s struggles, and he got a $100 pledge. It was not all about money, though. His family was also going through a rough stretch emotionally. Four of Deenie's relatives, including a close brother, had died from various causes during the past year, and Trotter's grief-stricken wife, writing to a friend in July, worried she might never "feel lighthearted again."

Then there was Woodrow Wilson. Trotter was increasingly frustrated about his inability to get the president's attention. He wanted Wilson to act on the detailed presentation he had made about Jim Crow in federal government during their November 1913 meeting. "May we have your response, and how soon?" he asked in a second letter written since their meeting, in which he included a packet of newspaper clippings about the government's discriminatory practices. One news item—about official action in Arkansas to begin keeping Negro and white mail clerks segregated—included unsolicited advice from Trotter that sounded more like a boss's order to an underling than an exchange with the president of the United States; typing in the margin, Trotter instructed Wilson, "Here is something important to work on." Getting no reply, he fired off a Western Union telegram two weeks later, urging the president "to set free government employees from the bonds of segregation." But all Trotter got back was the cold shoulder, and he was not someone to take lightly his being ignored.

Meanwhile, the NAACP's footprint continued to grow, in contrast to Trotter's political organization, the National Independent Political League, which had no staff and no budget. NAACP membership had doubled during the past twelve months; at the start of 1914 it had nearly three thousand members in twenty-four branches. The monthly circulation of the *Crisis*, the journal edited by W. E. B. Du Bois, now exceeded twenty-seven thousand. Expansion was not without growing pains—and worse, the latent racism of its progressive white leaders. By 1914, Oswald Garrison Villard and Du Bois were in regular conflict, not so much about ideology but governance. Du Bois, who came close to quitting, said no two members were "in closer intellectual agreement on the Negro problem than Mr. Villard and myself." The trouble was, Du Bois said, "Mr. Villard is not democratic. He is used to advising colored men and giving them orders and he simply cannot bring himself to work with one as an equal." For his part, Villard complained in his private letters about Du Bois and Negroes generally, saying at one point that when working with Negroes he often found himself struggling with "their easily hurt feelings . . . truly they are a child race still!" Even NAACP president Moorfield Storey, widely respected for his level-headedness, fell prey to this kind of thinking when he sought to comfort Villard by saying, "The difficulty which you call 'temperamental' in the case of Du Bois sometimes seems to me almost racial." To break the tension, Villard agreed to change leadership roles, from board chairman to the lesser position of treasurer. But the organization's ongoing internal strife stayed the hot chitchat in civil rights circles, gossip that Booker T. Washington, for one, savored. "Villard and Du Bois do not speak to each other," Washington wrote to a supporter in early 1914. "They have been at daggers points for a good many weeks." The men's argument reflected, too, a core leadership conundrum for the NAACP—whether white liberals or Negroes should be in charge. The association's annual report seemed to acknowledge the concern by including a line taken from Monroe Trotter's playbook, one he could have written: For the NAACP to succeed, the report said, "it must be increasingly supported by its colored members."

Certainly the NAACP was proving itself effective in ways small and large. The Boston branch, for example, was just as busy as Trotter in fighting the spread of Jim Crow in its city. "We are now making a very curious fight," reported a local official to the New York headquarters. "There is a color of cloth being sold in Boston called 'niggerhead.' We have said to those stores, 'You have got to take that cloth out or change the name.' Some have taken it out and others are going to change the name." When the lone Negro girl in her high school class was told she could not go on a field trip to the Museum of Fine Arts and would have to wait until a separate trip for Negro students was organized, the branch met with the school's principal, and the girl ended up accompanying her classmates. When a young Negro man, a longtime member of the Boston YMCA, was denied access to the Y's new swimming pool because of his color, the branch appealed to the Y's board, and eventually the color line was erased. In perhaps its most important achievement of the year, the branch persuaded the Boston School Committee in November to drop *Forty Best Old Songs*, a new songbook that had been compiled by the city's music director. Citing the explicit racism in many of the tunes selected for the book, the board was successful in ensuring that the 120,000-odd students in the city's public schools would not be taught to sing such lyrics as, "Now darkies listen to me," or the second stanza, composed in mock dialect, from the original 1848 version of American songwriter Stephen C. Foster's "Oh! Susanna":

> *I jumped aboard de telegraph,*
> *And trabeled down de riber,*
> *De Lectric fluid magnified,*
> *And killed five hundred Nigger.*
> *. . . "Oh! Susanna!"*

Nationally, the NAACP began developing political and legal strategies that became its hallmark in the decades to come. It sought help from supporters elsewhere in the country to be on the lookout for discrimination that might serve as test cases to bring to the courts—whether in education, the workplace, public places and facilities, or housing. In the spring of 1914, for example, the association targeted D. W. Griffith's boyhood hometown of Louisville, Kentucky, to launch one of its constitutional challenges to a residential ordinance enforcing racial boundaries—the kind of residential segregation law that was popping up frequently, especially in urban areas. The Louisville ordinance was signed into law on May 11, and soon after, the NAACP teamed up with a local white real estate agent, Charles Buchanan, who also opposed the ordinance as discriminatory. Together they staged a transaction that would result in litigation: Buchanan arranged for the sale that fall of a house in a white neighborhood to William Warley, a postal clerk and member of the Louisville NAACP branch. From this point the choreographed dispute involved a few ironic twists—because it was Warley, the Negro, who balked, refusing to complete his purchase, citing the race ordinance outlawing his move into a white neighborhood. It fell on the white Buchanan to go to court to sue Warley for breach of contract and to attack the ordinance as unconstitutional. Buchanan was backed by the NAACP and its Legal Bureau; Warley and the ordinance, by the city of Louisville, with its team of white attorneys. By June 1915, the NAACP would exhaust its legal challenge at the state level, when the Kentucky Court of Appeals rejected Buchanan's challenge and upheld the validity of the race-based ordinance. But the adverse ruling did not mean the case would end there; the NAACP appealed to the US Supreme Court.

The growing NAACP also emphasized creation of a strong branch in Washington, DC, to watch for any anti-Negro legislation and to join the protest against Jim Crow in Wilson's administration. Throughout the president's first two years in office, the NAACP had something Trotter did not—open lines of communication into the White House. Villard, in particular, wrote regularly to Wilson to complain about the spread of segregation on his watch. In one, he chided the president for allowing the creation in the US Treasury of a "nigger division" that he deemed cruel and un-American. In another, Villard reported to Wilson that the NAACP had passed a resolution calling on him to end the injustice of "segregation of colored employees in Federal departments." Wilson replied mostly with excuses, bromides, and requests that Villard and the NAACP maintain "a just and cool equipoise" rather than engage in "bitter agitation," asking Villard to appreciate his predicament. "It would be hard to make any one understand the delicacy and difficulty of the situation I find existing here with regard to the colored people," he said. "I want to handle the matter with the greatest possible patience and tact." Another time, the president told Villard the Jim Crow policies protected Negro federal employees: "I honestly thought segregation to be in the interest of the colored people, as exempting them from friction and criticism in the departments." Wilson's lip service aside, the ongoing exchanges in 1913 and 1914 seemed mostly to show a preference on Wilson's part for corresponding with a liberal white man rather than responding to entreaties from a Negro agitator like Monroe Trotter.

Trotter continued to feel miffed about being stonewalled time and again by the current administration. Wasn't he an early supporter dating back to Wilson's first foray into politics in the New Jersey gubernatorial race in 1910? Hadn't he pledged Negro support for Wilson's presidential run when they met face-to-face in July 1912 at the State House in Trenton, New Jersey? ("The governor had us draw our chairs right up around him, and shook hands with great cordiality. When we left he gave me a long handclasp, and used such a pleased tone that I was walking on air.") Hadn't he called out prominent social worker Jane Addams the next month, when she agreed to deliver the second nomination speech for Theodore Roosevelt at the Progressive Party's national convention in Chicago? (Do not do it, Trotter wrote Addams in a hastily composed nighttime telegram, do not "be false to colored race and betray cause equal rights by seconding nomination Roosevelt.") Hadn't their White House meeting the previous fall been a thoroughly respectful affair? Didn't all of this count for something, and didn't Wilson's position now signal a betrayal?

Trotter was not to be denied. He began putting into practice a lesson he had learned long before at Harvard and had tried when looking for job after graduation—to use any and all connections. Prior to his 1913 meeting with the president, Trotter had been in touch with US representative James M. Curley of Massachusetts, but to regain Wilson's attention one year later he undertook a full-court press. He started with James A. Gallivan, a former baseball star at Harvard and newly elected to the congressional seat Curley had vacated once he was elected to his first of four terms as Boston's mayor. In a letter to Gallivan, Trotter explained the Wilson problem: "Last year he told the delegation he would seek a solution. Having waited 11 months, we are entitled to an audience to learn what it is. Not only for the sake of his administration but as a matter of common justice." Two days later, on October 19, Trotter appealed to Andrew J. Peters, a former Massachusetts congressman and, like Trotter, a member of the Harvard Class of 1895. Peters was now working in the Wilson administration as assistant secretary of the US Treasury. "Dear Friend Peters," Trotter began, as he then explained Wilson's failure to grant "a return audience" from the 1913 meeting. "To refuse it is unfair, unjust, discourteous . . . Please get us a date in October." The next week, Trotter called on David I. Walsh, newly elected—with Trotter's support— as Massachusetts' first Irish and first Catholic governor, as well as Thomas C. Thacher, another Massachusetts congressman and also a fellow Harvard alum. To all, Trotter conveyed a sense of urgency about Jim Crow. Well publicized by this time were numerous instances of workplace separation, including separate toilets in the US Treasury and the Interior Department, a practice that Treasury secretary William G. McAdoo defended: "I am not going to argue the justification of the separate toilets orders, beyond saying that it is difficult to disregard certain feelings and sentiments of white people in a matter of this sort." It was not any better outside Washington, DC. Trotter's friend Ida B. Wells was busy fighting the everyday racism she encountered in Chicago. When she went shopping in June at one of the city's best-known stores, Marshall Field & Co., and a sales clerk ignored her, saying, "I don't have to wait on a black 'nigger' like you," Wells got the clerk fired.

Two congressmen, a governor, and an administration official. Trotter reached out to four men of power and all four, in turn, contacted either Wilson or Joseph P. Tumulty, the president's private secretary and key adviser.

"I am decidedly opposed to any condition existing in Washington or elsewhere that could be interpreted as discriminating against our colored population," Governor Walsh wrote Wilson on October 26. Congressman Thacher followed with a note to Tumulty, asking that he arrange for a Trotter-led group "to have a brief interview with the President this week." Of course, the president's plate was already and always full. He might have bumbled, and worse, on civil rights, but he was overseeing implementation of a "New Freedom" in the nation's economy—his campaign promise to restore competition and fair labor practices, and to enable small businesses crushed by industrial titans to thrive once again. In September 1914, for example, he had created the Federal Trade Commission to protect consumers against price-fixing and other anticompetitive business practices, and the next month he signed into law the Clayton Antitrust Act. He continued monitoring the so-called European War, resisting pressure to enter but moving to strengthen the nation's armed forces, which many advisers were advocating, including old friend Thomas Dixon. "I'm glad you have to bear the great responsibility of this solemn hour in our history while I am free to continue my work in my library in peace," Dixon wrote in

November. "The thing that weighs in my heart now is that sure conviction that the shock of the great war in Europe has opened a new era in the history of the world—an era in which only the nation prepared to *defend* itself can hope to survive." Wilson replied, "I think I feel as deeply as you do the necessity for national defense and for well-considered action in that direction." In addition to his needing to attend to the affairs of state, Wilson was in mourning: his wife, Ellen, had died on August 6 from liver disease. One of his advisers noted in his diary on November 6 that the president had told him "he was broken in spirit by Mrs. Wilson's death." On November 9 Wilson wrote an old friend about the void left by Ellen's loss. "We are sustained by the daily touch, the constant sympathy and union in little things, little things that make up the life that the world knows nothing about," he said. "It is a cold, barren region where these things are not. There is no getting any companionship out of the policies of a state or the fortunes of a nation!"

Around this time Wilson also instructed Tumulty that he would meet after all with Trotter and his group. Although it was not the October date Trotter had pushed for, the persistent editor and a contingent of Trotterites entered the Oval Office on November 12, 1914, for their long-sought, long-awaited follow-up meeting with the president. (Wells, who had been with Trotter during the 1913 meeting, was unable to accompany him this time.) Trotter came with a statement he had prepared, and the meeting began with his reading it as the president waited patiently. Trotter started with a reference to their 1913 meeting and to the petition he had presented, containing twenty thousand signatures "from thirty-eight states protesting against the segregation of employees of the national government." He listed the on-the-job race separation that had gone unchecked since—at eating tables, dressing rooms, restrooms, lockers, and "especially public toilets in government buildings." He then charged the color line was drawn in the Treasury Department, in the Bureau of Engraving and Printing, the Navy Department, the Interior Department, the Marine Hospital, the War Department, and in the Sewing and Printing Divisions of the Government Printing Office. Trotter mentioned the political support he and other civil rights activists had provided to Wilson, observing, "Only two years ago you were heralded as perhaps the second Lincoln, and now the Afro-American leaders who supported you are hounded as false leaders and traitors to their race." He reminded the president of his pledge to assist "Colored fellow citizens" in "advancing the interest of their race in the United States," and ended by posing a question that contained a jab at Wilson's ballyhooed economic reform program. "Have you a 'New Freedom' for white Americans and a new slavery for your Afro-American fellow citizens? God forbid!"

It did not take long for things to sour. When his turn came to speak, the president told Trotter what previously he had admitted only in private—that he viewed segregation in his federal agencies as a benefit to Negroes. Wilson said that his cabinet officers "were seeking, not to put the Negro employees at a disadvantage but . . . to make arrangements which would prevent any kind of friction between the white employees and the Negro employees." Trotter found the claim astonishing, and he immediately disagreed, calling Jim Crow in federal offices humiliating and degrading to Negro workers. Wilson dug in, and his comments only seemed to worsen matters. "My question would be this: If you think that you gentlemen, as an organization, and all other Negro citizens of this country, that you are being humiliated, you will believe it. If you take it as a humiliation, which it is not intended as, and sow the seed of that impression all over the country, why the consequence will be very serious."

Trotter was incredulous that the president did not get that when he separated workers based on race it "must be a humiliation. It creates in the minds of others that there is something the matter with us—that we are not their equals, that we are not their brothers, that we are so different that we cannot work at a desk beside them, that we cannot eat at a table beside them, that we cannot go into the dressing room where they go, that we cannot use a locker beside them." There was no letup as Trotter basically called the president a liar, saying that race prejudice was the sole motivation for Jim Crow and that to assert otherwise, to claim his administration sought to protect Negroes from "friction," was ridiculous. "We are sorely disappointed that you take the position that the separation itself is not wrong, is not injurious, is not rightly offensive to you." Wilson had heard enough. He interrupted Trotter: "Your tone, sir, offends me." To the entire delegation, he said, "I want to say that if this association comes again, it must have another spokesman," declaring no one had ever come into his office and insulted him as Trotter had. "You have spoiled the whole cause for which you came," he told the *Guardian* editor dismissively.

But Trotter would not be dismissed; he was not one to find being surrounded by white people and the trappings of power either alien or intimidating, having been the only Negro in his class at Hyde Park High School (where, regardless, he had been elected class president) and, at Harvard, having outperformed most white classmates, many of whom had since become governors, congressmen, rich, and famous. Instead, he tried to steer the meeting back on track. "I am pleading for simple justice," he said. "If my tone has seemed so contentious, why my tone has been misunderstood." He said they needed to work this out, given that he and other Negro leaders had supported Wilson's presidential run at the polls.

But Wilson was finished with Monroe Trotter, stating angrily that bringing up politics and citing Negro voting power was a form of blackmail. The meeting, which had lasted nearly an hour, was abruptly over. The delegation was shown the door—essentially thrown out. When the incensed Trotter ran into reporters milling around Tumulty's office, he began letting off steam. "What the President told us was entirely disappointing."

The reporters recognized right away they had a big one. They scribbled down Trotter's comments and then worked their White House sources to get Wilson's side along with other details about what had happened inside the Oval Office. The story about the dustup between the president and the *Guardian* editor went viral. Not since 1903 and the "Boston Riot" had Trotter been the center of so much national attention. Initial coverage stressed his conduct. The *New York Times'* front-page story was headlined, "President Resents Negro's Criticism," while the front-page headline in the *New York Press* read: "Wilson Rebukes Negro Who 'Talks Up' to

Him." But the larger point was that his tough-talking the nation's chief executive landed Trotter back on front pages everywhere. Now it seemed as if everyone wanted an interview with him. His direct style, while causing controversy, had certainly drawn public attention to Jim Crow—a result that did not go unnoticed. Of all people, even Trotter critic Villard seemed impressed, wondering whether "one has to be rude to get into the press and do good with a just cause!" If nothing else, perhaps Villard was beginning to acknowledge the value of a Monroe Trotter—that confrontation, direct action, or "radicalism" created room for another race spokesman sharing the same civil rights goals to step in and make inroads with the likes of Wilson, or any other opponent for that matter, who would be relieved not to have to be dealing with a troublemaker.

=10=

The Wilson
White House

With temperatures hovering around freezing on Thursday morning, February 18, 1915, D. W. Griffith arrived at Union Station in Washington, DC, lugging all twelve reels of the film still titled *The Clansman* but which he had decided to change to something sounding larger than life: *The Birth of a Nation*. The trip marked a return for the director to the city where, in 1907, his hope of becoming a great American playwright went bust after *A Fool and a Girl* bombed in its premiere at the Columbia Theatre. But that was then, and the present was both promising and hugely exciting. He was on his way to 1600 Pennsylvania Avenue, passing the famous Ford's Theatre on his way, for the first-ever showing of a feature film in the White House.

The screening had been Thomas Dixon's brainchild. He had written Wilson in late January, requesting a visit to ask a personal favor, and on Tuesday, February 3, had taken the train from New York City to the nation's capital, all for a thirty-minute meeting. The two began with small talk about their college days and mutual friends, and then Dixon made his pitch. He said there was a new film based on one of his novels that he wanted the president to watch. Dixon stayed away from giving a detailed description of the film's content. Instead he stressed that Wilson, as a scholar and historian, simply had to witness this amazing new form of media and, in particular, Griffith's film. "I told him that I had a Motion Picture he should see, not because it was the greatest ever produced or because his classmate had written the story and a Southern director had made the Film, but because this picture made clear for the first time that a new, universal language had been invented." Although Wilson was intrigued, he said there was no way he could be spotted at a public theater watching a movie. "Mrs. Wilson's death holds the White House in mourning." Wanting to help out his old friend, however, he offered a private screening inside the White House—Griffith could present his film to an audience of the president and his cabinet members, and their families. Wilson told Dixon to see his daughter Margaret to work out a date and other details, but insisted on one condition: "*Do not allow any use of the event by the press under these circumstances*" (italics added).

Dixon was ecstatic. "I assured him that we would permit no announcement to be made, and no press reports to be sent out afterwards." Before long, the date of February 17 was chosen. When he heard of Dixon's coup, Griffith, fully supporting of the private screening, agreed with the novelist that "If we could get the backing of the President we would have a powerful weapon." It could help inoculate the film from criticism—which its director had already gotten a taste of during its opening on the West Coast. The previews he had held over one weekend in early January at the Loring Opera House in Riverside, California, could not have gone better, but by the time of the official premiere in Los Angeles at Clune's Auditorium on February 8, he had experienced blowback from Negroes and their supporters. His friend Grace Kingsley, the film reviewer and entertainment writer at the *Los Angeles Times*, could not have said it better when she wrote, "And now . . . comes the protest of the darkies and the interference of the police against exhibition of the picture." The small L.A. branch of the NAACP had tried to get the Los Angeles Board of Censors to take action, and when that fell flat, had urged the Los Angeles City Council to order the police to prevent the premiere. "The Negro is made to look hideous," branch officials had written the councilors. To mollify city officials, Griffith had made a few trims, but he considered them minor and

part of the ongoing tweaking he did with every movie he made. Two
days before the film's debut, W. H. Clune, the prominent owner of
the theater, issued a press release to reassure expectant viewers:
"The unexpected opposition to the exhibition of this film has been
due to a misunderstanding of the great historical purpose of the
picture," Clune began. The film, he said, "a great motion picture
drama," was "not an attack of any race or section of the country.
It is a most powerful sermon against war and in favor of brotherly
love." For Griffith, the situation in California basically worked out.
From the day after its opening, the film got strong reviews in the
L.A. papers, lines began forming for tickets to sold-out showings,
and scalpers were earning more than triple the ticket face value of
$0.75. Negro opposition was still something the director needed to
consider tactically as he prepared to bring the movie to theaters in
the Northeast. But for now, he was excited about screening his film
at the White House, knowing full well that only good could come if
he won the backing of the president and other powerbrokers.

In helping plan the event, twenty-eight-year-old Margaret Wilson,
who served as acting First Lady since her mother's death, picked
the East Room, the largest room in the White House. With its high
ceilings, crystal chandeliers, and long rectangular space, this was
the preferred location for receptions, state ceremonies, and con-
certs. Chairs were arranged in rows on the oak parquet floor, and
two cumbersome Simplex projectors were set up to face a bank of
wooden panels, painted cream white, which would to serve as a
screen in place of a real one. The projectionists came dressed in
formal attire.

Griffith and Dixon were hopeful that President Wilson would
respond favorably. He was southern-born, of course, but more than
that, the subject matter played into his interests. During the academic period in his life, Wilson had produced the five-volume
A History of the American People. Its fifth volume, *Reunion and
Nationalization*, released in 1902, covered Reconstruction in the
manner popular at the time and that Griffith had now dramatized,
portraying the South as abused, overrun by ex-slaves who were
undeserving of freedom and by northern Republicans who were

President Woodrow Wilson surrounded by reporters.
COURTESY OF WIKIMEDIA COMMONS.

determined, "to put the white South under the heel of the black
South," as Wilson put it. In an appeal directly to the president's
ego, Griffith had drawn liberally from the book in writing intertitles, attributing the material to Wilson by name. Surely its author
would consider it flattering for his text to be quoted in an epic film
about American history, even if the excerpts presented, while true
in spirit, had been reworded to fit the card. And even if there were
no guarantees of enthusiasm from the White House, Griffith had to
feel bolstered by the good press he had gotten in L.A. *"The Clansman*, gigantic tale of race conflict following the Civil War," Kingsley
had written, "Bold indeed the director who attempts to picturize
the great moment of a nation. Yet David Griffith has done it in a
manner to startle the world."

The lights dimmed in the East Room as the president, Griffith,
Dixon, and other guests settled in. For Wilson, an evening spent, in
effect, at the movies was at once a novelty and an escape from the

pressures of his workload. The prior week England had suffered its first deaths from an air attack, when two German zeppelins bombed the country's east coast, killing four. Wilson and his advisers worried constantly about Germany's aggressiveness, in particular that Germany's submarine warfare would expand to include US targets. (Indeed, five days after the screening, on February 22, Germany's unrestricted submarine warfare would begin, and the very next day, two US cotton steamers, *Evelyn* and *Carib*, would be sunk in the North Sea.) The war in Europe was overtaking everything else, especially the "New Freedom" domestic agenda that had gotten him elected. There was, though, one recent action on a hot-button issue that had rallied Negro and civil rights activists of all kinds into a rare unity of purpose. The Senate, pushed by southern Democrats, had passed a sweeping immigration reform bill in early January that included a literacy test for all newcomers, plus an inflammatory provision to exclude "persons of the African race or of negro blood" from the country. The Senate vote was a lopsided 50–7. Within days, Booker T. Washington had called the bill "unjust and unreasonable" and Monroe Trotter blasted it during a speaking engagement in Chicago, Illinois. Wilson, too, was against the bill, despite the overwhelming Senate support restricting entry into the United States. By the time it came to his desk for his signature, the Negro exclusion clause had been rejected by the House and fortunately removed, but the president vetoed the measure nonetheless, given it still required a literacy test. Perhaps he thought his veto would show noisy civil rights activists, whom he viewed as increasingly intemperate, that he was not always the enemy.

Despite these and other pressing matters, Griffith's film proved captivating, even without the live orchestra to provide the musical score the director had worked on painstakingly and believed added unquantifiable power to the experience. Everyone in the room sat transfixed as the antebellum South was established, mainly through the northern Stonemans' trip to South Carolina to visit the Camerons. It was during this first part that key love stories began: Phil Stoneman fell for Margaret Cameron, and Ben Cameron was swept away by a photograph of Elsie Stoneman, who had not accompanied her family to the plantation. In the reenactment of the Civil War, during which the boys fought on opposing sides, one scene that was especially irresistible featured "Little Colonel" Ben Cameron who, though wounded, led a charge against entrenched Union soldiers and rammed a Confederate regimental flag into a cannon before collapsing. During the Los Angeles premiere the audience had risen to its feet to cheer the screen heroism.

The viewers in the East Room, including historian Wilson himself, seemed unfazed by the historical distortions and outright falsehoods. During the film's second part detailing Reconstruction, for example, Griffith made it seem as if Negroes took control of every state legislature in the South and then ran amok when, in fact, Negroes were briefly in the majority in only two states. The more accurate racial breakdown in state government was like that of Georgia, where in 1868 there were 186 white and 33 Negro legislators, or Alabama, where during that same year there were 106 white and 27 Negro legislators. Griffith's depiction of the Ku Klux Klan, too, was way off, crediting the fictitious Ben Cameron with forming the Klan to rescue the South from Negro crime and lawlessness and to heal a nation's sectional divide. In truth, the Klan's rise was not about public safety policing of criminal activity; rather, it was about the postwar repression of legal and constitutional freedoms of Negroes.

Everyone in the room seemed unbothered, too, by the film's portrayal of Negroes and ex-slaves as brutal, creepy, and villainous. To any Negro viewer in L.A., the film was a gothic nightmare. Even Griffith's maid had been shaken, telling her employer, "It hurt me, Mr. David, to see what you do to my people." Early on, for example, one scene showed abolitionists at a meeting before the Civil War, and during it Griffith had a white woman pick up a slave boy in her arms to cradle him. But once the woman got a whiff of the boy, she dropped him like rot, held her nose, and turned away in disgust. Demeaning to Negroes, this scene captured the hypocrisy and racism among liberals that Monroe Trotter had complained about, and to which several white NAACP officials had candidly admitted.

Instead of discomfort, there was applause and praise all around when the film ended and the lights went up. Margaret Wilson oversaw the serving of refreshments. "The effect on the picture in the White House was precisely what I knew it would be," Dixon said later. "Emotions were stirred to a depth, although there had been no interpretive music." He wrote President Wilson a note of thanks immediately, as did Griffith, who said, "The honor you conferred on us has brought to me so much happiness that I cannot refrain from expressing my deepest and most sincere gratitude." Never at a loss to seize a public relations opening, an emboldened Dixon proposed to Griffith that they do a second screening, this one to members of the other two branches of national government—the US Supreme Court and Congress. The filmmaker was on a roll of good feeling, so why not? He signed on, and the next morning the novelist called on Chief Justice Edward Douglass White, who was dismissive at first. White had never seen a moving picture before and considered the idea beneath him. But he was a southerner from Louisiana who had served in the Confederate army, and when Dixon finished describing the scope of Griffith's film—as well as sharing the fact that the president and his cabinet had already seen it—he succeeded in landing the chief justice. Griffith meanwhile had persuaded the National Press Club to sponsor a private showing at the swanky Hotel Raleigh on Pennsylvania Avenue, and by eight p.m. a screening hastily organized in less than twenty-four hours got under way in the hotel's ornate and expansive banquet hall.

This time, a bona fide screen had been procured. A few feet away from Dixon and Griffith, closer to the front and as the guest of honor, sat Chief Justice White and his wife. Near him sat the secretary of the navy, Josephus Daniels. Surrounding them were other justices of the court and members of Congress. Newspaper reporters, diplomats, and the "smartest society folk" filled the remaining seats. The turnout on such short notice had exceeded any reasonable expectation. To be permitted to attend, journalists had had to agree the film was off the record because it had not yet been shown publicly in the East, and, as one scribe pointed out, "The producer requested that no review of the master film be published." But the condition did not stop them from writing *about* the screening, coverage that stirred buzz in the nation's capital and thrilled Griffith and Dixon. "There were 500 spectators who cheered and applauded throughout the three hours required to show the gigantic picture," read the *Washington Post* account of Saturday, February 20.

The stories made no mention of the White House screening, and it seemed Wilson's insistence on a press blackout might hold up. But Griffith took care of that, his "deepest and sincere gratitude" apparently was not so deep after all, at least not when it came to choosing between a presidential decree and drumming up even more buzz for his film. He had gone ahead and leaked Wilson's viewing, contacting his favorite entertainment reporter immediately after leaving the White House on the night of the screening, so that she would have a scoop. Three thousand miles away, *Los Angeles Times* writer Grace Kingsley led her next column, the popular "At the Stage Door," with this hot item: "President Wilson and his Cabinet members viewed 'The Clansman' yesterday in Washington, D.C., according to telegram received last night from David Griffith."

It took the *Washington Post* three days to catch up, reporting that Griffith, while in Washington, had shown "the mastadon of the movies, *The Birth of a Nation*, at the White House." That *Post* story led to others, and even though neither Wilson nor Tumulty would discuss the special screening with reporters, continued mention in the press in the weeks and months to come became a source of personal embarrassment—given the president's public display of bereavement—as well as a political irritation once the civil rights crowd got hold of it. Even more troublesome from Wilson's perspective was the zinger of a quote that became part of any discussion about the White House event, where it was said he had praised Griffith's tour de force as "history written in lightning." No comment, again, from the White House when reporters pressed, but the absence of confirmation proved no obstacle for D. W. Griffith, who was soon aiding and abetting the circulation of the remark. *"The Birth of a Nation* received very high praise from high quarters in Washington," he told one reporter. In a marketing ploy rivaling Dixon's, Griffith coyly avoided saying the president's name, but anyone could tell whom he meant. "I was gratified when a man we all revere, or ought to, said it teaches history by lightning."

Events in Ohio, however, punctured Griffith's elation over his success in Washington. On Tuesday, February 23, the US Supreme Court issued its ruling in Mutual Film Corporation's challenge to Ohio's censorship law. D. W. Griffith, his partners, and film industry leaders—all of whom had been closely following the case—got hammered. The court flat-out rejected Mutual's bid to piggyback movies onto newspapers and the claim that the Ohio law trampled free press rights guaranteed in the state constitution and the First Amendment. The film company, in its legal briefs, had argued movies and newsreels were "as much a press enterprise as are *Harper's Weekly, Leslie's Weekly,* the *Illustrated London News,* and countless other periodicals." But the high court declared, "The argument is wrong and strained which seeks to bring motion pictures and other spectacles into practical and legal similitude to a free press and liberty of opinion." Movies, deemed the court, were nothing like the press. Instead, the panel—which included Chief Justice White and other justices still fresh from a night spent watching Griffith's film—lumped them in with circus shows, the theater, and "other shows and spectacles" that had long been subject to regulation in the interests of public safety and morality. "Moving pictures is a business pure and simple, originated and conducted for profit," the court said.

To be sure, the justices acknowledged the technological wonder of motion pictures—a revolution in media that was still relatively new and changing all the time—and agreed that films can have an educational and missionary purpose. "But they may be used for evil." The court then cited the unprecedented reach and influence of films—that on any given day thousands of viewers filled hundreds of darkened theaters around the country: "Their power of amusement, the audiences they assemble, not of women alone nor of men alone, but together, not of adults only, but of children, make them the more insidious in corruption." That capability for evil, and the power of film for it—"greater because of their attractiveness and manner of exhibition"—was ample basis for government supervision. In their landmark ruling, the justices concluded unanimously that because motion pictures were not equal to newspapers, and therefore had no constitutional free press protection whatsoever, they were instead subject to censorship boards, such as Ohio's, as valid exercises of a state's police powers to ensure public safety. It was a ruling validating a handful of state boards, as well as film censorship agencies in up to one hundred municipalities around the country, legitimizing, as one legal expert later observed, "an extensive regime of state and local film censorship that existed until the mid-twentieth century."

This was bad news for not only D. W. Griffith but other filmmakers. Making matters worse was word out of Washington the same week, that Georgia senator Hoke Smith's bill calling for a federal motion picture commission had won unanimous approval before the House Committee on Education. If enacted, the bill would give President Wilson the power to appoint five commissioners to serve six-year terms. The commission would be charged with reviewing every new film, although no specific standards to assess the movies were spelled out in the bill, and it included only the language typically found in censoring statutes—that a film or show was to be permitted unless it was found "obscene, indecent, immoral, inhuman. . . . [to] tend to impair the health or corrupt the morals of children or adults, or incite to crime." Although the bill ultimately would be defeated, its progress through Congress attracted much attention and reflected the deep and widespread unease with the growing popularity and power of motion pictures.

Griffith was in New York City when these developments broke, and, with his movie readying for its East Coast premiere in that city, he took the offensive, publicly criticizing the Supreme Court's result in the Ohio case. But he moved away from making references to freedom of the press as the basis for constitutional protection of film, now that, on the federal level, it was a failed argument. Instead, he trumpeted a position that came easily to him, one he had been making for years—that movies, at least the way he produced them, were art, guaranteed by the First Amendment as instruments of free speech and expression. Speaking at an afternoon meeting of the League for Political Education, he devoted his topic to this very point, deploring censorship of "any art form" to an audience at the Cort Theatre. He also drafted a new intertitle for the start of the film, "A Plea for the Art of the Motion Picture," in which he said film deserved the "same liberty that is conceded to the art to which we owe the bible and the works of Shakespeare." This became a main talking point for him, and the next year he even took time to prepare and publish a pamphlet titled "The Rise and Fall of Free Speech in America." His argument, pure and heartfelt, naturally appealed to social progressives and free speech advocates—although many in this crowd were also beginning to line up with Negroes opposed to Griffith's new movie for its racism, and thus were faced with a vexing dilemma of protecting expression and limiting it.

Coincidentally, too, while Griffith was pitching film as free speech, activists in New York City were up in arms about trouble flaring on a different location of the free speech spectrum. They filed into the Special Sessions Court in the Yorkville Police Court earlier in February for the arraignment of artist William Sanger on charges that he had violated the Comstock Law in the distribution of obscene material; to wit, his wife's birth control pamphlet *Family Limitation.*

Leonard D. Abbott—a socialist and president of the Free Speech League—and other radicals were there in force to protest Sanger's arrest. The aging Anthony Comstock appeared in court as well, bringing the agent he had used to ensnare Sanger as part of his larger plot to get Sanger's fugitive wife, Margaret, to return from England, which would enable Comstock to pursue the obscenity case still pending against her from March 1914. His agent took the stand and told the judge how he had gone to William Sanger's studio on East Fifteenth Street in December and, posing as a friend of Mrs. Sanger, lied that he wanted a copy of *Family Limitation* to translate and distribute to the poor. Sanger had then rummaged around his apartment and given the agent a copy—and his arrest soon followed. Based on the agent's evidence, the judge ordered Sanger held for trial later in the year. Sanger vowed to "fight the case to the finish." The Free Speech League attacked Comstock's sting operation, insisting Margaret Sanger's materials were constitutionally protected free speech. The league started a defense fund for Sanger and lined up a prominent lawyer, Gilbert E. Roe, a close friend of the national progressive leader Robert M. La Follette.

"Mr. Comstock doubtless thought he could railroad his victim to jail in quick order, but he found that he was mistaken," editorialized the radical monthly publication the *Modern School* in its February issue. The "free William Sanger" defense throng, situated in the edgy, antigovernment, and even revolutionary wing of civil liberties, eventually drew in such avowed anarchists as Emma Goldman and Alexander Berkman, who within weeks of the court hearing were declaring "war on Anthony Comstock, the supermoralist," and planning protests in New York City to get him fired.

Despite the legal setback for the film industry in *Mutual Film v. Ohio*, Griffith arrived for a luncheon at a Broadway hotel a few days later, acting as if he had not a worry in the world. He was meeting a reporter from the *New York American* for what in journalism was called a "setup" piece about his film, which was opening in the city in five days, on March 3. "The biggest man in the moving picture business today is a curious mingling of the man of leisure, man of the world, and the dreaming poet," wrote the journalist afterward.

The interviewer was fawning in his praise of Griffith and the movie, which was now officially titled *The Birth of a Nation* and ready to go at the Liberty Theatre around the corner on Forty-Second Street. The fancy program featured the new title and was designed in such a way that pages could be added to list high praise as it came in from reviewers and important persons. The booklet was intended to serve as both a souvenir and a reinforcement for viewers that the film was a big deal. Several pages summarized the plot; others contained still photographs from various scenes—including pictures of hooded Klansmen on horseback. Still another page was devoted to "Facts About the Picture," although many of the "facts" were not true ("18,000 people and 8,000 horses were utilized in making the narrative"). But they did serve to help justify the unprecedented price Aitken and Griffith had decided to charge for tickets—two dollars. The amount itself had drawn jaw-dropping publicity, and, again, fed the buzz of the movie's epic proportion.

The reporter may have found Griffith remarkably calm and upbeat, but the director's carefree air masked the aggravation he, Dixon, and the producers had been going through to repel interference from the NAACP. The annoyance was not over, either, but would continue for weeks to come. Griffith and his people had smartly gotten initial approval for the film from the National Board of Censorship in late January, prior to the Los Angeles opening. But after NAACP officials caught wind of the approval, they began causing trouble. Griffith received a letter at his New York City office from May Childs Nerney, secretary of the NAACP, who wanted "an advance performance of the moving picture" for her and others. He did not respond. But the NAACP eventually did manage to win over the board's chairman, Frederic C. Howe, to revisit approval and to arrange for another screening. Internal politicking began, with all sides pushing their interests. The Griffith forces certainly had to be pleased when they learned the board had told NAACP officials on the very day in March when the filmmaker was presiding over a screening that the twelve tickets originally set aside for the NAACP had been reduced to two tickets—and the two persons who used them had to be white.

It all proved a nuisance more than anything else. Griffith screened the film a couple more times for the board's General Committee—and during the second, members actually stood up and cheered him when he entered the room. He promised to make a few adjustments to two scenes the NAACP had objected to in the portion about Reconstruction: the attempted seduction of Flora and Elsie by ex-slave Gus and the northern mulatto Silas Lynch, respectively. Trusting Griffith to make the changes, the board gave its blessing to the film in a 12–9 vote. NAACP secretary Nerney immediately complained that her organization had been mistreated by the board and voiced her outrage that the National Board of Censorship "should unqualifiedly approve such a pernicious and dangerous film."

The NAACP then turned to New York City mayor John Purroy Mitchel to complain that the film was "an offense to public decency" and urge that he order the entire second part about Reconstruction to be scrapped. But both Griffith and Dixon met with the mayor and his staff, and once again the director promised to adjust the two scenes causing the most consternation. Ultimately he made only cosmetic changes, which the NAACP only realized when members saw the film at the Liberty. Further complaints went unheeded, and the New York run that began on March 3 was, overall, a smashing success. "We spent hectic hours and days—yes, weeks—with our lawyers, before various committees," Griffith recalled. "It kept us on the sleepless jump for a long time, but finally the mayor of New York city broke the ice and allowed it to be shown."

No aspect of this complication—still in its early stages—came up during Griffith's Broadway luncheon with the arts reporter from the *New York American*. To the contrary, their conversation was entirely upbeat, the reporter positively reverential. He asked the director at one point, "Why call it *The Birth of a Nation?*" and Griffith smiled before answering. "Because it is," he said simply. "The Civil War was fought fifty years ago. But the real nation has only existed the last fifteen or twenty years, for there can exist no union without sympathy and oneness of sentiment." The journalist came away unable to contain his superlatives. "The most poetic, the most daring, the most artistic, and the most stupendous works have had their inception in his brain," he told his readers the next day. "This week there will be shown at the Liberty Theatre the largest film drama ever conceived."

For all the good cheer, however, Griffith knew—but was not about to mention—that the "largest film drama ever" was in for more Negro opposition, fiercer than anything he had faced so far. In this regard, it probably made sense to see Los Angeles and New York City as a warm-up for the main event—Boston, Massachusetts—and that in preparing a ground game, he factor in the city's abolitionist legacy, the fact its incumbent mayor James M. Curley was the king of censors, and, finally, that Boston was home to one William Monroe Trotter, the most radical newspaper editor and Negro activist of the day. Griffith was not about to get into any of this with a New York reporter and spoil the love-in, but if he had, he might have cast the battle-in-waiting this way: If he were able to confront and defeat opposing forces mustered in Boston, then he would come away confident his film could play anywhere.

═11═

Trotter Rides the Rails

Monroe Trotter had stuck around in the nation's capital after the White House clash on Thursday, November 12, 1914, while President Wilson took off to New York City for the weekend, accompanied by his daughter Margaret, to stay at the East Side apartment of his confidant and foreign policy adviser, Edward M. House. Wilson's secretary, Joseph Tumulty, had chastised Trotter for his public remarks immediately after the fireworks in the Oval Office: "Mr. Trotter, you have violated every courtesy of the White House by quoting the President to the press." But Trotter was not about to be silenced. He was the keynote speaker on Sunday, November 15, at the Second Baptist Church at 816 Third Street, NW, where the standing-room-only crowd—estimated at two thousand—cheered for more than five minutes when he stood to speak. Then, staring down at reporters seated in the front row, he spoke slowly to be sure his first words could be written verbatim: "I emphatically deny that in language, manner, tone in any respect or to the slightest degree I was impudent, insolent or insulting to the President." Speaking for ninety minutes, he then denounced Wilson's practice of federal segregation, frequently interrupted by outbursts from the audience ("Put him out!" some yelled about Wilson). Trotter sought to tone down the rowdiness: "Don't show any disrespect for the office of President; I respect the office," he said. But news had been made: "Negroes Hoot Wilson's Name, Cheer Trotter," was a typical headline the next day.

Trotter had then taken the train home to Boston, arriving at South Station on Monday afternoon. Eager to capitalize on new and widespread attention, he spoke briefly to reporters before heading off to the South End for the regular monthly meeting of the Boston Literary and Historical Association that he had cofounded in 1901. Even though a speaker was slated to discuss the so-called Bacon-Shakespearian controversy, everyone who gathered in an assembly room of St. Mark's Congregational Church on Tremont Street wanted to hear from Trotter about his dustup with the president of the United States.

As was its custom the association's meeting, "called to order at 8:20 p.m.," began with a prayer, a reading of the previous meeting's minutes, and two hymns sung to the accompaniment of a piano. At the conclusion of the literary lecture, Trotter was finally "introduced and gave a detailed account of his recent meeting at the White House in Washington, when he was denounced by President Wilson as insulting and insolent," according to the minutes of the meeting. He told his Boston friends that the significance of the White House face-off was having the president confirm publicly for the first time that race segregation in the national government was an administration policy. Wrapping up, the group gave Trotter its full backing, voting to "endorse without reservation everything Mr. Trotter and the other members of the delegation did at the White House."

Despite the late hour that first night home and disregarding any cumulative road weariness, Trotter was back at it again late the next night, arriving at eleven p.m. to deliver what the newspapers described as a "fiery attack" before a "mass meeting of colored people" in Roxbury at the Twelfth Baptist Church to more than nine hundred Bostonians. To this assembly Trotter dropped any pretense of diplomacy, saying Wilson was a "long-jawed, slab-faced man" who, as a result of their contentious encounter, "had been brought to state his position and admit that segregation did exist." Then, in a run of epithets, he called the chief executive a "Deceiver" and a "Pledge-breaker" who since taking office had proved to be "the most dishonorable man that has ever been President of the United States." He insisted, likely without a straight face, that he was not looking to insult the president; rather, he had just been so shocked during their meeting "to hear a master of the English language use his intelligence to defend the degradation of a race." Trotter also mocked the complaint he had been rude. "I am so glad that the White House has told the world that a colored man has insulted the President I don't know what to do." He closed with obvious delight in the trouble he had caused. "We began the fight right under the White House roof and will continue it. President Wilson will never be elected President again."

Trotter was just getting started. The Boston talk kicked off a nine-state speaking tour of no less than ten cities on the East Coast and in the Midwest. It began with a second speech in Washington, DC, and a quick turn-around back to Boston where, on Monday night, November 23, he was the main speaker at Faneuil Hall before seven hundred listeners. "I have been taught in the Massachusetts schools and in one of her colleges that the President of the United States is not a King and is not to be approached with cowering spirit or with any wavering," he said emphatically. He was scheduled to appear at a New York City event in late December that was advertised in several city newspapers until petty Negro politics intervened. Unhappy that the *Guardian* editor, rather than Booker T. Washington, was garnering so much press, a prominent Bookerite named Charles W. Anderson strong-armed the event's organizers and persuaded them to cancel the speaker. Afterward, in a smarmy bid to make inroads at the White House, Anderson informed Tumulty that he had squelched Trotter's talk and then, a week later, on December 29, wrote to Washington, reveling in his anti-Trotter handiwork and hoping it would score points with the president. Referring to Wilson, Anderson said, "It won't hurt to have 'our friend' know that we were able to serve in this connection."

But the New York cancellation hardly slowed Trotter. In Chicago, old friend Ida B. Wells heard that his invitation in New York had been rescinded and immediately summoned him. She saw Chicago as a crucial stop in his regained fame. Trotter, she said, "had never been West, and I thought that he needed to get out

in this part of the country and see that the world didn't revolve
around Boston as a hub." She wanted him to deliver the "emancipation speech" to her local group, the Negro Fellowship League.
"We thought that the race should back up the man who had had
the bravery to contend for the rights of his race." Viewing this as
a huge opportunity, Wells rented the ornate Orchestra Hall, built
in 1904, which could hold more than two thousand spectators.
But the evening turned out to be one of the few disappointments
of Trotter's tour. Two Chicago mayoral candidates did appear to
make brief pitches for the Negro vote, but far too many seats went
unfilled. The first problem was Wells had scheduled the speech for
New Year's Eve, and many who normally would have come were
either celebrating or attending special church services held on the
last day of the year. A second issue was she had had to charge
admission to cover the rental fee and Trotter's costs, and this was
a break in custom—usually such talks were free and open to the
public. Before the event had even begun, just to get the manager to
open the doors to the hall, Wells had had to solicit a white patron
in attendance to pay a deposit. One audience member was a local Bookerite, George Cleveland Hall, a Chicago doctor at a black-
owned hospital, who conducted the kind of monitoring that had
long been part of the Negro leader's operational strategy. After the
abysmal showing he happily informed Washington, "Trotter meeting at Orchestra Hall was a frost . . . They closed the doors until
Ida got a white woman to stand for $200—his audience was just
180 people by actual count." Hall said Wells was still working on
raising $100 for Trotter, and, as for Trotter, "Never saw a Man so
hungry for money and cheap notoriety."

Despite the rough start, Trotter went on to give a series of
smaller talks his host had arranged—at the A. M. E. Zion Church,
for example, and then the Grace Presbyterian Church, the Frederick Douglass Center, the Quinn Chapel Church, St. Mark's Church,
and of course, Wells's own Negro Fellowship League. The pastor at
St. Mark's added a creative twist by announcing an essay contest
with prizes going "to the young lady and gentleman who write the
best essay on: 'Did Mr. Trotter Insult President Wilson?'" During
his time in Chicago, Trotter even made headlines when, on January

2, he showed up to deliver a speech to the Irish Fellowship Club's luncheon meeting at the La Salle Hotel but was rebuffed at the ballroom door. It turned out some members did not want to hear him criticizing President Wilson (who was expected to address the club on St. Patrick's Day). The ensuing front-page stories quoted officials as saying that Trotter then tried to force his way into the hall, with Trotter insisting he had taken his rejection "cordially" and left.

Trotter ended up staying with Wells and her family for ten days, and it was during this time that their partnership in race matters deepened. He joined Wells one night at a meeting of her Chicago group to discuss the inflammatory "negro exclusion clause" in the Senate's just-adopted Immigration Reform bill. Trotter spoke first, and the group passed a resolution calling on members of the Illinois congressional delegation to work to defeat the Senate bill. In addition, they launched a letter-writing campaign against the controversial measure (a version of which President Wilson ultimately vetoed). They also fought, along with the NAACP, to beat another bill to ban interracial marriage in Washington, DC. Wells then sent Trotter on his way on the nation's railways. "We made engagements for him as far north as St. Paul, Minnesota; as far west as Omaha, Nebraska; as far south as St. Louis, Missouri," she said. Trotter also traveled to Pittsburgh and Baltimore to give talks. "When Mr. Trotter returned East it was with the assurance that the West had approved his course and upheld his hands."

Wells was even able to round up some expense money for Trotter from sources other than the disappointing Orchestra Hall event. "We succeeded in giving him the one hundred dollars I had promised," she said. But at this point in his career, Trotter was used to money shortages. It had become a fact of his life to always be on the lookout for donors. In the *Guardian*'s November 21, 1914, issue, which covered the White House clash, he made an unusual appeal to readers on the weekly paper's editorial page. In addition to publishing their letters to the editor, he literally solicited a penny for their thoughts. "THE NEED," he headlined the request. "What is now needed is money to maintain *The Guardian* and the work. Pray come to the rescue." And around the same time, he cited a personal reason rather than the *Guardian* for needing money—Deenie's dental care. Concerning her teeth, he wrote a friend, "She needs them fixed badly."

Wilson's most loyal backers, meanwhile, reached out to reassure the president. Within days of his meeting with the Negro delegation, he received word from Julius Rosenwald, the wealthy president of the Illinois-based Sears, Roebuck & Co., who had read in the Chicago newspapers, with what he called "sympathetic interest," about the sharp exchange with Trotter: During the summer of 1914 he, too, had had an unpleasant interaction with the Boston editor. Trotter had upbraided him for supporting a YMCA exclusively for Negroes, saying such a facility would foster segregation. Trotter, warned Rosenwald, was "a notoriety seeker whose methods are dismaying to the conservative members of this race." But Wilson realized almost instantly the error of his ways, for by becoming unnerved in the face of what he considered Trotter's impertinence, he inadvertently had given the editor a platform. The matter came up during a meeting in the White House with his navy secretary, Josephus Daniels, who commented on the president's run-in. "Never raise an incident into an issue," replied Wilson, who had clearly conducted a postmortem analysis of the situation. "When the Negro delegate (Trotter) threatened me, I was damn fool enough to lose my temper and to point them to the door. What I ought to have done would have been to have listened, restrained my resentment, and, when they had finished, to have said to them that, of course, their petition would receive consideration. They would then have withdrawn quietly and no more would have been heard about the matter. But I lost my temper and played the fool."

Plenty was heard about the matter, however, as newspapers around the country rushed to cover and editorialize about the Trotter-Wilson exchange. The commentary ran the gamut. In his *New York Evening World* editorial, owner and NAACP official Oswald Garrison Villard said Trotter's manners were lacking but that Wilson should have focused instead on the "genuine wrongs" Trotter had presented. The editorial also sharply disagreed with Wilson's moan that Trotter had tried "political blackmail" for suggesting Negro voters would turn against him when, in truth,

Trotter was simply employing "the time-honored American way of showing disapproval of an elective official's conduct." To no one's surprise, southern newspapers had a different take. Some, like the *Baltimore Sun*, were comparatively civil. "William Monroe Trotter, of Boston, and others of his kind are rendering their people a notably bad service by such insolent performances as that at the White House." More typical, however, was the *El Paso Times*, which called Trotter a "Jamaica coon," and the *Beaumont (TX) Enterprise*, whose editorial writer did not mince words: "The little bunch of Boston niggers that made the 'protest' against the attitude of President Wilson in refusing to be called down by them, do not represent the respectable, self-respecting, law abiding colored people of the United States, who are not worrying about 'race equality.'" Trotter read as much as possible, with friends sending him clippings, and took the attacks as a badge of honor. "I have been denounced as being discourteous and insolent by all the North and the South, too," he said, "but it is a compliment to be denounced by the South."

The Negro press was largely supportive. W. E. B. Du Bois wrote in the *Crisis*, "William Monroe Trotter is a brave man" who had "voiced the feelings of nine-tenths of the thinking Negroes of this country." Du Bois, now one of the most prominent civil rights leaders in the country, did not mention Booker T. Washington by name but likely considered Bookerites to be among the one tenth who thought differently about Trotter and his in-your-face tactics. Indeed, one key Bookerite, an educator named Robert Russa Moton who would soon become principal of Washington's Tuskegee Institute, was quick to curry favor with the president after the Trotter affair. "I want to say that the Negroes, generally, do not in any way approve of Mr. Trotter's conduct at the White House," he wrote. Moton reminded Wilson about Trotter's arrest in 1903 in the "Boston Riot," for "breaking up a meeting in which Dr. Booker T. Washington was speaking in the interest of race co-operation," and he offered his apology on behalf of "ninety-nine percent of the thoughtful Negroes of this land at Mr. Trotter's attitudes and words." Wilson replied that it was "particularly delightful" that men like Moton and Washington who "have the interests of the negro people most at heart" truly understood his "real temper and disposition."

Moton quickly bundled the letters and sent them along to his mentor, Booker T. Washington, looking for praise for his political initiative and also to make the tactical point that Wilson's hostility toward Trotter could be exploited to their advantage. "I think he is in such a condition now that we may be able to make an impression on him," Moton wrote. Left unsaid and unacknowledged, of course, was that Trotter's style had created an opening for Negro leaders who, while positioned elsewhere on the civil rights spectrum, were working nonetheless to advance Negro life.

The maneuverings illustrated once again a splintered civil rights movement, even as all factions worked in their own way against Jim Crow in federal government, and against such legislation as the Immigration Reform bill and proposed bans on interracial marriage. By 1915, Booker T. Washington's long-held supremacy was in decline, as W. E. B. Du Bois and the nascent NAACP took over the lead in the movement, And then there was the radical newspaper editor Monroe Trotter and his band of followers who simply would not go away and, in fact, had reclaimed center stage. The blowout at the White House had certainly restored Trotter to the forefront, as he became the talk of the nation and the subject of heated praise and criticism. But a fractured movement, one that featured spying and other subversive acts, was hindering the overall cause. Racists and political opponents certainly gloated, and a leading Negro newspaper, the *Chicago Defender*, addressed the disunity in its first issue of the year 1915. Its editorial that day was tantamount to a New Year's wish regarding the three kings of the civil rights movement: "Wouldn't it be a glorious thing if the Booker Washington faction, the Du Bois faction and the Monroe Trotter faction would get together on a common ground and fight unitedly for the things that they are now fighting singly for?" The infighting helped no one but its foes, the newspaper said. "While we are squabbling among ourselves for some petty honor, what we have gained is being taken from us."

Trotter had been staying with Ida B. Wells when the editorial was published, and the *Chicago Tribune* ran a letter by Booker T. Washington in opposition to the Senate's Immigration Reform bill at around the same time. Trotter had read about Washington's statements against the bill and seemed caught up in the spirit of one-for-all and all-for-one on the night of the Orchestra Hall event, where he had spotted George Cleveland Hall in attendance. Trotter had gone over to Hall and unfolded a newspaper clipping he had with him reporting Washington's opposition. Remarking to the Bookerite that, for once, he and Hall's chief were "agreeing on the same thing," he hoped that "all factions might learn to stand on a common platform" as a result of the fight against the bill's Negro exclusion clause. What a fine thought, Trotter said, if Washington, Du Bois, and himself were "to appear in [the nation's capital] arm in arm fighting against the measure." Wishful thinking on Trotter's part, for sure, but there was another matter in the offing that would come awfully close.

In early January 1915, the NAACP delivered its official response to the White House affair, sending President Wilson a formal letter, along with several newspaper editorials. "This Association does not for a moment CONDONE any rudeness or lack of courtesy to you," wrote board chairman Joel E. Spingarn, "but wishes to place itself on record as agreeing with Mr. Trotter that the slightest discrimination against colored people in the federal service is a grave injustice." Simultaneously, NAACP officials were realizing a new firestorm was developing—D. W. Griffith's *The Clansman*, with its announced February opening in Los Angeles and (retitled *The Birth of a Nation*) New York City run beginning in March. The organization's leaders scrambled to mobilize its opposition, and one problem was figuring out where the filmmaker was taking his movie next. Griffith was not about to notify the NAACP of his schedule, and a cat-and-mouse game began, the association sending out telegrams to its branches alerting them to be on the lookout for any publicized runs in their locale. The first negative reviews had begun to appear, most notably in the March 20 issue of the *New Republic*, which ran a lengthy analysis by Irish writer Francis Hackett who, while agreeing that "as a spectacle it is stupendous," concluded "the film is aggressively vicious and defamatory" to the Negro race.

Then, in late March, before any public announcements were made, intelligence surfaced about Griffith's plans for a Boston run

to start sometime in early April. The information came to light
when Rolfe Cobleigh, associate editor of the liberal Boston-based
magazine the *Congregationalist*, wrote to Griffith after reading
about the movie in the New York newspapers and also hearing
from friends who had seen it there. Although he had not yet viewed
it, Cobleigh wrote to ask Griffith about the film's false history, alleged glorification of lynching, and incitement of race prejudice. But
Thomas Dixon, not Griffith, was the one who took up the epistolary
sword and replied. "You surely could not have seen our picture—or
you wouldn't write the letter in that tone," Dixon said. "The only
two scenes any *sane* man can object fill just two minutes of a 3 hour
entertainment." For the next several weeks, the two engaged in a
war of words through letters and a meeting, during which the novelist cited multiple endorsements from important people, including
Wilson—name-dropping that only added to the president's misery
that his favor to Dixon had caused him. In fact, the same week
Dixon and Cobleigh had begun their tangle, Joseph Tumulty fielded
a letter from a wealthy Washington, DC, matron, daughter of the
late James G. Blaine, former Republican governor of Maine and
Speaker of the House of Representatives during Reconstruction.
Harriet Blaine Beale had just returned from New York City, where
she and her sister had seen the movie—which she found to be "cal-
culated to arouse the worst form of race hatred and to send every
ignorant white man away with a feeling that every negro should be
lynched." She asked Tumulty about the rumors of a White House
screening. "We were told that the President and the Chief Justice
had seen the film before it was shown to the public and had given
it their heartfelt endorsement." The letter was the kind of political
headache Wilson did not need, but talk about his involvement in
Griffith's film only continued to nag him throughout the spring.

In the byplay between Cobleigh and Dixon, however, the reference to Wilson's endorsement was just a juicy morsel in the pair's
deepening debate, and the most important piece of information Cobleigh obtained was that Griffith was bound for Boston. Moreover,
he learned that Dixon and Griffith saw Boston in a different light,
regarding the city "as the critical point for their enterprise, that it
was more likely to object to such a play than any other city and . . .

that if they could get by in Boston they would be able to go anywhere else in the country."

The opposition strategies began unfolding as works-in-progress,
and Monroe Trotter would soon move to the forefront as the Boston
resistance crystallized. From the start he, Du Bois, and other leading NAACP officials all recognized that to complain about Griffith's
epic only added to the unprecedented marketing plan that the
filmmaker and his backers had developed for the movie's rollout.
Griffith and Harry Aitken had created a separate company, Epoch
Producing Company, to take *The Birth of a Nation* on the road,
and had assembled an advance team of public relations agents to
feed local reporters the inflated "facts" about the making of the
movie, which were repurposed in flattering feature stories about
the director. In one of many marketing tricks, they prepared flyers
and cards to distribute outside theaters, listing putative endorsements from well-known Americans, in a bid to inoculate the film
from criticism and to influence moviegoers before they had even
watched a second of the action. (Many of the so-called endorsements were later shown to be a mix of fiction and hyperbole.) They
even hired detectives to provide security in Boston and to track the
movements of some of the movie's leading opponents there.

In short, openly opposing the film would likely boost ticket sales.
"Much of the publicity resulting from our fight against *The Birth of
a Nation* has helped the photo play," an NAACP official acknowledged at one point. It certainly furthered the ends of marketing
schemer Thomas Dixon, who had years of practice stirring up publicity for his novels and had once tried to provoke Booker T. Washington into a debate to spike sales of a new book. During one of his
heated exchanges with Cobleigh, Dixon made the same point as
the NAACP after the Boston opposition got under way, taunting,
"The silly legal opposition they are giving will make me a million-
aire if they keep it up!" Booker T. Washington, on the other hand,
suggested a muted approach and warned to proceed with caution
regarding any public statements. "I hope our friends will be very
careful not to be used in a way to advertise the play," he wrote a
Bookerite in Boston, to whom he summarized the run-in with the

novelist. "Our friends in Boston want to be sure the same trick is not played on them." But for Trotter and the Boston NAACP to not respond, to stand by and stay silent, was not only unacceptable but seemed irresponsible, especially in consideration that *The Birth of a Nation* marked a pivotal and historic moment for the fast-evolving medium of film by showcasing moving pictures' enormous reach and power to shape public opinion. For opponents, it was sheer anti-Negro propaganda, tantamount to a miscarriage of justice that Griffith had prosecuted in the court of public opinion. By manipulating the evidence, the director had framed the Negro race, and it was now up to Trotter and others to undertake a public appeal and crusade to overturn that wrongful conviction.

But it also meant trying to stop the movie in its tracks—by censoring it. Its opponents had the apparent backing of the nation's highest court in fighting against Griffith's film, even if civil rights activists were likely not giddy with enthusiasm. For one, they were deeply aware the Supreme Court did not always get things right. The 1896 "separate but equal" ruling in *Plessy v. Ferguson* was an anathema to them, the legal foundation upon which Jim Crow in the twentieth century was built. Moreover, a censorship strategy was discomforting for many civil rights leaders who, ordinarily, were as vociferous about the civil liberties of free speech and expression as they were about equal rights. The censorship strategy brought about a dissonance where usually there was harmony, a tension that one journalist in Chicago noted in an article about the NAACP's role in pursuing it. The strategy, the reporter wrote, "must have embarrassed those members of the association who, like [Chicago NAACP member] Charles T. Hallinan, have always fought censorship of any kind. Liberals are torn between two desires. They hate injustice to the negro and they hate a bureaucratic control of thought."

Monroe Trotter, as a newspaper editor and activist, was certainly mindful of free press and speech rights—they were at the heart of his failed trial defense following the 1903 Boston Riot—and fighting speech with speech would have been the preferred course of action, rather than silencing expression. In the months to come, the NAACP, in fact, tried to help get a competing film going to rebut

Griffith's. In the *Crisis*, W. E. B. Du Bois announced the initiative, reporting that Elaine Sterne, an accomplished playwright, screenwriter, and novelist, was at work on a "new movie-picture play, *Lincoln's Dream*," which would serve as an alternative narrative to *The Birth of a Nation* and offer a true depiction of "slavery, the Civil War and the period of Reconstruction." The NAACP created a Scenario Committee to work with Sterne and also to assist in raising the $10,000 producers said was necessary as part of a development deal with the Universal Film Company to produce a twelve-reel film budgeted at $60,000. The committee lined up meetings with potential investors in Boston, New York City, and Chicago, and sent out a pitch letter that had "CONFIDENTIAL" typed in bold atop the document. "*The Birth of a Nation* with its anti-Negro propaganda has captured the imagination of hundreds of thousands of people in the United States," the letter said. "If this goes unchallenged, it will take years for our propaganda to make any impression unless we do something really spectacular." Sterne threw herself enthusiastically into the research and the writing, telling an NAACP official at one point she was "working like mad" and that "Griffith may put poison in my beef tea before I get through."

For all the effort and fervor, however, the fund-raising effort failed utterly, as NAACP officials faced the insurmountable hurdle that Booker T. Washington, and not their own rank and file, was the one with access to white money. For example, a possible investor, Sears, Roebuck president Julius Rosenwald, who had come to Wilson's defense against Trotter, was aligned with Washington. "I supposed," wrote the NAACP's May Childs Nerney, "Rosenwald would be hopeless because of the B.T.W. influence." The idea of pitting film against film eventually proved unsustainable.

Censorship therefore became the chief option, so that Trotter and his NAACP counterparts began working the edges of the First Amendment, seeking ways to limit expression deemed hateful and racist, in order that D. W. Griffith's *The Birth of a Nation* could be suppressed. The effort served, in effect, as a prequel to national free speech controversies later in the twentieth century over the scope of the First Amendment. In one, a New Hampshire man named Walter Chaplinsky was charged with breach of peace for shouting at another man that he was a fascist. In 1942, the Supreme Court supported the conviction, creating a "fighting words doctrine," ruling that speech likely to result in an immediate violent response may be prohibited. In another, in 1969 the justices upheld the rights of the Ku Klux Klan in Ohio to stage a rally, based on their finding that the bigoted messages delivered during the rally had not created an imminent threat of violence. In a third, the late 1980s and 1990s saw hundreds of American colleges and universities adopt what became known as "hate speech" codes, forbidding bigoted expressions based on race, ethnicity, gender, or sexual orientation. More than forty states, meanwhile, passed laws criminalizing various forms of offensive speech.

Then, in 1992, the Supreme Court stepped in to rule that these "politically correct" restrictions had gone too far. The ruling was made in a case from Minnesota, where a white teenager had burned a cross on the front yard of a St. Paul home owned by a black family. Instead of charging the youth with criminal trespass and arson, prosecutors accused him of violating the "hate speech" ordinance— whereupon the Supreme Court ruled that the ordinance was unconstitutional. Fighting words were one thing, but restrictions on ideas—however offensive—violated the basic First Amendment right to "communicate messages of racial, gender and religious intolerance." Wrote Justice Antonin Scalia, "Let there be no mistake about our belief that burning a cross in someone's yard is reprehensible, but St. Paul has sufficient means at its disposal to prevent such behavior without adding the First Amendment to the fire." Eleven years later, though, the Supreme Court took another look at cross burnings as protected hate speech and tweaked its earlier position, ruling that if Virginia authorities could prove a cross burning had created imminent fear and intimidation, then the offender could be prosecuted, but absent that, the burning itself warranted First Amendment coverage. "A State may choose to prohibit only those forms of intimidation that are most likely to inspire fear of bodily harm," Justice Sandra Day O'Connor wrote in 2003.

Back in 1915, Trotter, the NAACP, and D. W. Griffith were embroiled in an early chapter of the still ongoing legal quarrel over when speech and "artistic" expression that are hateful may be restricted. As nettlesome in principle that censorship was to civil rights opponents of the film, back then it was, tactically speaking, the weapon du jour.

By the end of March 1915, Monroe Trotter was winding down his speaking tour and heading back east. On Thursday night, April 1, to an overflowing crowd in the Ward A. M. E. Church in Peoria, Illinois, a city located along the Illinois River and about 165 miles southwest of Chicago, he talked about his run-in with Woodrow Wilson and about the dangers of "self-segregation" in seeking separate YMCAs. In Chicago, meanwhile, Ida B. Wells and local NAACP officials were just realizing D. W. Griffith's agents were quietly securing a permit to screen *The Birth of a Nation* by going through the office of the city's lame-duck mayor, Republican William H. Thompson. The news set off lobbying efforts to get the mayor to stop the film. Trotter knew Thompson from when Thompson had attended his talk in Orchestra Hall prior to taking office. The controversy about the on-again, off-again Chicago showing swirled around the Windy City for the next several months.

When Trotter was back home in Boston three days after his talk in Peoria, rumors of a Boston debut of *The Birth of a Nation* were confirmed publicly. Griffith's team kicked off its marketing campaign on Sunday, April 4, with the first of a continuous run of newspaper advertisements. The ad in the *Boston Sunday Post* announced that the film would premiere on Saturday afternoon, April 10 and that in four days, advance ticket sales to the Boston run would begin—at nine a.m. at the Tremont Theatre box office across from Boston Common. "A Dramatic Triumph, Dwarfing All Records," declared the advertisement that featured such eye-catching (false) filmmaking factoids as "8 Months to Make it," "18,000 people," "3,000 horses," and "Cost $500,000.00."

Immediately the war of words expanded beyond the private exchanges between Cobleigh and Dixon and burst into the public arena. On the morning of April 5 Boston lawyer Moorfield Storey, president of the NAACP board and Trotter's sometime ally, wrote a letter against the movie, which the *Boston Herald* published the next day. Referring to the Sunday announcement and quoting from negative reviews about the film's "pernicious caricature of the Negro race," Storey hoped "the public opinion of this city will assert itself, and that the authorities will exercise their power to prevent the proposed performance." He called the movie a greed-inspired attempt to exploit "the prejudices and passions of the spectators."

Griffith's business agent and key public relations operative, J. J. McCarthy, already in town to get ready for the opening, did not waste a second in firing back. He composed a retort defending Griffith that the *Herald* published the next day. "We deny in toto that we are inculcating race prejudice," McCarthy insisted. He also came up with a stunt—to put money where his mouth was—as part of the film company's rebuttal to the allegation that Griffith's masterpiece falsely retold the history of the Civil War and Reconstruction. "Mr. David W. Griffith will give to Mr. Storey or to any charity he may name the sum of $10,000 in return for pointing out any such distortion." While all of this was getting going, the Boston Literary and Historical Association held its monthly Monday night meeting at the South End church. Trotter was in abstentia when the meeting began at nine p.m., but Deenie Trotter was newly elected to serve on the Executive Committee. Members caught one another up on the fast-breaking developments involving Griffith's movie. The association had joined the Boston NAACP branch in asking Mayor James Michael Curley to hold a public hearing, seeking to ban the film from the city's theaters. Word had just come back from the mayor's office that a hearing would be held at City Hall on April 7—just two days away. Everyone was urged to round up people to attend, and then they voted on a resolution to send to the mayor, condemning *The Birth of a Nation*. They strategized "as to the best method of procedure at the protest meeting," and several members suggested that with Mayor Curley—and his reputation as culture czar—"the best way would be to attack the play on the grounds of immorality."

Monroe Trotter, meanwhile, needed to get back to Boston. He had been notified first of the Sunday advertisement and then about the upcoming City Hall hearing. But he had to fulfill a prior commitment—as the Literary and Historical Association members met Monday night, he was giving his last talk on the "now famous interview with President Wilson" to an enthusiastic crowd in Baltimore. The pastor there praised Trotter as a "fighter for the rights of the race," and Trotter made a point during this particular speech to emphasize the president's disloyalty to Negroes, reminding his audience that prior to his election, Wilson had "promised the Colored people of this country a square deal." He and many Negroes "had ardently supported his candidacy on the strength of this belief." But once in office, Wilson had betrayed them. Negroes, said the editor, were being "discriminated against in every way," a perverse turn of events requiring more than ever that they "fight manfully" all forms of bigotry.

Immediately after the event Trotter boarded a train bound for Boston. In making loyalty a theme of the Baltimore talk he might well have been looking ahead to the hearing before Mayor Curley in two days' time. If so, Trotter had to be feeling confident the fate of this monstrous new film was falling into the lap of the forty-year-old Democrat and political party boss. He and Curley had a history—which included that both were "jail birds" at the Charles Street Jail within months of each other in 1903 and 1904. More important, of course, was their more recent involvement. Trotter had contacted then congressman Curley in 1913 for help in arranging his first White House visit with Wilson. Curley, on behalf of one "William Monroe Trotter, a prominent colored citizen of Boston" then contacted presidential secretary Tumulty to express Trotter's concern over the "segregation of the colored employees of the Post Office Department." The next year, Curley had won election to his first mayoral term, with Trotter serving as a vocal member of a successful coalition that consisted of supporters from the city's fifteen-thousand-strong Negro population, and the Irish and other working-class immigrants. Curley, his record showed, understood loyalty, and Monroe Trotter knew that.

Moreover, Trotter knew James Michael Curley took seriously his role as guardian of morality when it came to the city's artistic and cultural life—and in Boston, the mayor's office was no paper tiger with regard to fulfilling this function. Ever since 1908, when the state legislature passed a law exclusive to Boston, authority to police the city's theaters rested with the mayor. It meant that a mayor, or his agent, such as the police commissioner, could pull a theater's license if he found "any part of the show obscene or immoral." Once he took office, Curley had appointed staffer John M. Casey as City Hall censor, to assist him. The pair became Boston's equivalent of legendary national censor Anthony Comstock.

In fact, the mayor had just exercised his powers in this regard just the week before. On March 29, he and Casey had gone to consider a new movie by director Lois Weber called *The Hypocrites*. Set partly in medieval times, one plotline showed a monk killed by a mob for making a nude statue to symbolize "Purity." The film's producers were hoping for a Boston run, but within minutes Curley was on his feet. He stormed out of the theater and announced the film was banned, plain and simple. Casey told reporters that the mayor only needed to see two scenes "before he became so disgusted that he quit." One scene, Casey said, showed "a wood nude fairy sliding to and fro" and that was basis enough to take action. Curley later remarked that he found the film "so obscene that I would not for a moment consider any compromise in the matter." He said he expected "moving picture houses here to respect my wishes" and had instructed Casey to be on the lookout. *The Hypocrites*, he declared, would never play in Boston so long as he was mayor. "Under the law," he said, "I am empowered to stop any immoral exhibition."

This decisive action was fresh news on the eve of a hearing on *The Birth of a Nation*. The task for the movie's opponents was clear—they needed to show Griffith's film was as immoral as any stage play or moving picture that the mayor routinely censored. In this light, who could argue with Monroe Trotter if he felt upbeat as he headed home, thinking he had D. W. Griffith right where he wanted him.

PART IV

1915

Tremont Theatre

=12=

Curley's Our Man,
or Not?

When the year 1915 began, the nationally acclaimed journalist Ray Stannard Baker decided to travel the countryside, North to South, to gather information for a magazine story chronicling the sorry state of race relations, the spread of segregation in government agencies and everyday life, and the spike in ghastly mob violence against citizens whose skin color was not white. Lynching, he found, was on the rise again—six months into 1915, there were thirty-four hangings, or thirteen more than in the same period during the previous year. "Some of the more recent lynchings, involving women and even whole families, have been peculiarly barbarous," he said. Competing for most barbarous was the hanging of Will Stanley, a murder suspect who was taken from police custody in Temple, Texas, in the middle of a summer night and dragged to the town square. Before a crowd that grew to ten thousand, Stanley was hanged and cremated on a makeshift pyre. One enterprising observer thought to snap a photograph of the corpse, which he then made into a postcard that soon was selling briskly for ten cents apiece in surrounding cities and towns. Meanwhile, racist thought in popular culture and the arts proliferated. Early in the year a new poem by Stephen Phillips titled "The Black Peril" debuted in the *Los Angeles Times*:

> *Beware the black blood with the white!*
> *The skull of brass, the hands that tear!*
> *The lecherous ape, not human quite,*
> *The tiger not outgrown his lair!*

The final stanza served as a warning to white women:

> *And him no shout upraised can fright,*
> *Nor lighted bon-fire scare away;*
> *Restless as he crouches day and night,*
> *Leaps! and a woman is his prey.*

Encountering the spread of Jim Crow in President Wilson's administration, Baker commented that the reversal of fortune constituted a profound betrayal for Negroes because, ever since the Civil War, "Uncle Sam was their friend and protector." Noting that a Negro migration from South to North was now well under way, he said the trend, along with advances in education, had heightened racial tensions everywhere, as many whites felt threatened by a Negro population now exceeding ten million and making up a tenth of the country's overall population. His reporting became the basis for an article, "Gathering Clouds Along the Color Line," which appeared in the monthly magazine the *World's Work*, in which he built upon a 1908 piece of his that was one of the first examinations in the white media of Negro politics—about W. E. B. Du Bois and the Monroe Trotter faction in the civil rights movement, and the fact Booker T. Washington did not speak for all Negroes. In the earlier article Baker had described "Two Great Negro Parties," one in the South, led by Washington; the other, based in the North, led by Du Bois and Trotter. Now, revisiting the matter seven years later, he detected a significant power shift. The bitter infighting and decisiveness had certainly continued, but his update revealed Booker T. Washington's emphasis in individual duty and self-improvement had lost considerable ground after twenty years of popular support, including that of white southerners who saw Washington's way as producing "a kind of super-servant." Baker found, instead, changing Negro public opinion in favor of more "agitative organization—the

emphasis being upon rights rather than upon duties." New civil
rights leaders, such as Du Bois and Trotter, wrote the journalist,
"have shown an increasing impatience and boldness of tone."

Monroe Trotter arrived home from Baltimore to find the region in
the throes of a drought—the worst in seventy-five years, according
to the weather bureau; instead of a normally wet March, in 1915
Boston had seen only a few "fugitive flakes of snow." Manufacturers
dependant on waterpower worried that without rain, they might be
forced into plant shutdowns in the fall, and Bostonians complained
about the nasty dust and dirt on the city's streets. One newspaper
reported just days before Trotter's return, "The clouds of street
dust, popularly supposed to be laden with germs that cause influenza, grippe and colds generally, have been unprecedented for this
time of year during the last two days."

Early in the afternoon of Wednesday, April 7, Trotter emerged
from this sand and fog to climb the white granite steps of Boston
City Hall, an ornately built, three-story structure in French Second
Empire design. He passed the ornamental columns, walked through
the huge front doors composed of different woods and inlayed with
a marble circle, and entered the large first-floor lobby. His destination was the aldermanic chamber on the second floor, where Mayor
James M. Curley had scheduled a hearing on short notice, at the
request of Trotter's literary group and the Boston chapter of the
NAACP, on the fate of *The Birth of a Nation* in Boston.

The moment marked the first time Trotter and D. W. Griffith
had ever appeared in the same room together. The Boston militant was an earnest-looking man of medium height dressed in a
white shirt, a dark tie, and his trademark coal black suit, which,
as usual, could have used a fresh pressing. Trotter did not make
any kind of public pronouncement about it, but the day marked
his forty-third birthday. He had filled out a bit since his Harvard
days, wore a mustache, and his hair was turning a striking iron
gray. Joining him to argue against the film were a number of prominent civil rights activists and Boston clergy, including lawyer
Moorfield Storey and a local NAACP leader named Butler R. Wilson, also a lawyer, as well as settlement house worker Mary White

Old Boston City Hall. COURTESY OF WIKIMEDIA COMMONS.

Ovington, a cofounder of the NAACP. Ovington, the one in charge of the NAACP's Scenario Committee that was trying, futilely, to develop a competing film, had rushed by train from New York City just in time for the hearing. Contrary to the findings of journalist Ray Stannard Baker about a splintered movement, this side of the hearing room was picture of unity.

The Birth of a Nation's creator, whom the press was calling the greatest American filmmaker ever, was taller than Trotter probably expected—an athletic-looking six-footer, with an aquiline nose, who favored stylish pinstriped suits and often sported a derby hat. Griffith, now forty, seemed comfortable in public, projecting an almost regal bearing befitting a prominent director and a southerner with aristocratic pretensions. He, too, had come ready for battle, standing with his attorney, John F. Cusick; business manager, Henry MacMahon; and John B. Schoeffel, manager of the Tremont Theatre, where the film was to open in three days.

The hearing room was large—forty feet square with twenty-foot ceilings—but not large enough for the nearly two hundred spectators, mostly Negroes, who had turned out. Those unable to find a chair sat on windowsills, leaned against the perimeter walls, and stretched out into the wide corridor near the mayor's office. Several Boston police officers were on hand, and shortly after three p.m. Curley silenced the chattering so that the hearing could begin. The first thing he did after calling the session to order was to read the state statute that empowered him to forbid a show if he found it indecent or immoral. Because Trotter and fellow opponents had called for the hearing, they went first, and for the next two hours a series of witnesses presented their case against the film.

Lawyer Wilson began by submitting letters from Jane Addams and other notable figures who had seen and were opposed to the movie. In brief remarks he said the film "excited hatred for colored people" and that, in its entirety, "is suggestive of sensual excesses and an offence against common decency." As their first witness they chose Ovington who, freshly arrived from New York City, was able to provide a firsthand account of the film's content. She had viewed it twice at the Liberty Theatre, she told the mayor, and, in an attention-grabbing start, said that while leaving the theater afterward, she had overheard white patrons spewing anger. "I would like to kill every nigger," she quoted one as saying. "I would like to sweep every nigger off the earth," she quoted another. Then, knowing full well Curley's s penchant for policing nudity as the apex of immorality—indeed, his "barefoot ban" was part of the city's vernacular—Ovington emphasized Griffith's portrayal of "colored women," their "sensuous" looks, their champagne drinking, and their "décolleté gowns."

But Curley did not take the bait. He interrupted her, and for the remainder seemed at once to have sport with the pious-sounding liberal and use her as a vehicle to strut his self-taught mastery of literary classics. He asked whether high society women also wore low-cut gowns in fashionable hotels. Ovington, taken aback, said she was not much for high society, but noted that even if what the mayor said was true about their dress, high society matrons "don't wear the bestial expressions on their faces that are seen in the play."

Ovington then tried to score points by describing one of the scenes that opponents had begun citing as most objectionable, where the ex-slave Gus, played by a white actor in blackface, his eyes leering and mouth foaming (an effect created by the use of hydrogen peroxide), chased the virginal white Flora, who "to escape his clutches throws herself into an abyss."

Curley initially seemed more interested in the young maiden than in a Negro character shown as a lustful animal. "Was the girl sufficiently dressed?" he asked. "No," Ovington replied curtly, her manner suggesting that, to him, nothing was afoul "as long as the girl kept her shoes on." But then he did tackle Ovington's focus on the Negro characters' facial expressions as putative evidence of indecency, although he conveyed interest in the form of cross-examination.

"Are you familiar with Shakespeare's plays?"

"Modestly," Ovington replied, adding she knew some of his works.

"You have seen, then, where Lady Macbeth commits murder?" Curley was leading the witness to subjects familiar to him, for he worshiped Shakespeare—and not just for his plays. He admired the playwright's hard-luck story, featuring a ruined father and a childhood spent in poverty, as it reflected his own tough start, which worsened with his father's death when Curley was only ten. Then there were the plays themselves, and Curley had read them all, some while in the Charles Street Jail, and he had come to rely on Shakespeare, as a biographer noted, "as a kind of political consultant, summoning quotations from memory to garnish his speeches or to put opponents in their place with a barb from the Bard." The latter was the purpose for which Curley presently invoked the master writer.

Ovington replied that she knew the Lady Macbeth scene.

"Was there not an awful expression on her face at that time?"

Ovington dug in. "Not as horrible as Gus."

"You have seen *The Merchant of Venice*?" he asked. "Don't you think the Jews have as much right to protest this play as you have to oppose the moving picture of the Negro? Was not the expression on Shylock's more horrible than the face of this Gus in the picture?"

"No," Ovington said, "the face of Gus was much more horrible."

The mayor seemed to tire of Ovington. He suggested her problem with the film might be rooted in her mind. "You imagine that a Negro wishes to attack a white girl because he chases her through a wood until she hurls herself from a cliff. This is not sufficient grounds for me to disallow the production of the play."

"What your imaginations tell you is not sufficient," Curley concluded.

Despite being outnumbered, D. W. Griffith surely had to like what he had seen so far. Indeed, right away Trotter and other "protestants" began sensing Curley was not simply playing devil's advocate but was leaning against them and that his generous concept of moral depravity might not include racist and hateful film material. During the next presentation, Moorfield Storey addressed this worry head-on. Storey opened making the point *The Birth of a Nation* was a planned libel against the Negro race. "This picture is for political purposes," he said. "It is to discredit the Negro all over the country." But, again, Curley dipped into Shakespeare for an analogy as a counterpoint. If those were grounds for suppression, he said, the English "could enter just such a protest against Shakespeare's *Henry VIII*," given that drama's harsh view of the Episcopal Church. Storey disagreed and said the mayor did not get it, that Griffith's film was incomparable to Shakespeare, that if *The Birth of a Nation* was allowed to play, "white people who see it will want to kill every Colored man in the United States."

Curley then tested the basis for the lawyer's sweeping conclusions: had Storey seen the film? Storey had to reply he had not. The admission hurt. The mayor behaved dismissively and mockingly toward the distinguished attorney from that point on. Curley said, "According to you the production of almost every comedy on the stage should be prohibited because of the Irish, the Dutch, the Germans and the Jews." Storey, now smoldering, said they were not discussing satire or comedy, but race-baiting propaganda. He repeated— the singular goal of Griffith's film was "to discredit the Negro race."

The two were on the verge of an argument. When Storey interrupted him an irritated Curley looked out at the audience and said melodramatically that he should have asked the upstart's permission to speak during a hearing at which he, the mayor, was presiding.

Fuming, Storey responded, "Go ahead, if you represent the other side."

"I don't represent any side," said Curley with a glare.

Following Moorfield Storey, a Boston architect named Joseph P. Loud, also a member of the Boston NAACP, and several clergy gave brief presentations. Loud seemed to suffer a bout of stage fright and was unable to speak without referring to his notes. When he described the way Griffith had made heroes out of the Ku Klux Klan, his voice grew shaky. But Loud had something over the two clergy; he had seen the movie in New York City. For that reason Curley seemed attentive as Loud focused on the film's polar portrayals of Negroes and whites—the former as bestial and the latter as noble. Loud reiterated the scantily clothed condition of women in the movie, and emphasized again the so-called Gus chase scene, saying the sight of the Negro's chasing the white girl until she jumped from the cliff was horrible. It was as Loud spoke that Curley, in an almost offhand way, finally conceded a possible shortcoming, but he was stingy even saying that much, calling the chase scene "the only thing of an objectionable nature" he had heard so far. The two clergy, meanwhile, made only generic objections, as one insisted any picture based on Dixon's *The Clansman* had to be "vindictive" and the second mainly wanted to introduce their next speaker, someone the mayor actually knew—someone "who had rushed from Baltimore to be in time to protest."

Monroe Trotter had been saved for last, and so after nearly ninety minutes of other testimony, he stood in the crowded chamber to deliver the equivalent of a closing argument at trial, bidding to sway the mayor with a speech that pulled together the evidence others had presented while embroidering his own to it, so that his words built to a climax and left a final and indelible impression, to leave Curley with one option and one option only—to ban Griffith's film. Trotter began by telling the mayor he had read Dixon's novel and, also, that he had seen *The Birth of a Nation*, the point being

Walter Lang in blackface as ex-Union
Negro soldier "Gus" in *The Birth of a Nation*.
COURTESY OF THE MUSEUM OF MODERN ART, NEW YORK.

that he spoke credibly with firsthand knowledge. But if Trotter had already seen the movie, this marked the first public indication. It is also the only reference to a viewing found in the historical record. Given his travels, as well as the fact the film had only just begun in Los Angeles and New York City, it is hard to determine where and when he had had the time. There is no way of knowing, in the end. But if he had not seen the movie, and was engaged in a histrionic bluff, this much was true: Trotter had done his homework, because for the next hour he spoke with a detailed familiarity of the movie and a honed sense of horror at its depiction of Negroes.

Trotter reiterated the opponents' position that the whole purpose of the movie was to "disparage the Colored race." He charged that portraying the Negro as obsessed with "preying upon and raping white girl children" was propaganda, pure and simple, to "convert the North to belief in the South's repression and disenfranchisement."

He then backed up rhetoric with evidence, zooming in on numerous specific scenes, citing, for example, when Silas Lynch, the acting lieutenant governor during Reconstruction, locks Elsie in his room, and ties and gags her to force her into marriage, or when guffawing Negro legislators celebrate passage of a law permitting interracial marriages in South Carolina. These scenes, he argued, "were all so worked as to rouse the passions of white men to a hostile, retaliatory, even murderous feeling toward Colored men."

Trotter enlarged on his argument, describing the societal context in which the film was debuting, "the extreme degree of segregation even in border states and the denial of civil rights in Northern states." It was a performance garnering both negative and favorable reviews, one reporter afterward calling it "a lengthy and lurid speech," another saying Trotter delivered "an impassioned appeal." Likewise, one Boston NAACP member on hand criticized the presentation as suffering from "too much Trotter," whereas Ovington, of the NAACP's home office, said the editor had been "eloquent" and that he had made a "very fine impression."

Trotter then turned his focus onto Curley himself, as if it were just the two of them talking politics and personalities—all of it being local. He asked the mayor to remember back to when he was a congressman, when Curley had made all Bostonians proud for the stand he took against bigotry and denounced lynching "to the faces of Southern members of Congress." For that, Trotter had rallied Negro voters to turn out en masse to help elect him mayor. And for that, reminded Trotter, Curley had promised to protect them. Now, he said, with the arrival of *The Birth of a Nation*, the Negro was depending on the mayor to deliver on that promise. He urged Curley to "construe with liberality" the censorship law, particularly the clause addressing the morals of the community, because a film inspiring racial hatred, retaliation, and injury "certainly were moral feelings and lowered the morals." Trotter then stepped away from the table and, to gain greater intimacy, moved in closer to the mayor. It was a signal that the editor of the *Guardian* was reaching his finale, in which he said the controversy marked a new kind of civil war requiring Curley to draw the line against a film "by a Southerner seeking to flout Boston and her abolitionists." The mayor, he said, must "stand up for his home city and her great men, and protect his Colored friends."

With that, Trotter rested.

Trotter and the others had used nearly two hours. It was after five p.m., and the mayor indicated the film group could have thirty or so minutes to respond. Griffith's attorney, John F. Cusick, rose first, and he made a few quick points. He insisted, for example, the film was based on historical fact and that Griffith was not ridiculing the Negro race. The lawyer's main defense strategy, however, was to impress Curley with approvals for the work, and he began ticking off a who's who of the film's supporters. He mentioned the National Board of Censors' endorsement but, without question, his heaviest firepower was the alleged approvals of powerbrokers at the highest levels of government in Washington, DC. Ignoring the pledge Thomas Dixon had made to Woodrow Wilson to keep the White House screening a secret, in grand fashion Cusick told Curley that *The Birth of a Nation* had been shown in the East Room. "The first production of this photoplay," he said, "was before President Wilson and the members of his cabinet. They declared it wonderful."

The moment Cusick mentioned the president—Trotter's adversary—hissing started in certain quarters of the room. Instead of being a momentary and isolated outburst, the hissing caught on and spread all around. The room was suddenly in an uproar, with any semblance of decorum gone. Reporters knew in an instant the leads for their stories—"Negroes Hiss Wilson's Name," was the headline in the *Boston Journal*, one journalist characterizing the hearing as "one of the most sensational gatherings of its kind ever held in Greater Boston." The coverage would add to Wilson's ever-deepening consternation over ever becoming involved with the movie. Curley pounded the gavel, calling for order, as the hissing only grew louder. Boston patrolmen Dougherty and Leary leapt into action, moving quickly around the room and ordering spectators to calm down and to show the proper respect.

"To think that this would happen in the good old Democratic city of Boston," quipped Cusick, looking toward the mayor and smiling. Resuming, the lawyer disclosed that there had been a second viewing in Washington at the National Press Club, where the chief justice of the US Supreme Court, other justices, members of Congress, and key members of the press had all praised the film and said that Griffith's work, "instead of being degrading, was of especial educational, instructive and of moral value." The news triggered a second round of hisses, but Curley squelched the noise before it could move again like a wave around the room.

The presidential name-dropping and its attendant outburst seemed to overshadow what was left of the hearing. Cusick turned to introduce the famous director so he could share a few thoughts of his own, but the moment seemed anticlimatic. Griffith, poised and ever courteous, said he could not help but respond to the opponents' charge of anti-Negro bias and to question, even if true, which he insisted it was not, how that could be construed as a basis for censorship. If that were the case, he said, then Indians could win suppression of many western films, given that most cowboy scenarios show Indians killing white men. Then, to score a second point, Griffith made a transparent appeal to the mayor's Irish Catholic heritage. He pulled out a letter from a Catholic priest affiliated with the *Columbia*, the Knights of Columbus newspaper, and read aloud the man's praise for the movie. But that was not all, Griffith said. He had brought along for Curley's consideration letters from three Catholic clergy in New York City, letters he had received on Monday just before he had left for Boston. In them, the director said, the priests explained how they would like to take the children in their parish schools to see the movie at the Liberty Theatre. Emphasizing his movie's educational purpose, he also mentioned that six New York City school principals had contacted him about taking students to *The Birth of a Nation.*

Curley had a question—about what everyone was calling the Gus chase scene. The opponents' repeated protest about its vulgarity had apparently stayed with him, and he wondered about Griffith's flexibility: would he consider eliminating that scene? Griffith replied he would, if the mayor insisted.

That said, Curley made clear he had heard enough. "My power is limited in this matter," he announced. Then, alluding to electoral politics and politicking, he said, "I do not want to make political capital out of it, and I do not want to hurt a legitimate firm doing business." He turned to Trotter and the others and said, "You people seem to want everything pertaining to the Negro cut out of this picture. Are there not good Negroes and bad? Are there not bad whites as well as good?"

Good Negroes and bad? Trotter, agitated by the turn of events, stood up. The complaint with *The Birth of a Nation* went far beyond basic character development—and, as far as he was concerned, if Griffith's movie had battered the Irish the way it had the Negro, James Michael Curley would be the one leading the charge to run the film out of town. But Trotter did not get into that kind of comparison. He focused on reminding the mayor of the political support Negroes had given him.

Curley paused for a moment. First Moorfield Storey had interrupted him, and now Trotter. "You have stated your case," he said firmly. "You have introduced no evidence that I could use in stopping at least one performance." The film, he ruled, could continue with its scheduled opening on Saturday at the Tremont Theatre. "This photo-play will be produced," declared the mayor.

Then came the *but*. Despite the interruptions, and in seeming deference to Trotter and his side, Mayor Curley ordered D. W. Griffith to screen *The Birth of a Nation* in two days' time, on Friday night, to which presentation he would send his censor John Casey as well as a police department official. Curley stressed that morality, and not race portrayals, was his measuring stick: "If this film violated the law it will be stopped." He then abruptly adjourned the hearing and left for his office.

The hearing, which had lasted three hours, concluded around six p.m. The two sides huddled in the wake of the mayor's hasty departure, assessing the outcome and whether it constituted a win or a loss. Undoubtedly Trotter, having mustered every argument he could think of and executing a bravura performance, was disappointed. He had wanted nothing less than a clear-cut ruling to stop the film, and Curley had not come through. But however betrayed the *Guardian* editor felt, he knew to suppress his outrage, because the mayor had left open the door to a ban that might follow the special preview. He, Storey, Ovington, and the others were thus left in limbo. Griffith and his group, meanwhile, seemed pleased to have gotten past such a public hurdle, especially in view of Trotter's appeal for a return on the Negroes' political investment in the Boston mayor. The filmmaker's publicity machine got cranking right away preparing a press release. "We regret very much that on our first appearance in the city of Boston we should be engaged in such an unpleasant dispute," Griffith began. But if he must do battle, he said, then "Boston, the very beginning of the liberty of the American people" was a most fitting venue—"Boston, whose very name is synonymous with freedom." The statement seemed a retort to Trotter's use of Boston—and its abolitionist legacy—to argue in favor of a ban, as Griffith redeployed the city for his own rhetorical purpose. The editor and director, in addition to locking horns over the legal right to show *The Birth of a Nation*, were now also in a fight about what the city stood for. Griffith said, "I have little fear, when asking for the privilege of free speech in Boston, that that privilege will not be granted—granted honestly, squarely and surely."

The two groups made their way out of the aldermanic chamber and were in the second-floor corridor, when Moorfield Storey got it in his mind to challenge Griffith. He was thinking about the latter's assertion that the film depicted history accurately and his much-ballyhooed offer to donate $10,000 to charity if anyone found a single historic inaccuracy. Storey, with Trotter and the others nearby, strode up to Griffith and got the director's attention. Was it historically correct, he asked, that the acting lieutenant governor of South Carolina during Reconstruction—the mulatto character Silas Lynch, in the film—had locked a white maiden in a room to force her into marriage?

The unflappable Griffith dodged the interrogatory. "Come and see the play," was all he said. Then he offered his hand to Storey, but the lawyer drew back.

"No, sir," he said, turning and walking away.

Everyone cleared out of City Hall. Ovington wrote about "the little bout" between Storey and the filmmaker in a single-spaced typewritten letter to NAACP board chairman Joel E. Spingarn of

New York City. In her thorough summary of the hearing, she referred to Curley as a "very kindly Irishman" who, while "ready to hear all we had to say against the film seemed prejudiced against" the opposition. Her report conveyed profound disappointment that the mayor was allowing the film to open that weekend, an outcome she said foreboded trouble.

"I think something will happen Saturday night."

But nothing did—at least in the way Ovington had insinuated.

Instead, in the forty-eight hours building to the special screening, the two sides fought in the court of public opinion while continuing to lobby the mayor privately. Trotter was at his desk in the *Guardian* office on Cornhill Street the next morning, to pull together a package of newspaper clippings and opposition letters to *The Birth of a Nation*. He composed a letter that he and Rev. Montrose W. Thornton signed under the auspices of their political action group, the National Equal Rights League (NERL), and delivered what Trotter called the "documentary argument" to Curley at City Hall two blocks away. In the cover letter, the editor told the mayor that the film was "a Southern attack upon Boston, her moral leaders of the past generation," writing, "Our home city of Boston will never again be for us what it is if this play is presented." Trotter and Thornton also led a group that met with Boston Police officials, given that a representative from the force would be attending the screening the next night, and once again presented the claim that Griffith's film was immoral for "fostering a spirit of lawlessness and race hatred." Thornton added a comment intended to get the officials' attention: that the "production might lead to a riot and violence."

D. W. Griffith, meanwhile, was already rolling out huge ads in the city's newspapers, designed to smother the Trotter opposition with a litany of approvals for *The Birth of a Nation* from clergy, elected officials, and critics in New York City who had seen the movie. The ads carried a headline: "Tremendous Volume of Praise Completely Drowns Out Antipathy of a Few Opponents." As part of the Griffith strategy to quickly confront opposition, by either letters to newspapers, paid advertisements, or in person, Thomas

Dixon had arrived in town, too, and on Friday morning he paid a personal visit to pen pal Rolfe Cobleigh, editor of the *Congregationalist*, the magazine of the National Association of Christian Congregational Churches, at the latter's office. Dixon came armed with testimonials lauding *The Birth of a Nation*. "He tried to convince that it deserved my approval," Cobleigh said later. But a conversation that began with Dixon's emphasizing Griffith's artistry devolved quickly into a heated debate about the film's treatment of the Negro race. Cobleigh provoked the novelist into a rant that a Negro's "dominant passion" was to have "sexual relations with white women," and that a core purpose of the movie was "to create a feeling of abhorrence in white people, especially white women against colored men." He further asserted that the KKK was formed to save the South from the Negro, protect white women from Negro heathens, and restore power to white men. Afterward, Dixon vehemently would deny having made those admissions, but Cobleigh came away with plenty of copy to work with, and his account of the morning he spent with the author was soon published as an article in the *Congregationalist*. The Griffith team also hired Pinkerton detectives to gather intelligence about plans or actions Trotter and other opponents might be hatching. "We were all subject to the annoyance of being followed by plainclothes men," said pro-Trotter testifier Loud. "We understand twenty-four men are so engaged, and I was followed to the country by them."

Then came the screening on Friday night. Originally imagined as a small, private affair mainly for Curley's censor, it was suddenly transformed into something else, as Griffith threw open the doors of the Tremont Theatre and invited many of the city's opinion shapers—newspaper arts reviewers, select public officials, and Boston society types. The evening took on the markings of a high-profile setup for Saturday's premiere rather than a last-minute assessment of the movie's moral fiber, as 1,500 attendees took their seats to view a film its maker hoped would be embraced as the spellbinding epic that it was. The timing of the screening was a publicist's dream— April 9, 1915, marked the fiftieth anniversary of Robert E. Lee's surrender to Ulysses S. Grant at Appomattox Court House—and, as Griffith liked to tell reporters, he had painstakingly re-created the interior of the Virginian home where the surrender occurred, had researched to get the costuming of the two generals exactly right, and had even uncovered previously unknown details, namely that General Lee had had to borrow a pen from a soldier to sign the paperwork because no pens were found in the house.

The move paid off. Rave reviews began appearing the next morning in nearly all of the Boston papers. "I cannot describe this picture in a half column, or a column; a page would not do it justice," wrote Frederick Johns of the *Boston American*. "It is impossible to keep from bursting into admiration at the marvelous way the author has woven the great incidents of the war into his film. He is an amazing impressionist; his scenes flash the story at you with never a rest. You sit overpowered by the beauty and magnitude of the pictures." If those words were not enough acclaim for Griffith, Johns's comments about the way the movie "deals boldly with the negro excesses during reconstruction" had to be icing on the director's cake: "I am quite sure," the critic said, "nobody last night left the theatre feeling inflamed against the respectable and industrious colored population of Boston."

Most of the mainstream press in Boston was as unequivocal in its praise. The lone contrarian was the *Boston Traveler*'s Salita Solano, a woman in her twenties who only the year before had been promoted from cub reporter to art critic. Despite her relative inexperience, Solano's review came across as a balanced counterpoint. She gave high marks for the film's production qualities: "Never has there been a photoplay shown in this city which combined such beauty and artistry with such a powerful dramatic appeal and fidelity to details." However, she pulled no punches in her criticism of Griffith's "Southern viewpoint" in which slavery was presented without any of its inherent cruelty—no whipping posts, no auction blocks, no brutal overseer, no maltreatment of any sort. "On the contrary, we see the 'happy cullud folk' dancing and making merry." Solano knew she was being a spoilsport, noting the movie was "most enthusiastically received" at Friday's screening and that it "will doubtless have a long run." But she could not help rue the bigotry upon which its success was built. "The more the pity that its lesson is so insidious," she wrote.

The biggest surprise was that, at the screening Griffith had so swiftly and successfully turned into an invitation-only social spectacle, the mayor himself turned up to accompany his censor, John Casey, and a police representative. The next morning he issued a statement: "With the desire that the fullest possible measure of justice be accorded the colored citizenship of Boston, I attended the production last evening." After conferring with his censor, he said, he had found no legal basis to ban the film—no immorality or indecency. But Griffith had agreed voluntarily to soften parts the mayor had found unduly harsh in its treatment of Negroes. Curley wanted the opening intertitle seemingly blaming the Civil War on Negroes dropped altogether. "The bringing of the African to America in the seventeenth century," the card read, "planted the first seed of disunion." He also asked that the Gus chase scene and a few others be trimmed, scenes "that while not immoral or obscene, yet might be offensive to certain of the public." Otherwise, he said, the show was free and clear to open in Boston.

Griffith's producer Harry Aitken, renting an entire train car for the occasion, arrived at South Station with a large party of friends. He joined the director, Dixon, and others for the gala premiere, as crowds surged to attend the first public showings on Saturday afternoon and evening. The three-story Tremont Theatre, built in 1807 and adapted to a movie house in 1913, had long been considered one of the most elegant venues in the city. The original brick and brownstone front was now mostly obscured by awnings and the giant marquee jutting out onto Tremont Street, but the interior still featured ornate Renaissance decorations and delicate coloring. Ushers dressed in period costume were on hand to distribute programs. The young women, or "usherettes," their hair styled in flowing curls, wore puffy crinolines and pantalets under their gowns, while the young men wore the uniforms of the Blue and Gray.

Both Saturday performances were sellouts—with tickets ranging from twenty-five cents to the unheard of price of two dollars ($46 in 2014 dollars). For Griffith, riding a wave of rave reviews, the weekend was turning out to be as successful an opening as he could have hoped for, given this was Boston and that earlier in the week the deck had seemed so stacked against him and his blockbuster film. "Griffith and His Associates Are Delighted with Boston's Verdict Regarding the Wonderful Picture Drama," read the *Boston Globe*'s headline about the first screening.

For Trotter, momentum was headed in the wrong direction. The mayor had continued to disappoint. Sure, a war of words continued throughout the opening weekend, but mostly under the radar of largely glowing headlines. Cobleigh kept on writing against the film, as did other like-minded liberals. One of the best lines—or sound bites—was coined by Boston lawyer, legislator, and NAACP member Albert E. Pillsbury, who wrote that Griffith's film was "history upside down." During this epistolary combat, Griffith became infuriated when one of his invitees to the Friday screening the next day produced a lengthy censure. It was as if the filmmaker had expected everyone in the invited audience to fall under the spell of his technical magic, no matter their predisposition. But not J. Mott Hallowell, whose father had commanded one of the all-Negro regiments in the Civil War from Boston, the 54th. Hallowell, a Harvard graduate and former state attorney general, called on Curley to condemn the movie as a "slanderous assassination of a race." Piqued, Griffith returned fire, charging Hallowell with social misconduct. "Permit me to thank Mr. Hallowell for an original departure of manners," he began, sarcastically. "He attended the private performance of the play, as he says, by invitation, whereupon he proceeds to thrust a stiletto into the back of his host." He should pay for his ticket, the filmmaker said.

The big story around the globe was the European War, as the United States was being drawn inexorably into the conflict. The same weekend *The Birth of a Nation* opened at the Tremont, a relief steamer that had left the city's port bound for Belgium was sunk. The Germans had promised safe passage for the ship carrying gifts and supplies rounded up from New Englanders for the Belgians, but instead torpedoed it. Early reports said twenty crew members were killed, including the captain. The film controversy, however, was the dominant preoccupation of the people of Boston, and by Monday morning Monroe Trotter was headed back to City Hall.

Trotter had learned Griffith had not made the cuts he had promised, and wanted the mayor to do something about it. The editor and a delegation of about twenty supporters arrived with diminishing confidence, however, worried that Curley was holding a finger to the winds of public opinion and leaning in the direction it was headed—and the movie was already a box office smash. The session, which included Griffith's lawyer in attendance, grew testy at times, as Trotter questioned Curley persistently about his lack of action. The mayor's responses seemed all over the place, as if he were trying to please everyone. He offered criticisms of the film, his first since viewing it on Friday night, but said he thought both whites and blacks were not treated very well in the dramatization. When Trotter continued to press, however, Curley finally went further, commenting that Griffith's portrayal of Negroes "was an outrage upon the colored people of the country."

"That is all we want, Mr. Mayor," Trotter said, sounding like a police detective who had just gotten a confession. "Throughout the country the word is being spread that you favor its production. We are pleased to see that you do not."

Trotter shifted to the cuts Griffith had promised. What about those? The mayor turned to attorney John F. Cusick, Griffith's stand-in, who disclosed Griffith was en route to Hollywood—having left town the victor. Cusick's demeanor seemed less conciliatory compared to his behavior at the previous week's hearing, when the movie's fate hung in the balance. He assured Curley that Griffith had tweaked the film prior to his departure, and stood firm in saying his client would not be making any further changes, in light of the official city ruling that "there was no violation of the law in the photoplay." The message was clear—any cosmetic changes made so far had been voluntary; Griffith could play nice, seem cooperative, but need not do anything.

Trotter and his delegation were getting little out of the meeting, save for the cold comfort of Curley's quote. The *Guardian* editor showed his frustration and Curley stiffened, telling him that if he and his comrades were so dissatisfied, they ought to head over to the state legislature on Beacon Hill and get the Boston censorship law changed to give him, as mayor, "more arbitrary powers in such matters." But as things stood he was impotent, because in his view the film had passed the morality test.

He had thrown Trotter a bone of sorts—hinting that if he did have broader powers—"more arbitrary powers"—he would act against *The Birth of a Nation*. Trotter, of course, thought that Curley had plenty of authority under the existing statute. Even so, he took note of the mayor's comment. In fact, he and others were already a step ahead of City Hall investigating alternative options.

Griffith and his team might think the game was over, but it was not.

━13━

Bringing Down
the House

D. W. Griffith and his team always seemed to be working the angles for marketing opportunities—chief among them publicizing plaudits and endorsements from important people. The name-dropping scheme caught up with them in Boston, however. Trouble was already brewing two days before the Curley hearing, when Chief Justice Edward D. White wrote to President Wilson's aide, Joseph Tumulty, to take issue with all of the "rumors about my having sanctioned the show." The nation's top judge, clearly angry, said, "If the owners were wise they would stop the rumors." If they did not, he would publicly deny them and say, "I do not approve the show." When the Griffith team bragged about the White House screening during Curley's hearing, tensions exploded. Wilson and Tumulty began receiving newspaper clippings quoting Griffith's lawyer as saying the president loved the film; and Wilson began fielding queries from his liberal friends, supporters, and members of Congress, asking whether it was true.

The movie had become a full-fledged political nuisance at a time when Wilson constantly had war and peace on his mind. He was preparing a keynote address for the annual meeting of the American Newspaper Publishers' Association and the Associated Press in New York City, at which he uttered the slogan "America First" while reiterating a determination to keep the country neutral in the European War. But given all the fireworks in Boston over *The Birth of a Nation*, he decided he had to say something. But there was a rub—Monroe Trotter. Wilson advised Tumulty to find a way to squirm out of his appearing to support the film, yet without seeming to align himself with the agitation stirred up by "that unspeakable fellow." He decided to use the query from former Massachusetts congressman Thomas C. Thacher as the vehicle to make known a version of the event that played down his backing, and had Tumulty write Thacher, saying the following: "It is true that *The Birth of a Nation* was produced before the President and his family at the White House, but the President was entirely unaware of the character of the play before it was presented and has at no time expressed his approbation of it. Its exhibition at the White House was a courtesy extended to an old acquaintance." By the end of the month, the Thacher communiqué had landed on the front pages of Boston newspapers following its release by the White House, thus silencing Griffith and his team—at least insofar as their proclaiming presidential approval for the movie.

The filmmaker's marketing tricks were not simply reserved for a national bang, either. Local publicity stunts were manifest once the Boston campaign got rolling. Two in particular became public controversies. In their advertising blitz for the special Friday night screening, Griffith's team had listed George Foster Peabody as one of the film's fans. The name jumped out at many Bostonians—Peabody, a philanthropist with deep ancestral ties in New England, had grown up in Georgia, lived in New York, and was a longtime Bookerite. Many progressives and NAACP officials in New York and Boston knew him, and counted on his support. To see his name in the ad in praise of Griffith's "film art," was a disconnect, and Peabody soon fired off a letter to the *Boston Herald*, saying he was surprised to have learned he had been quoted approving the movie. Rather, he said of the film, "The gross caricatures of the Negro were so evidently unfair." Having grown up in Georgia, he added, "I especially deplore all such wicked teachings of race prejudice."

Even more cunning was the ensnaring of two locals, Phillip J. Allston, a Negro druggist, and Dr. Alexander Cox, a Negro dentist, both prominent members of the Boston chapter of Booker T. Washington's Negro Business League. The men were given free tickets to the movie's Saturday night opening, the idea being that unlike that lout J. Mott Hallowell of the Boston NAACP, they would come away impressed. Griffith, along with his business manager, Henry MacMahon, and his publicist, J. J. McCarthy, made a point to schmooze with the two in the lobby after the show, the gist of their talk being that the film was hardly intended to harm the Negro race but was mainly a love story in the context of an epic chapter in the nation's history. The director also said how much he admired Washington's Tuskegee Institute and mentioned he would like to film the school someday to publicize its work.

The two men seemed to enjoy thoroughly the Hollywood attention. Allston told Griffith he would be honored if the director could find time in his hectic schedule to drop by his store across the Charles River in Cambridge. Within a day, too, the druggist wrote Booker T. Washington a quick note describing the film's impressive premiere and said that Griffith—*the* Mr. David W. Griffith— had asked about "reproducing in pictures Tuskegee." Allston told Washington that, in his personal opinion, any such project should not proceed without some financial benefit, but that it did sound like a terrific opportunity to promote the school.

Griffith seemed to have the two Boston Bookerites in his pocket. Following Allston's note to Washington, and while Monroe Trotter and others renewed their opposition during their follow-up meeting with Mayor Curley, Allston and Cox next tried to get the Boston chapter of the Negro Business League to endorse *The Birth of a Nation*, introducing a resolution praising the film at a special meeting of the chapter's executive committee. But then came a fierce reality check. Other members were shocked, the resolution was crushed, and everyone in the group worried about the disgrace that would befall them if word got around about the two men's foolishness. Griffith's publicity men took care of that, however, circulating news of the two Bookerites' support. "I am glad to say that our efforts are appreciated by some of the colored people," Griffith executive MacMahon wrote in a letter to the *Boston Post*, as a setup to outing Allston and Cox as alleged film fans. The disclosure set off an angry backlash against the two men as well as the league—with Monroe Trotter among the most vociferous, blasting the pair as "colored traitors."

Bookerites scrambled to control the damage. "Indignation runs high against these two men," reported Dr. Samuel E. Courtney to Washington. "It has been considered dangerous for them to show themselves on the street. Not only are they condemned by the colored people but by the whites as well." Courtney, Washington's most loyal Bostonian, bemoaned the two members' misconduct and "the embarrassing position in which our Business League has been placed." He worried, too, about the impact of the brouhaha on plans for Washington's appearance at the league's late summer convention, to be held in Boston. "I am afraid if these two men are not asked to resign from management of the August meeting, Boston will be a cold spot for our National Meeting."

To date, Washington had been noticeably silent about *The Birth of a Nation*. But he could no longer ignore the film. Upon receipt of Courtney's letter he composed a telegram that was to be used as a press release. "From all [I] can hear is vicious and hurtful play," he commented. "Glad to hear people in Boston are against play and hope their efforts to stop it will be successful." In short order, too, Allston issued a statement refuting the Griffith team's account of his encounter in the theater lobby, saying he had only spoken briefly with the director. Washington made sure Allston and Cox were not forced to resign from the Boston chapter of his league. He needed them; they both were playing crucial roles in organizing the upcoming convention.

From Griffith's perspective, Washington's breaking his silence was an unintended consequence in the exploitation of two Boston Bookerites. But any marketing missteps—whether involving the president or a couple of local Negro businessmen—were small brushfires that had little impact on the movie's buzz. "By far the most impressive spectacle ever brought to Boston," raved the *Boston Journal*; "Motion Pictures on a new scale of magnitude," praised the *Boston Evening Transcript*; "It is a great work, first, last and

all the time, and it stamps Mr. Griffith as a master artist," hailed
the *Boston Globe*. During the movie's first week, the theater decided to add matinee shows on weekdays, while tickets sold briskly
for performances weeks in advance. No amount of marketing controversies seemed to make any dent in the film's splash—that, apparently, was the challenge for Trotter and the Boston NAACP to
accomplish one way or another.

"The center of the fight has been Boston," W. E. B. Du Bois told
readers of the *Crisis*, as he drew national attention to his NAACP
cohorts in Boston and his former associate Monroe Trotter who
were "fighting race calumny." In the days after the unsatisfying
meeting with the mayor on Monday, April 12, Trotter went to work
organizing a rally for Thursday night at a Baptist church in the
South End, where the pastor, Rev. Aaron W. Puller, was one of his
key supporters. Much of the city was focused on big league baseball, with the Boston Braves opening their season as defending
World Series Champions at Fenway Park—which the team was
sharing with the Red Sox. Players participated in the pregame
ceremony, escorting Mayor Curley to the flagpole, where he raised
"Old Glory." The Braves began on a sour note, however, losing in a
shutout to the Philadelphia Phillies, 3–0. Trotter, meanwhile, was
preoccupied with turning up the heat on Griffith's film.

He took the dais of the packed People's Baptist Church at nine
p.m., joining Puller, two grandsons of abolitionist William Lloyd
Garrison, and a female militant named Dr. Alice W. McKane who
was, in effect, Boston's equivalent of the more famous Ida B. Wells
of Chicago. McKane, a relative newcomer to Boston, had a long
track record in fighting for race and gender equality. She had
grown up in Pennsylvania, earned a medical degree there, and
then worked in Georgia as the only female doctor in the state. She
and her husband, also a doctor, later moved to West Africa, where
she trained nurses and helped start a hospital. Moving to Boston
in 1909, she and her husband had become close friends of Trotter
and his wife. Alice McKane joined the couple's literary club and
Trotter's political organization. She also joined the Boston NAACP

chapter, and in that capacity served as a bridge of sorts between two Boston civil rights groups that were often at odds.

McKane had viewed *The Birth of a Nation* during its first week at the Tremont Theatre and provided the several hundred spectators with a vivid accounting. The so-called history of the Civil War and Reconstruction, she said, was riddled with "malignant errors." Following her attendance, she said she had wept. "It's a crying shame," she said, "that the managers of this theatre should be permitted to cram down the throats of white people the bundle of lies contained in these pictures." Moreover, she and the others complained that Griffith had still not complied with making the cuts he had agreed to at the mayor's request, and there were persistent reports of box office discrimination, Negroes often being denied tickets.

Puller introduced Trotter as the keynote speaker. Trotter noted the "strange coincidence" that their protest meeting was being held on the fiftieth anniversary of Lincoln's death from a bullet wound in his brain. Lincoln, Trotter said, was the great emancipator of the Negro race. He motioned to two of the men on the platform— grandsons of Garrison, the crusading journalist for emancipation and race equality. The *Guardian* editor then focused on the business at hand—the need to stop Griffith's movie, a virulent screed of race hatred and violence. He said he deeply regretted that Mayor Curley, whom he and many Negroes had supported at the polls, had so far allowed the film to appear in Boston.

The hissing started the moment Trotter mentioned Curley. The mayor had gone from much beloved to betrayer in less than a week—joining President Wilson in the lineup of white men who had made promises to Negroes, only to break them. But Trotter immediately sought to halt the derision. The fight was not over, he said, and he had not yet given up on Curley. Instead, their message should be that they are watching: "Keep him still on trial," he said. "Of him and of all other public officials we will demand that they do their duty. If they refuse, then we will find some way of recording our verdict on their public career." He then led the audience in the unanimous passage of a resolution calling on the mayor, on record now saying the film was an outrage against Negro citizens, to request that the theater discontinue the run. The resolution emphasized that they were asking him only to do what he had done plenty of times previously: to take "the same sort of positive action that you have in opposing other productions you considered harmful."

In calming the crowd and steering it toward the resolution it was not as if Trotter was going soft. To the contrary, he knew other plans were percolating that might render moot Curley's role in the fate of the film. Overtures had been made to Governor David I. Walsh, a liberal Democrat, adversary of race inequality, and the first Irish Catholic to be elected governor of the state. The previous day, on Wednesday, Walsh had summoned Boston's police commissioner, Stephen O'Meara, to the State House for a debriefing on the Curley hearing and efforts to ban the film. Walsh could order the commissioner to do that because he, and not Boston's mayor, was O'Meara's boss, due to a political quirk that dated back to the mid-1880s, when the Massachusetts state legislature, a fading bastion of Brahmins troubled by the ascendency of the Irish, wanted to remove control of Boston police (and liquor) from the city itself. In 1885, a new law gave the governor the power to appoint the city's police commissioner.

Word of the hour-long session between the governor and the commissioner leaked out, and even though O'Meara had reported nothing could be done to censor the film—due to Curley's ruling the movie was not obscene—Walsh let it be known he was deeply concerned over the production. That was when lawyer Moorfield Storey, of the Boston NAACP, came up with an alternative theory for legal action, one that would rely instead on a state law making it a crime for a theater to feature any show affecting the morals of young people. The law had been passed just five years earlier, in 1910, and it read in part: "Whoever, as owner, manager, director, agent or in any other capacity prepares, advertises, gives, presents or participates in any lewd, obscene, indecent, immoral or impure show or entertainment . . . manifestly tending to corrupt the morals of youth, shall be punished by imprisonment for not more than one year, or by a fine of not more than $500."

Forget about the city's censorship law. Forget about Griffith himself. The new target was the manager of the Tremont Theatre, John B. Schoeffel, for showing the film.

On Friday, April 16, the morning after Trotter's church rally, Storey hastily prepared his idea in a letter delivered to O'Meara the next day. (It was too late to reach Walsh; he had left to spend the weekend in New York City.) Griffith's film, wrote the attorney, "will exercise a baneful influence" upon the "multitudes of children and young people who know nothing of the truth" and will "make them hate their neighbors." Even though the police commissioner had already gone along with Curley's findings, the state law seemed broad enough to cite the theater for the movie's harmful impact on youth and also, arguably, as a public nuisance generally. The mayor did not even have to be involved. This could be viewed as a police matter involving a state criminal statute.

Monroe Trotter was certainly privy to these developments, and indeed was helping to advance them. Moreover, he, Storey, and others were considering lobbying legislators to tinker with Boston's censorship law as another line of attack. But by week's end, in addition to these legal strategies, Trotter was working up an altogether different kind of idea involving crime and punishment, one that played off the question the mayor had posed at his City Hall hearing to one of the other opponents to the film—whether any "physical clashes" had marred its showing in New York City. This remark, made almost in passing, was largely overshadowed by the arguing over immorality. Besides, it had had little practical relevance in Boston, where at the time the movie had not yet opened. But by raising the issue, Curley was acknowledging that violence was a potential factor—that a film inspiring lawless action might be considered differently. Now, a week after the premiere, Trotter had become emboldened to add direct action to the protest.

The morning of Saturday, April 17, 1915, the *Boston Post* published the final installment of a six-part series about the Lincoln assassination, a retelling that served to honor the slain president and his presidency. The last part was titled "Reconstruction—After Lincoln." The article's muted tone, its measured history of freed slaves and their political rights, the northern "carpetbaggers," the public corruption that followed the war's end, and the rise of the KKK and southerners' "reclaiming" their states after the withdrawal of federal forces by 1877, was in stark contrast to the passionately pro-South rhetoric and anti-Negro story showcased daily at the Tremont Theatre in the form of Griffith's epic *The Birth of a Nation*. The article concluded, "Marked by more turbulence, more retaliation, more bitterness than Abraham Lincoln would have countenanced, the reconstruction was at last accomplished; 4,000,000 slaves were free; the seceding States had again been brought into their proper practical relations; the Union was secure."

Meanwhile, around the corner from the *Post*'s offices on Newspaper Row, Monroe Trotter was recovering from the previous night's frantic scramble to put the latest issue of the *Guardian* to bed and print it for distribution on Saturday morning. In addition to the nearly all-consuming task of fighting Griffith's film, he still had the weekly slog of putting out his paper, and now, more than ever, his wife and his sister were proving indispensable. Not surprisingly, the issue hot off the presses that Saturday morning was devoted to the Boston film war. Under the masthead ran the banner headline "Fight Against Birth of Nation Continues." Stories on the front page and inside the paper rounded up the week's developments— coverage that included reprinted news stories that had appeared in the daily papers; opposition letters, such as the one J. Mott Hallowell had written after seeing the movie; and reports of the pivot in protest strategy from City Hall to the State House, where Trotter and Boston NAACP officials were hopeful Governor Walsh would join their cause.

Then, around midafternoon, a letter arrived, containing the mayor's response to the resolution passed Thursday night at the church rally that had called on him, once again, to stop the film. In it, Curley curtly reminded the editor "there is no way legally" for him do anything, "until such time as the State Legislature changes the existing law," as well as that he had nonetheless done what he could to help, which was to request that Griffith modify the movie. "Eliminations originally requested by me have been assented to," he wrote. For Trotter, it was as if the resolution had been his way of giving the mayor a last chance to do the right thing, as he first had contained his own shock at Curley's ruling following the hearing and then contained the hissing on Thursday night. But this correspondence reiterating a virtual do-nothing position was a breaking point.

The litany of grievances against the Griffith team was growing, not shortening. All week long, Trotter and other opponents had fielded complaints about illegal discrimination at the box office. Just that morning, his friend William D. Brigham described his experience with the "color line" when he had gone to see the film the night before. Brigham, who was white, watched as the ticket seller told a Negro in line ahead of him that the only seats remaining were the pricey two-dollar seats. Unwilling to pay that much, the Negro turned away and left. But when Brigham stepped up to the ticket window, he was told plenty of the seventy-five-cent seats were still available. In addition, there was the matter of the alleged cuts that Curley kept asserting he had secured and seemed so proud of. To *Birth*'s opponents, nothing substantive had been altered. Worse, to Trotter, who had seen the movie at the Tremont during the past week, the many objectionable scenes had "been enlarged rather than reduced." It was as if Griffith was mocking them all—the protesters, the city, Curley—and Curley in his reply had seemed to be dodging reality with words signifying nothing. The mayor, Trotter said, had not kept his word. Curley might be willing to play Griffith's fool, but Monroe Trotter certainly was not.

W. E. B. Du Bois had rightly and enthusiastically noted Boston was the center of the protest action, even if back at NAACP headquarters, at least one key official was discouraged by the way things had gone the first week. "I never believed myself that this thing would be shown in Abolition Boston," May Childs Nerney said on Saturday, the same day Trotter received Curley's dismissive response. Further, she was incredulous that *The Birth of a Nation* was being shown there without any demonstration whatsoever against it. Nerney, of course, had no way of knowing that within hours of writing a letter with those thoughts, this would change. Word was going around in certain quarters of Boston during the fading light of the early spring day, and around six p.m., the telephone rang in the newsroom of the *Boston Globe* on Washington Street. The anonymous caller was a "colored woman" (the newspaper never explained how it identified the woman's race) who advised the newspaper to hurry and dispatch a reporter over to the Tremont Theatre a few blocks away.

"There might be something interesting happen [*sic*]," she said.

It was around 7:15 p.m. and nearly dark when Monroe Trotter walked down Tremont Street to the Tremont Theatre, located across from the Boston Common at its southeast corner and near the Boylston Street intersection. Having been alerted beforehand, reporters from the *Globe* and the other dailies had already arrived, and what they saw was wave upon wave of Negroes joining the civil rights leader as he approached the front of the theater. They came from every direction, and estimates varied, with some reporters putting the gathering of "colored men and women" at about two hundred, while others said the number was closer to five hundred. Either way, journalists agreed that over the next couple of hours, the crowd continued to swell until about two thousand people had turned out. Nearby in the compact Theatre District, movies and stage plays of all kinds were playing at the four other cinemas and the fifteen-odd theaters. *Tillie's Punctured Romance*, for example, a comedy featuring Charlie Chaplin, had audiences in stitches at the Bowdoin Square Theatre, while Paramount Picture's *The Eternal City*, a melodrama set in Rome, was being shown at the Boston Theatre. But nothing in town compared to the spectacle at the Tremont where, with that night's performance set to start at 8:10 p.m., the marquee lights in front were ablaze with the theater's name in a fancy cursive style and each side of a large awning jutting out over the sidewalk featured the name of the current show in hand-posted block lettering: *The Birth of a Nation*. The sidewalk in front and the lobby inside were already abuzz with the arrival of moviegoers, some holding tickets purchased in advance and others lining up to buy them. In making his approach to the theater, nothing appeared out of the ordinary to Trotter. Even the sight of uniformed Boston police officers was not a surprise; since the film's opening the past weekend, the theater had paid for a special detail of up to ten officers.

In fact, though, preparations for the current screening were very different. The Boston police and Tremont manager Schoeffel had both received information that trouble was brewing. Police superintendent Michael H. Crowley never disclosed his source's identity but said that during midafternoon, a reliable informant had warned of a possible disturbance, and so he immediately ordered the day shift from the district station around the corner on Lagrange Street to stay on for special night duty, as well as summoned officers from nearby stations to assist them. Schoeffel said another theater manager had called him with word of a plot "arranged by a certain gang of colored men to raid the theatre and destroy the film." At 4:30 p.m., Crowley had laid out for Schoeffel the beefed-up security plan he had devised, assigning more than sixty policemen to take up seats inside, dressed in plainclothes, with another complement of one hundred uniformed officers out of sight and on standby at the nearby station, ready for action.

By the time seven o'clock approached, or just before Trotter arrived at the theatre at 176 Tremont Street, Crowley's forces were in place. Some occupied the entire first row of seats in front of the orchestra pit. Their assignment was to block anyone from reaching the movie screen. Others guarded the operating booth, with a few from that contingent responsible for protecting the wire leading from the booth into the cellar.

The remaining plainclothes officers were scattered in the first and second balconies, the gallery's reserved section, and in the front lobby. Trotter detected none of this—all he saw was the typical detail of ten or so patrolmen milling about.

Then, with the arrival of what one reporter described as a "large body of colored men led by William Monroe Trotter," Schoeffel did two things. The first was to make a quick telephone call to notify Crowley. The second was to order suspension of ticket sales for that night's show. The only tickets to be issued from the box office, said the manager, were to patrons who had reserved them in advance. The goal was to impose a lockdown of sorts in the lobby; yet despite the order, box office employees continued selling tickets—and they did so discriminately. Mrs. Mary E. Moore, a Negro housewife from the Roxbury neighborhood, was rebuffed and then watched in disbelief as the white woman next in line purchased a ticket. Another white woman who had witnessed the disparity stepped forward and bought two tickets. She turned and handed one of hers to Moore. When People's Baptist Church pastor Puller tried to buy a ticket, he was told, "Nothing doing." By now Trotter and his followers had piled into the lobby, ignoring calls that they show their tickets. Crowley also appeared on foot from the station just minutes away, accompanied by a police captain, and saw the lobby was jammed to capacity. Outside, too, the crowd continued to grow—comprising mostly film protesters, Crowley said later, but also including curiosity seekers eager to observe the commotion. Immediately the superintendent called the police station. "Get 'em all down here," he barked. People in the lobby continued to clamor for tickets. In reply, theater employees announced the show was sold out, that "the ticket rack was clean and they could not even sell any more stand-up admissions." But Trotter and everyone else saw this was a canard, as white patrons were still being ushered inside.

Surrounded by supporters, the *Guardian* editor began pressing forward to reach the ticket window. Although far outnumbered, the police on hand ordered everyone out. "We won't leave," Trotter said. "We demand our rights to buy tickets." Schoeffel said later that he heard Trotter yelling that if the movie could not be suppressed through legal means, it would be shut down by force. Police accounts said it was a man standing near Trotter who next shouted, "If we don't get justice from the white man we will take the law into our own hands." For his part, Trotter was determined to confront the ticket seller, arguing that if the show was sold out, then why not post a sign outside saying so. "I demand my rights," he said, holding up a half-dollar and insisting the box office employee sell him a ticket. "You are selling to white people," he roared.

Around 7:30 p.m., police reserves arrived from around the corner—more than a hundred men "on hand in a twinkling," as one reporter wrote, and the action accelerated quickly. Crowley ordered the officers to clear out the lobby, and that was when the pushing and shoving began. Police, targeting Trotter as a ringleader, tried to move in on him, but supporters, many of whom were women, had encircled him as his bodyguard. The lobby was suddenly a thick, rocking mass of protesters and policemen, jockeying elbow to elbow. Amid all of the noise and confusion, the officers were having difficulty getting to Trotter. Dennis Harrington, dressed in plainclothes and appearing to be a civilian, wiggled his way close to Trotter and tried to seize him. When Trotter pulled away and would not budge, Harrington slugged him in the jaw. The assault stunned Trotter and seemed to freeze those around him in place, creating a kind of pause that other officers exploited to rush in and grab hold of him.

Boston Police sergeant Martin King and a second officer wrestled with Trotter, who struggled to hold his ground but was no match for his larger, stronger opponents. The editor demanded that police arrest the man who had punched him but was told they would not—because he was a policeman, too. The officers then hauled him out from behind the railing near the box office and toward the entrance. The Roxbury woman who earlier had been denied a ticket until a white woman gave her one, rushed over to the men who were restraining Trotter.

"What are you doing?" she shouted. "Why are you arresting him?"

"Shut up!" Sergeant King yelled, pushing through and threatening to arrest her.

Others screamed at the police, "Don't you hurt him!"

Outside, Trotter saw not only hundreds of protesters all around but also cordons of police—the majority of nearly two hundred officers now on the scene were lining the sidewalks to keep them clear. Most protesters were assembled on Boston Common across Tremont Street, contained behind a wall of police to prevent anyone from getting near the theater. Trotter could hear shouts of support along with angry denunciations of the police and the film, but he also heard scattered racial epithets and cries of "Nigger." Although the protesters never broke through the police line en masse, for the next several hours they hung around, defying officers' attempts to make them move on. The time immediately following Trotter's arrest was tense, turbulent, and seemingly on the verge of a race riot. At one point someone in the Boston Common crowd threw a projectile that barely missed hitting an officer, but when police rushed over they could not tell who had done it. When a newspaper photographer took a picture, the camera's sudden pop and flash of light was mistaken for gunfire, and women screamed. Police said that as King emerged from the theater with Trotter in tow, a Negro woman ran up to hit the sergeant in the face several times, but King chose not to take her into custody.

There were other arrests, however. Puller, also targeted as a ringleader, was arrested in front of the theater after Trotter was brought outside. Police said Puller and a second man had refused an order to clear out and kept demanding to go inside to see the film; the pastor was charged with disturbing the peace. He disputed the police version, insisting he was there to help *keep* the peace when officers began pushing him around and King yelled, "Lock that nigger up!" He said police choked him and ripped his collar, and that he lost his bag with his Bible in it when they began dragging him to the station. Joseph Gould, a social worker, was then arrested on charges that he ran up and kicked one of the officers holding Puller. One of Trotter's staunchest allies, Rev. Montrose W. Thornton, was also arrested, but a search of his pockets turned up a movie ticket.

Meanwhile, as the arrests started, Mayor Curley was notified about the tumult at the Tremont. He was at the Copley Plaza Hotel in Copley Square, less than a mile away, attending a Knights of Columbus banquet. Reporters caught up with him there, too, and he did his best to dodge questions about the large Negro street demonstration at the theater. "The matter is entirely in the hands of the police, it being a disturbance," he said. Pressed about the film, he said there was nothing he could do. Pressed further, he confirmed that Monroe Trotter had been in contact to ask him again to help stop the screening. "I told them today that I could not do so and they threatened to go to the Governor, and I said that they might." Curley scoffed at the suggestion he had encouraged Trotter to demonstrate or knew anything about a protest being in the works.

Held tightly by his captors, Trotter saw not only the one police cordon across the street but another that snaked around the corner intersection toward the district police station on Lagrange Street. Two officers had fallen in behind as a rear guard for the cluster pulling him along. Because they were stronger and taller, he had trouble keeping up, and he was being partly pushed and partly dragged down the street past the two lines of armed guards on each curb. Trotter squirmed and complained, "If you let me go, I'll go along." Despite the large show of force, several of his supporters broke through the line and ran ahead toward the police station. He arrived there within minutes, and awaiting him was his friend Joshua A. Crawford, a bail commissioner, and member of Trotter's literary group. Crawford posted Trotter's $50 bail after Trotter, Puller, and the two other men were booked. The editor was told to report to Boston municipal court on Tuesday for his arraignment. Upon release, he hurried back to Tremont Street. There he became part of a cat-and-mouse game with police, as protesters gathered around him and others to hear their fiery commentary only to be broken up by advancing officers looking to avert violence by dispersing clusters before they enlarged. In one such impromptu assembly Negro lawyer Allen W. Whaley put his hand on Trotter's shoulder and bellowed, "My friends, this is William Monroe Trotter, who is the hero of the evening. He has been arrested simply because he sought his rights guaranteed under the Constitution of the United States." Police chased them off before anything further was spoken, but no one seemed in the mood yet to leave the area for good. Hundreds of Negroes continued to mill around the Common and on the streets surrounding the Tremont Theatre, alternately cursing, yelling for the film to stop, defending their right to demonstrate, and accusing police of excessive force.

With Trotter's arrest police had secured the lobby, and they barred anyone, including the press, from entering from that point on. The film, even with all the disruption outside, was able to begin basically on schedule. But some protesters had made it inside the darkened theater, either entering as ticketholders beforehand or slipping past police during the commotion. Their shouts and complaints were heard periodically throughout the screening, especially after the start of the film's second part, Griffith's rendering of Reconstruction that was chock-full of racist content. One protester was a twenty-six-year-old Boston man named Charles P. Ray, who had smuggled in eggs and four small boxes containing "odiferous bombs." Seated in about the tenth row, he managed to toss a few of his stink bombs while remaining undetected by the plainclothes police seated within the audience. But that ended when the film got to the part where the ex-slave Gus chased Flora through the woods. The young man stood up and threw one of his eggs, which landed smack in the middle of the screen. Everyone could see its drippings. Police rushed over to the standing Ray, took him into custody, and marched him down to the Lagrange Street station, where he was charged with malicious mischief. But no real protest action made much headway during the screening, due to the suffocating police presence.

When the movie ended around eleven p.m., however, another round of trouble ensued. Masses of people were moving at crosscurrents as the audience began exiting the Tremont, and the demonstrators outside, who had been marching back and forth, suddenly swarmed the main entrance. Police shouted at demonstrators to clear the way so that patrons could leave, but the crowd stood fast. Three Negro women in particular blocked one door like football linemen and refused to budge. Several officers rushed and shoved them back. One of the women, Clara Fosky, only twenty-two years old and living in the Negro neighborhood on the west side of Beacon Hill, flew at one of the policemen, shouting and flailing at him. She reached to remove a pin from her hat, but was stopped when the officer, assisted by colleagues, wrestled her into custody. They pulled the young woman out into the street to take her in, when three of her friends tried to rescue her, grabbing at the officers. More police moved in, and the three—two men and a woman who lived next to Fosky on Beacon Hill—were also arrested. Fosky was charged with assaulting a police officer; the other three, with attempting to rescue a prisoner. The army of police toughened and kept after the remaining protesters to keep the street clear. In response, they faced rounds of furious jeering and name-calling, an ad hominem lexicon that five decades later would have included the word *pig* but in

ARMY OF POLICE NIP THEATRE RIOT IN BUD

11 Arrests Follow Attempt of Colored Citizens to Purchase Tickets for "Birth of a Nation"—Theatre Refused Seats, Claiming None Left—200 Policemen Clear Lobby and Wild Excitement Follows—Tremont Street Blocked by Big Crowd

Arrest Man Who Threw Egg at Screen During Show

Two Colored Spectators Manage to Get Inside

One Opens Up Noxious Bomb to Break Up Performance

Riot attended last night's performance of the photo-play, "The Birth of a Nation," at the Tremont Theatre, when several hundred colored people stormed the box-office and demanded tickets.

Refused, on the grounds that the house was sold out, they claimed discrimination, maintaining that white people were securing tickets, and resisted the police efforts to clear the lobby.

Two hundred police officers

The *Boston Post* cover page headline printed on April 18, 1915, featuring Boston police lined up outside the Tremont Theatre at a screening of *The Birth of a Nation.*

this 1915 incident went unspecified and was characterized by an eyewitness reporter this way: "Frequently discourteous remarks were made to and about the police officers." James L. Dunn, for one, shouted loudly while hustling up and down Tremont Street as the Fosky foursome was taken into custody, and once officers had heard enough, they arrested him as well on a charge of profanity.

In addition to altercations between protesters and police, the night's large-scaled demonstration also featured an occasional shouting match between groups of Negroes and whites, although no arrests resulted from confrontations occurring before and during the film's screening. Instead, around 11:30 p.m., or more than four hours after the protest began, the scene at the theater started winding down, as the crowd thinned and headed home. In all, eleven people—ten Negroes and one white—were arrested, and most observers and reporters heaped kudos on police for smothering a situation seemingly primed for spontaneous combustion. "With all the makings for a real race riot at hand serious trouble was averted, and at last the crowd died away," said the *Boston Globe*.

Nearly missed, however, was an outburst of true bloodletting—perhaps because of its later timing and its location away from the theater. Around midnight, or thirty minutes after everything had died down, three Negro men who had left the Theatre District and were walking home to Roxbury clashed with a group of white men who were also at the protest. Police responded quickly to reports of a brawl in progress, but not before the Negro men, each carrying a razor, had wounded four white men. The injured were taken by ambulance to Boston City Hospital, where they received stitches for lacerations on their necks and treatment for abrasions on their heads and bodies. The Negroes were jailed on charges of assault with knives, and, when searched, one was found to be carrying a loaded, .38 caliber pistol in his pocket. Only two of the seven daily newspapers managed to learn about the bloodshed in time to include a brief sidebar story in their Sunday morning edition.

"Race Riot in the South End," was the *Boston Post*'s headline. The article continued, "Two hundred police officers battled the crowds in the lobby and on the streets, before and after the show." "As a racial demonstration probably nothing like it has been seen in Boston since the Civil War," reported the *Boston Globe* in its front-page story.

The night's events hardly needed such exaggeration, but that did not stop Thomas Dixon from later writing a fantastical account in which he had hundreds of "misguided colored men" charging the Tremont Theatre, only to be confronted by an army of one thousand Boston police officers armed with clubs and revolvers. "Night sticks whistled and the first ranks of the riot leaders fell in a wave of groaning terror," Dixon wrote. "The men behind turned in panic and ran for their lives." In his purple prose rendition of the street fighting, Dixon used hyperbole in the same way Griffith's promotion of *The Birth of a Nation* relied on such claims as needing eighteen thousand extras for the filming of Civil War battles.

Monroe Trotter, in a series of impromptu press conferences after he was bailed out and had returned to the theater, vehemently denied plotting the disturbance. "I know nothing of any planned demonstrations," he said. "I came downtown tonight to see the performance as an individual." Few believed him. There was, after all, the call to the *Boston Globe*'s newsroom about an hour before Trotter's appearance—a trick to drum up press coverage that also resembled something out of Griffith's marketing playbook. Then there was the tantalizing statement Trotter supporter William D. Brigham made later that night, when reporters reached him at his Dorchester home to ask whether the protest was planned. "You can see for yourself," he replied. "I don't think a formal vote was taken, but the word may have been passed along." Brigham defended the evening's mass protest, even if his words were in denial of the actual scope of the mayhem. "Such a mild demonstration as this," he said, "where no clubs were drawn and nobody was injured, is necessary to impress upon the people of Boston that this show is objectionable to the colored people who live here." Especially incredulous of Trotter's denials was Griffith's business manager, Henry MacMahon, who was at the theater all night. He issued a statement reassuring the public's safety and attacking the protesters as unrepresentative of the majority of law-abiding Negroes in Boston. "Their leader, Munroe Trotter [sic], is certainly not representative of the best sentiment." He and the theater's management pressed Superintendent Crowley to charge Trotter with conspiracy, but Crowley said that lacking hard evidence of preplanning, he could not.

Trotter's denials notwithstanding, the direct action, ahead of its time, brought a heavy dose of Trotterism to the Boston protest against Griffith's film. In his remarks to the press, Trotter was livid about the massive police action. "The way they treated us is shameful," he said. "It's an outrage." Most of all, he unleashed anger at Curley. The *Guardian* editor did not believe his claim that Griffith had cut parts of the film, and insisted that was why he came to the theater. "I came down tonight to see for myself," he said. Trotter then fired off a double-barreled attack on the film and the mayor. "It is a rebel play," he declared hotly, "an incentive to great racial hatred here in Boston. It will make white women afraid of Negroes and will have white men all stirred up on their account. If there is any lynching here in Boston, Mayor Curley will be responsible."

The gloves were off. Trotter had broken publicly from the mayor, and he continued his fierce criticisms the next afternoon, Sunday, when he, clergy, and Boston NAACP officials staged an old-style "indignation rally" at Faneuil Hall, the historic meeting house, which drew an overflow crowd of more than two thousand Negroes and another three hundred white supporters. Trotter's friend Thornton, fresh from the Tremont Theatre protest, said this was their time. "I urge you to be as courageous as those who were arrested last night," he shouted. "So help us God there's going to be a lot more of the same sort. We have resolved, if it takes the very last drop of our blood, to continue our protest against this outrageous film." The leader of the city's Irish National League, Michael J. Jordan, also stood on the dais. "I would be untrue to the Irish race if I did not come here to join in this protest with you," he said. When Trotter's turn to speak came, he announced a plan for a march to the State House first thing the next morning to take their fight against the film to Governor Walsh, and then he took direct aim at Curley. "He admits that this film is a disgrace, but says his hands are tied," he said to the loudest cheers of all during the three-hour rally. Yet, noted Trotter, "If this was an attack on the Irish race he would find a way pretty quick to stop it.

"Where is the valiant Jim Curley of old," he asked, "the friend of the people—loveable Jim Curley, whom we colored people supported for the mayorality."

=14=

"We'll Hang
Tom Dixon . . . "

Monroe Trotter, the Negro clergy, women activists, and their allies at the Boston NAACP had had a momentum-building weekend that seemed to feed on itself—going into the movie's second week, more and more people, in Boston and around the country, were riveted by the swelling protest action. "Doubtless you have heard of the wild unrest of the colored people," Dr. Samuel E. Courtney wrote Booker T. Washington first thing Monday, April 17, a letter in which he included newspaper clippings about the mayhem at the Tremont Theatre on Saturday night and the mass meeting on Sunday at Faneuil Hall. Courtney was clearly impressed by the Negro solidarity against *The Birth of a Nation*, repeating the line used in the papers—that not since the Civil War had the city seen protests of such magnitude. He added, "The Negroes are a unit in their determination to drive it out of Boston."

For their part, Griffith and his team had known that by going into Boston, they would have a fight on their hands. But instead of its being a settled matter after a tense and contentious buildup to the first screening, they watched as the fight against their film had escalated dramatically, their opponents ever more determined. That first weekend Griffith had left town confident that, as a result of Mayor Curley's finding, he had won, but a week later it was clear the battle was not over. His team, alarmed at the troubles on Saturday and the protest's potential impact at the box office, hastily prepared a new ad for the film that began appearing in the Boston papers on Monday morning. Printed atop the ad was the headline "HIGHLY IMPORTANT," followed by the message: "The management has made special arrangements and extra precautions to insure that the convenience, comfort and enjoyment of its patrons will not be disturbed during the performances." The "special precautions" included a continuously beefed-up police presence—for the seven days after the Saturday night "near-riot," the number of Boston police detailed for special duty at the Tremont Theatre totaled 897. By contrast, the number of officers on special duty for the Ringling Bros. Circus parade in late May would be 94.

But apart from their general concern, one member of the team was positively energized. Tom Dixon, historically hotheaded, seemed to find a kind of perverse pleasure in the goings-on in Boston. He revealed this in a letter to Joseph Tumulty, after the president had been forced to comment about the White House screening because of its mention at the Curley hearing. The letter read as part-apology for entangling Wilson in the film's political controversy and part-explanation for his motivation behind the White House screening. The novelist confessed that in early 1915 he had not dared tell the president the real purpose of the film, which as far as he, Dixon, was concerned, was to foment racism and convert viewers against the Negro—"to revolutionize Northern sentiment" and to "transform every man in my audience into a good Democrat."

Conceding he had not told Wilson the whole story, Dixon insisted what he had said was unimpeachably true—his pitch having been that he wanted to show the president "the birth of a new art—the launching of the mightiest engine for molding of public opinion in the history of the world." On this point—film's transformative impact on modern media—he was at once prescient and irrepressibly enthusiastic. Dixon went off on a riff on the power of moving pictures by describing the expected reach of *The Birth of a Nation* once it got past Boston and was shown around the country. "Within one year 20,000,000 people will see it," he predicted, and, "before the next presidential election one-half of the voters in the U.S. will

Thomas Dixon Jr., a North Carolina novelist and legislator
best known for his play *The Clansman*, which inspired
Griffith's film adaptation *The Birth of a Nation*.
COURTESY OF WIKIMEDIA COMMONS.

have seen it." Imagine, he posited, the value of the big screen in
electoral politics: "The next political campaign may witness a revolution in political method," he gushed. According to Dixon, the old
media—meaning newspapers—were no match for emerging new
media in shaping public opinion. "We have launched a cyclone before whose beast the press is a zephyr."

In the rant Dixon could also not resist commenting on the topic
raging at that very moment—the movie's Boston run. "Every man
who comes out of one of our theatres is a Southern patriot for life,"
he boasted. The exception, of course, was the angry "opposition of
fools," as he termed the protesters, for whom he held unvarnished
contempt. "The more opposition we encounter the more tremendous our triumph," he wrote, "The play sweeps every audience off
their feet and every man and woman goes home laughing at the
asininity in its critics."

The experienced writer ended the three-page letter with a "kicker" he knew the president would savor, like dessert at the end of a three-course meal—about Monroe Trotter, the agitator he knew Wilson loathed. Trotter had "attempted to head a mob of 500 Negroes" into the Tremont Theatre but was arrested, Dixon happily reported. The best part, though, was that "a good Irish policeman gave him one solid rap in the coco!"

"This, I confess, pleased me much," he wrote. "I'm a sinful man!"

That Monday morning, just before eight a.m., Negro demonstrators began arriving in front of the Massachusetts State House atop Beacon Hill singly, in pairs, and in small groups, "from all points of the compass," as one reporter observed. Many of the protesters had attended the overflow Faneuil Hall rally the previous afternoon. Others had learned by word of mouth of the march on the State House and decided to join in. They began occupying the broad granite staircase leading to the elevated portico of the gold-domed building. In an hour they numbered about five hundred, and the number only continued to grow. By midmorning as many as five thousand people, mostly Negroes but "sprinkled" with whites, filled the staircase of the state capitol building and spilled out onto Beacon Street and into the Common across the cobblestoned street. Appropriately, on the corner of the Common stood a bronze relief sculpture honoring one of the all-Negro regiments from Boston that had fought in the Civil War—not James M. Trotter's 55th, but the 54th. The sculpture, unveiled in 1897, depicted the regiment and its commander on horseback marching down Beacon Street, heading off to war. Now, eighteen years later, troops of a different kind were mustering in a civil rights campaign against D. W. Griffith's film.

The morning skies were clear and sunny, with temperatures eventually reaching the low eighties—an unseasonably warm spring day that would hinder many of the runners competing in the nineteenth Boston Marathon. It was Patriot's Day in Massachusetts, the third Monday in April when the marathon was held and the first battles of the American Revolution in Concord and Lexington on April 19, 1775, were commemorated. In 1915, Édouard

Fabre, of Montreal's Richmond Club, would win the marathon in 2:31:41, a time that, as a result of the heat, was almost six minutes slower than his pace the year before, when he finished second. It was a day, too, where the Boston police force was taxed—stretched thin by the special details at the Tremont Theatre and now the marathon and a State House rally.

The early arrivals milled about, awaiting the appearance of their leader, Monroe Trotter. They talked about the Saturday night arrests and the Sunday speeches at the indignation rally, but were not sure exactly what to do, knowing only that as a result of the weekend's events they were bringing their protest to Governor David I. Walsh. Their numbers simply continued to grow, and included many women and also children who either played or were seated on the steps, resting and waiting. No one out front noticed, but shortly after nine o'clock, the governor arrived by car and slipped into the brick building by a side door to head up to his office on the third floor. He had just returned from New York City. His aides had advised him on Sunday night about the troubles back home and he had taken the night train back to Boston. With him as he entered the State House was his counsel, Judge Edward L. Logan, and his private secretary. Then, around 9:30 a.m., Trotter arrived out front, where he took charge, short on sleep but animated as he greeted those already assembled. He was dressed as most men were in those times, in a suit and hat, as a matter of course. Like everyone, too, he was anxious and uncertain about the prospects ahead. Every reporter on hand noticed the same thing— the crowd, while orderly, "was not in extremely good humor. It was excitable and nervous from the start."

This much Walsh knew: impressed by the protest actions, he wanted to help the fight against the Griffith blockbuster. But whether he could was the part he did not know, and so his first act after getting to his office was to send for a small group of legal advisers and police officials. Representing the Boston Police, Commissioner O'Meara and Superintendent Crowley arrived together by automobile. They hustled inside without taking questions from reporters. But the acting chief of the Massachusetts State Police,

George C. Neal, stirred interest when, on his way in, he paused long enough to comment about the state law Moorfield Storey of the NAACP had been pushing as a new legal tactic, the so-called immoral entertainment act, which targeted theater management. "It is my opinion that this play violates the law, so far as the scenes depicting outrages on white women are concerned," Neal said curtly. Then he bolted inside. "Great interest attached to Neal's opinion," a reporter wrote, "because it puts him on an opposite side to Mayor Curley and the Boston police authorities." The last to join the governor was Nelson I. Brown, the first assistant state attorney general, filling in for his boss who was spending the holiday in New Hampshire. The governor at first had thought to allow Trotter and his followers inside to wait in Doric Hall, the main reception in the State House on the second floor, but the swelling numbers of the editor's supporters made that impossible. Instead, Trotter was told that he could select representatives from the rally who would be admitted. Standing atop the staircase, he began calling out the names of ministers, heads of organizations and societies, and other prominent Negroes. This subset group—the "Committee of 60"— included the pastors of all the Negro churches, Mrs. Anna Phillips Williams, the niece of the abolitionist Wendell Phillips, and Dr. Alice W. McKane, who, it seemed, had been at Trotter's side at every major event in recent weeks. As they heard each name, members of the crowd cheered and made room for the person to pass. Then he shouted, "No more—pray for us!" and entered, too.

The waiting game began, with the Committee of 60 now in Doric Hall, a high-ceilinged room featuring ten Doric columns, which served as the setting for all kinds of official ceremonies and was decorated with historic memorabilia, including a marble statue of George Washington and a full-length oil portrait of Abraham Lincoln. Outside, the several thousand other protesters stayed in the growing heat. Meanwhile, upstairs in his chambers on the west side of the State House, the governor conferred first with his small circle of advisers and then with five Negro representatives he had asked to join them. The five included attorney William H. Lewis, the onetime Trotter ally turned Bookerite, and attorney Butler R. Wilson, a Boston NAACP leader. Trotter and Lewis had since mended their relationship, whereas Trotter and Wilson had never much got along. But all of that was put aside during the protest against Griffith's movie. Why Trotter was not in on this select group became the subject of later speculation, the gist of it being that Walsh preferred dealing with Negro leaders seen as more moderate than the unpredictable editor. Whatever the case, the pressure exerted by Trotter and his supporters had contributed hugely to the state's highest elected official's willingness to brainstorm ways to shut down *The Birth of a Nation.*

The governor emerged just before eleven o'clock to brief reporters, explaining the purpose of the caucus was to determine whether he had authority to act against the film—which, he emphasized, was something he wanted to do. The movie was breeding racial prejudice, he said, and no wonder Negroes were outraged. He had monitored the recent events and was amazed by the "considerable agitation" against *The Birth of a Nation.* "I was impressed at the start. The agitation did not center in a few people and was not sporadic, but was widespread and almost unanimous among one group of people of the State." Reporters tried asking the governor what he planned to do exactly, but he waved them off, headed back inside and simply reiterated his view that he found the protest against the film "extraordinary."

Walsh's remarks—a pledge of commitment diluted by uncertainty—heightened the excitement of the long morning. The large crowd outside hung in the balance, maintaining order but, by all accounts, anxious. To help pass the time, demonstrators sang gospel and other songs and listened to speeches that a few among them stood and delivered. Some started to sing, "America," but the hissing at it became so loud that the singers gave up. Hissing also accompanied "The Star-Spangled Banner" but not to the extent it interrupted the song. "Onward Christian Soldiers" went off without any interference. The one song that was heartily sung by all was a version of "John Brown's Body," the crowd substituting the name of *The Clansman*'s novelist for that of the Confederacy's president Jefferson Davis: "We'll hang Tom Dixon to a sour apple tree."

The song carried beyond the Boston Common to surrounding city blocks, and during one refrain Joshua Crawford, the bail

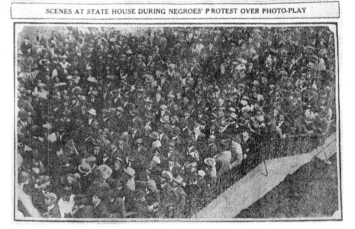

SCENES AT STATE HOUSE DURING NEGROES' PROTEST OVER PHOTO-PLAY

An image of a mass rally held at the Massachusetts
State House, in the *Boston Journal*, April 20, 1915.

commissioner who had posted Trotter's bail, received a big round
of applause when he announced they would start singing about
Mayor Curley, too, if "Curley didn't behave himself!"

Several women fainted from the heat as the morning wore on,
and they had to be taken to shaded areas to recover. Trotter periodically poked his head outside, spoke with those gathered atop
the stone staircase, and tried to break the tension. "Be orderly, but
firm," he advised, then joked, "No favorites played here; I can't let
you in just because you're good looking." Given the task of speaking
the longest while awaiting the governor's decision was Trotter's
friend Allen W. Whaley, the former New Yorker who had called
Trotter a hero the night of his arrest. Whaley's topic was an ambitious recounting of Negro history, from Africa to present-day
America. He paused when a new song broke out, but resumed once
the singing stopped, and his voice grew impassioned when he climaxed his history at the day's protest. "We are here not only to tell
Governor Walsh but the whole nation that we want justice," he
yelled. Thomas Dixon, he said, was an "absolute blockhead, time-
served hypocrite and a rogue," and he promised that the days of

the Griffith film's playing in Boston were numbered. "We do not propose to stop until *The Birth of a Nation* is removed from the stage, not only of Massachusetts, but of the United States."

Inside, the governor and his conferees reached a consensus fairly quickly. Key was that Commissioner O'Meara said he concurred with Moorfield Storey's suggestion to use the 1910 state law in a new challenge to the film—as outlined in the letter Storey had sent to him over the weekend. To get that going, a criminal complaint had to be filed against the Tremont Theatre in Boston Municipal Court, asking a judge to issue a warrant against its managers.

Discussed, too, was a second plan in the event the court option failed. Walsh wanted to have new legislation ready to push through the state legislature, changing the way film was regulated in Massachusetts so that *The Birth of a Nation* could be banned. How to do this was not settled upon at the meeting, but two approaches were floated. One was to expand the existing law authorizing suppression of immoral and obscene productions to include works that, as the governor described, "tended to raise race or religious prejudice"; in other words, to add what later became called hate speech to the kinds of expression that could be censored. Such an expansion seemed a response to Mayor Curley's complaint that the result of the city's review might be different if the censorship law provided him "more arbitrary power." The second idea was less about concepts and more about on-the-ground, head-counting politics—to change the makeup of Boston's review process so that, instead of the mayor mainly having the authority, a three-person board would rule on the moral suitability of plays and movies in the city.

Although the governor settled on both courses of action not long after his late-morning briefing with reporters, he delayed sharing it until he and his aides had time to compose a lengthy, prepared statement. It was nearly midday, then, when Trotter received word that the governor would like his Committee of 60 to head upstairs to the Executive Council Chamber on the third floor.

"I know the purpose of your visit," Walsh said as Trotter and the rest of the committee entered the chamber. Before getting down to

that purpose, he first thanked them for their patience and, referring to the throng outside, for standing in the heat "peaceably and
orderly."

The protesters were engrossed in the governor's every word,
anxious with anticipation—a state of suspense that his next statements only seemed to prolong. He recapped events that had led
to this moment, reminding everyone that under the current 1908
Boston censorship law, and following the mayor's ruling, *The Birth
of a Nation* was being presented "under legally licensed authority."
But he knew full well that many seriously questioned this finding,
and therein was the standoff: "We have public authorities on one
side," he said, "and an element of the community making conten-
tions that the facts are not well founded."

With that, the governor finally announced the outcome of the
summit, describing the 1910 statute and saying, "Your committee,
with the assistance of the Police Commissioner of Boston, will apply to the Municipal Court of Boston for a warrant." Everyone, reg-
istering his words, began clapping. "That is the first step." Walsh
then explained a plan to change censorship laws. He urged patience. "Let us in our own way work out this problem, and if there
is not any law, we will try to have some enacted." The committee erupted in cheers. "I sympathize with you tremendously," he
said. "I don't propose, while I am Governor, to allow any movement
arousing antagonism to any race of people in Massachusetts."

The cheering continued. Some wept. Others cried out, "God
bless our governor!" The moment seemed perfect and true—the
Commonwealth's leading political figure was so clearly and thoroughly on their side. Victory was at hand, if only a matter of time.
When the applause quieted, it was the governor's turn to hear the
Committee of 60 enumerate a litany of grievances against Griffith's
film. One man told him that the movie was "a menace to colored
people. Men and boys shout at us on the street as we pass by." The
good Dr. Alice McKane called the movie a "studied political trick" to
turn viewers against the Negro. Trotter pulled everyone's thoughts
together when he said to Walsh, "We are glad that you are our governor at a time like this," and, "we ask you to stand up and protect
the history, the name and the ideals of this Commonwealth." The

comments stirred Walsh to his strongest rhetoric yet: "I don't suppose there was ever a day before like this witnessed in the State
House in its history," he said. "Men and women coming here with
tears in their eyes, asking the Governor to protect them from race
hatred!" He pledged to serve as their protector and to "assert every
influence and power that I possess to keep Massachusetts free from
race or religious prejudice."

Trotter then suggested to Walsh that he end the drama for the
throng outside, but the governor hesitated. Not wanting to be accused of grandstanding, he authorized the editor to speak for him.
Trotter seized the moment as if he had planned for it, stepping outside on the chamber's third-floor balcony. Down below yet another
impromptu speech was under way, but its speaker stopped at Trotter's emergence, as people looked up, spotted their leader, and began pointing him out to others. Dramatically, Trotter climbed over
the iron railing. With his left hand gripping the rail and his right
hand raised, he leaned out and began, "Ladies and gentlemen—
your delegation has waited upon the Governor and he has assured
us that the management of the Tremont Theatre will be prosecuted
tomorrow morning in the criminal courts." The crowd roared in ex-
ultation. He explained the workings of the 1910 law and the warrant process, noting the significance that they were all standing
"within the very shadow" of the bronze-relief sculpture honoring
the all-Negro 54th regiment, and that they were fortunate to have
a governor who had just promised equal rights for all. Trotter spoke
for nearly twenty minutes, mixing in further attacks against D. W.
Griffith and his film, and rousing those assembled into repeated
cheers for the governor. Winding down, he asked that the hat be
passed around to raise money for the women arrested Saturday
night, in the event they were found guilty and fined.

The demonstrators began dispersing peacefully following Trotter's announcement, which further included cancellation of a
protest at the Tremont Theatre during the holiday matinee and
evening performances. He and other leaders advised against it,
urging a "calm and orderly manner" now that Governor Walsh
had joined their cause. Trotter, in effect, had committed himself to
the legal process, showing once again that while he was a militant

and agitator in his approach to civil rights, he was no anarchist. Even so, about a thousand people gathered outside the theater, although the turnout was largely white—curiosity seekers wanting to see whether any trouble occurred. But reporters had little to write about. "No thrills, no excitement, but the crowd still hung on," wrote one. Police, in uniform and in plainclothes, were everywhere, and they including mounted officers who kept the street out front clear. Commissioner O'Meara and Superintendent Crowley were both on hand. Newsboys, meanwhile, were selling papers announcing the governor's action. "Extra, extra!" they shouted. "Gov. Walsh's story of *The Birth of a Nation.*"

With the protest rally canceled, Trotter instead attended the Monday night meeting of the Literary and Historical Association, beginning at 8:35 p.m. It was just two days after his arrest, and the end of a long day of demonstrating at the State House. The group talked energetically about all that had happened, his friend Whaley predicting their success in stopping the film. Trotter, the main speaker, seemed exuberant as he described the scene inside the State House when the governor spoke to the Committee of 60. Trotter then took at swipe at Mayor Curley, saying Negro voters will "show up those politicians who go back on the Colored race." He was mostly excited, however, about the court action set to begin the very next morning, confident "the fight was won." But present, too, was Joshua Crawford. The bail commissioner had some concerns about the new strategies. "The trouble is that all this will take time," he said, and he may have been on to something: perhaps they were growing too confident, and perhaps Trotter, in his thrill, was acting in haste in releasing the pressure his persistent agitation and direct action had brought to bear on the protest against the movie. It had happened before, with President Wilson and then Mayor Curley, when the *Guardian* editor's commitment to work within the system and with its leaders had ended badly. Perhaps another mass rally at the Tremont would have been wise.

Crawford's concern was warranted. First thing the next morning, Tuesday, April 20, Commissioner O'Meara dispatched one of his sergeants to seek criminal complaints against D. W. Griffith and

Tremont manager John Schoeffel before Judge Thomas H. Dowd in
Boston Municipal Court. Griffith's lawyer, John F. Cusick, quickly
got the judge to approve replacing Griffith's name in the complaint
with that of his manager, J. J. McCarthy. Griffith was traveling at
that moment and thus could not appear, Cusick said, although an
unspoken reason might have been the attempt to spare the director the notoriety of a criminal charge.

The downtown courthouse proved a busy place for film-related
matters. In another courtroom that morning, Trotter and the others arrested at the theater on Saturday night were arraigned. Their
cases were all continued until the following week, but not before a
new charge of inciting to riot was lodged against Trotter. With that
procedural business completed, the focus turned to Dowd's courtroom, which Trotter, Boston NAACP officials, and several hundred
others filled, the overflow spilling out into the corridor. Reporters
noticed a bounce to the crowd, with one writing that those "who
have protested against the production of *The Birth of a Nation*
were quietly jubilant today over the progress of their case to date."

Judge Dowd's job was to hear evidence for and against the claim
that Griffith's film was either obscene or immoral and therefore in
violation of the 1910 criminal statute. He began the actual hearing
around two o'clock, taking testimony from several clergy, the acting State Police chief George Neal, and the NAACP's William H.
Lewis, who described at length what he called "scenes of brutality
and immorality." Their basic legal position was that the film's depiction of the Negro race and its glorification of the Ku Klux Klan
and lynching were immoral, which, according to various legal authorities, was defined broadly as "hostile to the welfare of the general public." Griffith's team refuted the claims, insisting the epic
portrayed history: "Mr. D. W. Griffith is not a sectionalist but an
artist." His supporters tried to remain diplomatic, however, saying,
"We firmly and strongly believe that those trying to stop the play
on the alleged ground of immorality are badly advised." But after
only two hours, the judge halted testimony, announcing he would
view the film himself that night, to decide.

On Wednesday, Judge Dowd, having attended the standing-
room-only screening on Tuesday night, issued his ruling to another

full house in his courtroom. This time, court officers had locked the main door and allowed entry only through a side door, an easier way to control the flow of people. From his perch on the bench, the judge ruled the only problem with the film was the Gus chase scene. "I will give management 24 hours to eliminate the objectionable scene wherein the degenerate Negro pursues the white girl, who throws herself from the top of a cliff, and if this is not done a summons will issue" for Schoeffel and McCarthy, in lieu of D. W. Griffith.

Further, the judge insisted, race was not a factor in his decision; he would have made the same ruling if the Gus character were a white man lusting after a girl with "an expression on his face which leaves no doubt of his state of mind. There is not any question of his purpose in pursuing the white girl." But other than that one "nauseating" scene, the judge said, he had enjoyed Griffith's movie, calling it "a splendid thing, one of the best I have ever seen." He continued, "There may be things which incite the colored people to protest, but these things are not covered by the statute."

The Trotter crowd remained orderly but was upset and outspoken in its displeasure. How could Judge Dowd have ignored race in his analysis, wondered the NAACP's Butler R. Wilson. What about "the scene wherein the Negro 'Lynch,' elected lieutenant governor, attempts to force the white girl into marriage; where she is tied to the chair, carried off by him, only to be rescued by her father"? he asked. That was immoral action, Wilson charged, with race an inextricable component.

Trotter, described by reporters as "the leader of the colored people," was likewise livid that the judge had made no mention of the Silas Lynch scene. "We might excuse the brutality of the uneducated Negro (Gus) in the excised scene, but the one showing the educated Negro full of the same instincts is a libel and a vilification."

The tensest moment, however, involved an exchange between lawyers Cusick and Lewis. Thanking the judge and clearly pleased, Cusick began waxing poetic about Griffith the master artist, how his epic movie was a work of unprecedented magnitude. "There are three miles of film," Cusick exclaimed.

"Three miles of film?" Lewis interrupted, "Or filth?"

Cusick, momentarily flustered, recovered. "Mr. Lewis," he admonished, "you are an educated colored man; you should not talk like that."

"You can cut out the colored," Lewis retorted.

The invective stopped at that, with the judge ending the session while the parties packed up to leave. Speaking for the absent Griffith, J. J. McCarthy afterward promised that "Judge Dowd's mandate will be obeyed to the letter."

Trotter and his allies had suffered a blow, a courtroom setback requiring they now focus on the state legislature and passage of a revised censorship law.

Victory and Defeat

Film still from *The Birth of a Nation*

═15═

Victory at Hand

James Michael Curley jumped back into the fray the same afternoon Judge Thomas Dowd issued his order that Griffith excise the Gus chase scene. The Boston mayor did so by releasing an official statement that was a curious mix of I-told-you-so gloating and venting his pent-up anger against reporters, protesters, and other public officials who were meddling in a film controversy on his turf. He said he was pleased Griffith and his team planned to comply and cut the contested scene, noting that this was his "original suggestion." In other words, Curley was taking credit for being correct about the movie—even if, to do so, he had to gloss over the fact that its director had agreed two weeks earlier to trim the scene after the City Hall hearing, but to date had not done it. Rather than dwell on Griffith's not keeping his promise, the mayor continued driving home his own importance, saying next that he was pleased the distinguished Judge Dowd's assessment of the film mirrored his own. "I am glad to learn," he said, "that the judge who has heard the evidence of both sides in the case has confirmed my view that only the scene in question could possibly be regarded as offensive in the eye of the law." Curley also could not resist answering his critics with a few cutting digs that displayed his legendary temper, all the while pointing out again that he was the smart one: "So much has been said in criticism of my action in this case, and so unjustly, that I request the press, in fairness to me, to emphasize the fact that the elimination, which has now been assented to, was suggested by me from the beginning." The mayor did not single out anyone out by name, but everyone knew he had Trotter, his allies, and Governor Walsh in mind when he ended his remarks with a bit of advice: "It would be well if all public officials, like the judge in the case, would decline to decide important questions offhand on the ex-parte statements of witnesses who are laboring under the stress of violent emotions."

That same Wednesday afternoon, April 21, film protesters pivoted from the failed judicial action to the State House. Trotter and about three hundred supporters marched from the court to Beacon Hill several blocks away. Their first stop was Governor Walsh's chambers. Trotter reported the breaking news about the Dowd ruling and that, with the governor's help, they now needed to get new legislation. Walsh urged the group to hurry to Room 240, where the Committee on Rules was considering whether to allow some late-filed bills into the current legislative session—one of which was a new censorship proposal submitted by a state representative named Lewis R. Sullivan, a Democrat from Dorchester and a Walsh supporter. Quickly drawn up following Monday's State House caucus, the bill sought to amend the 1910 law to add as a basis for censoring films "any show or entertainment which tends to excite racial or religious prejudice or tends to a breach of the public peace." The language certainly brought *The Birth of a Nation* into question—indeed, it was arguably extremely broad and subjective—but the Sullivan Bill at least got the process started, as long as the rules committee endorsed it for the legislature's further consideration. Trotter left the chambers and marched the group to the hearing room while debriefing everyone along the way about Walsh's continued support, saying the governor again pledged, "to use his influence on behalf of a new bill governing the censorship of plays."

Representing Walsh at the hearing was Lieutenant Governor Grafton D. Cushing, who urged the committee to permit the bill, saying that he, for one, opposed "anything that tends to stir up race hatred and prejudice." Trotter, whose crowd filled the room and beyond, also testified during the late afternoon hearing, as did Rolfe Cobleigh, several clergy, Butler R. Wilson, and William H. Lewis, who said that the Negro race was patient and long suffering, as a rule, but was aroused today as never before in Boston. The only person to speak against the bill was a Boston man named Richard A. Callahan, who rambled on briefly against the Negro race. Callahan claimed to have been mugged by a mob of Negroes in Boston after watching a prizefight film of Negro champion Jack Johnson. "Negroes were looking for trouble," he said and, dropping his voice a few octaves, added, "They were likely to get it." When he claimed the Negroes in Boston—not D. W. Griffith or his film— were the cause of the current unrest, Trotter and several others rose to their feet. Some began hissing, and for a moment it looked like there might be trouble. But the committee chairman called for order, cut Callahan off, and ruled that his remarks be stricken from the official record. Then the chairman called for a vote, and the Rules Committee voted unanimously to permit consideration of the Sullivan Bill to amend the 1910 state censorship law—a bill that decades later might have been dubbed the hate speech amendment but, in 1915, went by the formal legislative name of House Bill No. 2077.

The Trotter force had lost no time in making inroads at the State House. The Boston press might be characterizing Judge Dowd's ruling requiring a single scene be modified as a "partial victory," but the militants would have none of it. "The colored people want no compromise in this matter," attorney Wilson said. They had rebounded quickly from the court ruling and gotten the legislative ball rolling in the State House, and then, on Sunday, April 25, three large rallies were staged—one in Cambridge at the First Parish Unitarian Church in Harvard Square, a second in Boston at the Twelfth Street Baptist Church in Roxbury, and a third at the A. M. E. Zion Church in the South End. The afternoon Roxbury event marked the creation of a women's group specifically to fight the film. More than eight hundred turned out, considered one of the largest gatherings of Negro women ever assembled in Boston. Trotter was there to cheer them on, offering resolutions against the film. Mayor Curley was hissed, with some calling for his recall. "He is not worthy to sit in the chair of Mayor of Boston!" one speaker shouted. Dr. Alice McKane, elected to serve as the new group's vice president, was applauded when she exhorted everyone to fight against the film "to the bitter end, fight until the last drop of blood is gone." She said, "If we cannot get rid of it by fair means, we will get rid of it by foul."

A few hours later Trotter also appeared at the Zion Church indignation rally, which drew several thousand protesters and where a collection was taken to add to the defense fund for him and the others facing trial. The Cambridge event was largely NAACP-dominated, as officials from New York joined local members. Harvard's president emeritus Dr. Charles W. Eliot offered his public support for the first time, incredulous a film would ever glorify the Klan "as doing good work." The Klan, Eliot said, "stood as an example of lawlessness, cruelty and outrage." Others censured Griffith's work as "anarchistic propaganda." The choir from the nearby Baptist Church sang hymns, including "The Battle Hymn of the Republic," and William H. Lewis explained the activists' new mission on Beacon Hill: "We have got to work against these pictures, and when the Mayor and the police commissioner and the police court judge say that they are not obscene and immoral we have got to get the Massachusetts Legislature to tell them what is immoral and obscene and what tends to corrupt the morals of the young." Between them, the rallies served to reinvigorate protesters, ready them for the legislative battle over the Sullivan Bill, and nourish the notion that Trotter and his allies still had the momentum.

When did Monroe Trotter sleep? He seemed to be everywhere—editing the *Guardian*, hustling from one rally to another, convening strategy sessions, tracking censorship efforts in court and now before the state legislature, a relentless pace that did not go unnoticed. His militant "activities to have the photo play run out of the city have been unceasing," the *Boston Post* observed. Then, on Thursday, April 29, he faced a new judicial challenge back at the Boston Municipal Court—the start of his criminal case before Judge J. Albert Brackett on charges of disturbing the peace, inciting a riot at the Tremont Theatre, and assaulting a police officer.

Dispositions had already been reached earlier in the week in the other cases. Charles P. Ray pleaded guilty to throwing eggs at the screen, and Brackett ordered him to reimburse the theatre $20. The judge found Clara Fosky guilty of assaulting an officer with a hatpin, and he fined her $15. Lugenia Foster was fined $6 after Brackett ruled she had hit an officer with a handbag while trying to rescue Fosky, and he found two other protesters guilty of profanity. He then cleared the docket of the remaining cases with small fines or findings of not guilty, setting up the trial of alleged ringleaders Monroe Trotter and Rev. Aaron Puller.

The prosecution's key witnesses were Boston Police sergeant Martin King and the head of the theater's box office. King described the melee, testifying that Trotter not only refused to leave the lobby when asked, but urged the several hundred Negro protesters to stay put. The ticket seller described shutting off ticket sales to everyone and denied the claim that white patrons were allowed in while Negroes were blocked. When Trotter's turn came, his lawyer announced a plan to call one hundred witnesses to prove that tickets were, in fact, sold to whites but not Negroes—actions that were at once illegal discrimination and the cause of the rioting. The judge was not about to allow that; he ordered Trotter to "select a reasonable number of witnesses who can state calmly and clearly just what happened." Moreover, Brackett made clear that if Trotter succeeded in showing discrimination, it was not a defense to the charge of inciting a riot; rather, it would be weighed as a mitigating factor in the court's overall assessment of the evidence.

The trial lasted four days, each day drawing a packed courtroom of mostly Negro supporters but also a few observers from the Griffith team. Mrs. Mary E. Moore, the Roxbury housewife, testified about being refused a ticket only to watch a white woman purchase one, and then about Sergeant King's yelling, "Shut up," at her when she wanted to know why Trotter was being manhandled. Egg bomber Ray testified about watching the ticket seller telling a "colored couple no more tickets were for sale" and then selling a white couple a pair of 50-cent tickets.

The trial's duration overlapped another local story of note—the weather. A powerful thunderstorm on April 30 rocked the region and "played strange pranks" that included a lightning strike on a farm in Lincoln, where a bolt hit a wagon's forward wheel, traveled through it, and instantly killed the horse. Lightning strikes were reported in Woburn, where a trolley car and a barn were hit, and also in Winchester, Wakefield, and Danvers, where homes were struck. New Englanders were hopeful the 0.63 inch of rain signaled a turnaround from the small amount of rain in April and almost none in March.

Indeed, showers and unsettled weather continued into the following week when, on Monday, May 3, Trotter and Puller both took the stand in their defense. Puller described Sergeant King's use of force, adding that the officer had referred to him as a "nigger," and Trotter described being hit with "a powerful blow on the jaw" by plainclothes policeman Dennis Harrington. Trotter forcefully denied going to the show that night to cause a riot.

In rendering the verdict the next day, on May 4, Judge Brackett gave the two defendants a virtual sweep. Puller was acquitted outright, and two of the charges against Trotter—inciting a riot and disturbing the peace—were dismissed. Brackett did decide the editor had been guilty of assaulting a police officer, for which he levied a $20 fine. In explaining the verdict, the judge said Trotter "might have done better in counseling his colored friends to leave the theatre as officers directed" but that his conduct in the lobby did not rise to the level of "riotous." Ever the fighter, Trotter immediately vowed to appeal the lone conviction.

Perhaps most important, Brackett went after the government by attacking the credibility of its key witnesses, namely the ticket seller and the police; he ruled the theater had discriminated against Negroes at the box office; and that this bias, more than any other factor, had been the trigger for the unrest that followed. "When he testified here that he sold no more after being ordered to stop, I hoped to believe him," the judge said about the Tremont's ticket seller. "But subsequent testimony convinced me his statement was not a fact." He was referring to Mary Moore and other Negroes, whose testimony he had found credible. Brackett said, "His acts were unreasonable discrimination against a respected part of the community, and I am not afraid to give such criticism in a public place. I believe the ticket man was largely responsible for the trouble."

Nor was the judge afraid to single out police misconduct. He called Harrington's slugging of Trotter an act that "did much to aggravate affairs" and called on department officials to censure the officer for using excessive force. But Brackett also reserved a few parting words for Trotter. While avoiding direct comment on whether he believed, as few did, the editor's claim of having no prior role in planning the massive rally, Brackett did say, "Mr. Trotter's conduct was not what it should have been considering his influence with his brethren." He then told Trotter that the latter's methods—direct protest action and agitation—were ones he did not consider acceptable. If Negroes—or "his people," as the judge phrased it, "had wrongs, they should seek redress later in the Legislature or the courts."

This was exactly what Trotter and the NAACP Boston officials were doing in the days leading up to his trial, following the failure to find "redress" in court before Judge Dowd. During Trotter's criminal trial, hearings on the Sullivan Bill were held regularly before the House Judiciary Committee. On Monday, April 26, more than two thousand onlookers—the largest crowd yet—filled the State House. In addition to Trotter and local clergy, the NAACP was throwing its increasingly substantial weight behind the Boston protest against the bill that, combined with several court cases testing broad civil rights issues, made 1915 a game-changing year for the national civil rights organization. In the area of residential segregation, for example, Boston's Moorfield Storey was splitting time between the movie protest and readying briefs in *Buchanan v. Warley*, a case heading to the Supreme Court that challenged the city of Louisville's race-based ordinance forbidding the sale of property in white neighborhoods to Negroes.

In a few more weeks, the NAACP would claim victory when the Supreme Court issued a ruling defeating a popular ploy in southern states to restrict Negroes' voting rights through the use of literacy tests and "grandfather clauses" that exempted whites from the tests. Storey had argued against Oklahoma and Maryland rules to grandfather those persons eligible to vote before 1868—*and their descendents*—as exempt from newly enacted state literacy tests.

The racism was blatant: whites qualified for the protected, or grandfathered, class of voters, whereas Negroes, mostly ex-slaves and illiterate, faced having to pass the new test in order to vote.

The Supreme Court ruled the grandfathering clauses unconstitutional, with Chief Justice Edward D. White, a former Confederate soldier and, more recently, a secret but upset fan of D. W. Griffith's *The Birth of a Nation*, writing the court's unanimous opinion. In *Guinn v. United States*, White said that to even argue the point that states had a right to engage in such suffrage shenanigans was absurd, because to do so would render the Fifteenth Amendment—which guaranteed voting rights could not be denied on account of race, color, or previous servitude—"wholly inoperative." The June 21 decision sent segregationists scurrying back to state legislatures to work on devising new Jim Crow laws aimed at disenfranchising Negroes.

But as galvanizing as these high court test cases were, they could not match the angry outcry against Griffith's movie in terms of mobilizing support across the country for the nascent group. In the Boston chapter alone, membership was on its way to doubling in a single year, to a total of 764, and many of them joined Monroe Trotter that Monday to wage ideological warfare against the filmmaker over free expression and hate speech.

In arguing for the Sullivan Bill and, more broadly, that free speech was not absolute, it was Rolfe Cobleigh who perhaps best framed the philosophical conundrum. "Dixon and Griffith plead for free speech for themselves," said the editor of the *Congregationalist*, "but they forget that there is a point where liberty becomes license, and where law says it must stop, a point where the weak become victims of the strong and where liberty becomes anarchy."

Then it was the turn of the Griffith team to push back against the bill, attorney John F. Cusick leading the presentation to the Judiciary Committee. As in the *Ohio v. Mutual Film* case before the Supreme Court, the crux of his argument was that film, as art, was protected by the First Amendment's guarantee of free speech and expression, and that Massachusetts would be wading into "very deep waters" if it decided "to drag race or religion into the realm of censorship." If it did, where would censorship stop? Would any expression or idea that was discomforting be subject to official suppression? Cusick called a parade of witnesses who praised *The Birth of a Nation* as high art and attacked the film's protesters. Rev. Chauncey J. Hawkins, for example, testified he was against "placing any race above criticism" and dubbed the proposed bill "Russian censorship." Hawkins, the white pastor of the Central Congregation Church in the city's Jamaica Plain neighborhood, had been making news as an outspoken fan of the movie, citing the Gus scene in particular as not immoral; rather, as a true representation of "the dread under which the Southern woman constantly trembles, the horrible fear of rape."

Other speakers at the legislative hearing accused Governor Walsh and high-ranking state officials of coddling the Negro. "If a race is to be pampered and protected from criticism it will never grow up," one said. Thomas Dixon, not to be outdone, weighed in with a public statement attacking the proposal and defending the film's showing at the Tremont. "I cannot believe that the supreme lawmaking assembly of the state will deliberately deny to a Southern white man freedom of speech on Boston Common merely because a few Negro agitators differ from his historical conclusions," he said.

In addition, Griffith had gathered the backing of film studios and the Society of American Dramatists and Composers, as well as from some labor unions that worried about the loss of work at area theaters were stricter censorship to result in fewer shows. Not surprisingly, editorial boards at Boston's mainstream newspapers began lining up in opposition to the bill, also on grounds of the First Amendment. "The Sullivan petition would deliver a blow at religious freedom, the rights of the individual and the liberty of the press," opined the *Boston Transcript*. In an editorial titled "Free Speech and the Sullivan Bill," the *Boston Journal* said that however slanted its portrayal of Reconstruction and the Negro race, "there can be no possible harm in letting Bostonians see the Southern side." The newspaper continued, "What should we think of a Southern city or State that forbade a film of *Uncle Tom's Cabin* to be presented? The suppression of *The Birth of a Nation* would be just such a narrow act of bigotry on our part." The *Boston Herald*, calling the bill "far too radical," went after the protesters. "The agitation," it said, "has induced hysterical conditions in many minds, one of the symptoms of which is this petition offered in all seriousness by Mr. Sullivan."

The *Herald*'s commentary drew a response from one of the most respected liberals in the city, Rev. Charles F. Dole, the seventy-year-old Unitarian minister at First Church of Jamaica Plain. In a letter to the editor he praised the paper's opposition to "hasty legislation" drafted to confront the "vexing question of wicked films." He, like Trotter, might oppose Griffith's work, but censorship was not the solution. "I think we may at times greatly deplore the misrepresentation produced by a book or a show without being justified in forbidding people to see it." Instead, he wanted protesters to take the high road. "Isn't this really a good opportunity to rally the Negroes to play the part of men," he said, "and not to make fools of themselves, because a rather evil-minded white man plays the fool?"

The conservative *Herald* pounced immediately on Dole's missive as a means to taunt Trotter. On its editorial page it highlighted the minister's lengthy civil rights record on behalf of "the dusky races" and then, after publishing the text of Dole's letter, added its own tart editorial remark aimed squarely at the militant *Guardian* editor: "Good deal of sound sense here—think it over, Mr. Trotter."

Pettiness aside, the larger point was that such liberals as Dole were not comfortable with the curtailment of free expression as represented in the Sullivan Bill. The year 1915 may have been a time when censorship was commonplace and not the libertarian bugaboo it would become later, particularly in the cutting-edge context of exploring possible limitations on racially offensive and hateful expression, but many liberals found themselves confronting the dilemma of being at once against the film's racist message and against censorship as the response to it. There is no surviving evidence that Trotter was particularly responsive to this quandary, but two Boston NAACP officials were. As the week of April 24 unfolded and as the Judiciary Committee wrapped up its public hearings, William H. Lewis and Butler R. Wilson became aware of eroding support for the Sullivan Bill from their usual constituency. In response, they began working the back channels at the State

House, aided by other film protesters, such as J. Mott Hallowell, lobbying new ideas for a censorship overhaul that would be more palatable politically. They were not alone. Griffith's team, through various legislators, filed its own competing bills, so that suddenly the whole pool was muddied with a grab bag of bills.

The House Judiciary Committee, after meeting privately for two days in executive session, announced its decision on the last day of the month. Few were caught off guard when members rejected the Sullivan Bill, given the drift of the debate. But the committee did more than reject that bill; it reported an altogether new one that took just about everyone by surprise. The lawmakers, in a proposal that would now go before the Joint Committee on the Judiciary for consideration, abandoned tinkering with the 1910 state criminal statute that had been the preoccupation of film protesters ever since their conference with Governor Walsh. Instead, it returned to the original statutory source for censorship in Boston, the 1908 law. But even bigger than that unexpected move was the way in which the House committee wanted to overhaul the earlier law. Removing from the Boston mayor, in consultation with the police, the authority to ban entertainments, a new board would place three key city leaders—the mayor, the police commissioner, and the chief judge of the municipal court—in charge of "revoking and suspending licenses for theatrical exhibitions, public shows and amusements in the City of Boston." The proposal—known as House Bill 2127—further provided that the panel would have to act unanimously in ruling on a petition to ban a show. Most significant, however, was a change in the criteria for censoring. Gone was any language addressing a production's immorality or obscenity—wording that was part of the current statute. Nor was any language added directed at hateful expression based on race or religion—wording that was at the heart of the rejected Sullivan Bill. The committee dodged all of those hot-button topics by inserting, in the last line of Section One of the bill, new language that the panel, acting unanimously, "may revoke or suspend such license *at their pleasure*" (italics added). Noting the novel turn, the *Boston Globe* reported, "The new measure is entirely distinct from any of the other seven which were presented to the committee by those desiring to stop *The Birth of a Nation* or those interested in the production."

The press began calling it "the triple-headed board" proposal that would give a panel "unlimited power over theatrical productions in the city." The Griffith team was none too happy, while the Trotter forces and the Boston NAACP were encouraged even if, as the new bill moved through the legislature, they would have liked to see it fine-tuned so that a majority, rather than a unanimous, vote was the rule.

Then, less than forty-eight hours after the committee's action, and to maintain the edge, the antifilm movement kicked into overdrive. That Sunday, May 2, circulars were distributed at nearly every Negro church, with clergy devoting their sermons to attacking the movie. Its protesters, meanwhile, staged two more massive downtown rallies. The early afternoon event inside a Baptist church on Tremont Street featured white liberals denouncing the movie to a largely Negro audience. *Congregationalist* editor Cobleigh spoke, as did the former Harvard president Eliot, who received a standing ovation when he was introduced. "From the galleries colored women waved their handkerchiefs and cheered him," wrote a *Boston Post* reporter in attendance. Negro militants and clergy were in charge of the later event, held outdoors on the Boston Common in a biting wind. Trotter, looking ahead at a reconstituted Boston panel, had begun talking about the need to win back Mayor Curley, but most speakers were interested in stoking fire and fury.

"If *The Birth of a Nation* continues something similar to the human barbecues of the South is going to happen on yonder hill," Rev. Montrose W. Thornton, referring to lynching and burnings of corpses, yelled to applause. Thornton, who had been with Trotter the night of the latter's arrest, said so far there had been no justice in Boston. "The difference between the courts here and Georgia is that in Boston they say 'Mister' to the defendant and in Georgia they say 'Nigger.'"

The Griffith team made a last-ditch effort to turn things around. Neatly engraved invitations were delivered to all the members of the Massachusetts legislature, requesting their presence at a private screening of *The Birth of a Nation*, and on Monday, May 3, the doors at the Tremont Theatre were thrown open at 10:30 a.m. for the elected officials and their families. Even while Trotter was taking the witness stand a few blocks away at the start of his defense in his criminal trial, the capacity crowd at the Tremont was bearing witness to Griffith's spellbinding masterpiece. "When the Legislature shuts up shop and attends a photo-play in a body to judge the merits of disputed films the situation must be acute," one reporter said. "It was a novel event. It marked an epoch in public amusements."

In brief remarks prior to the show, the Griffith team explained the screening was a chance to present its case to "the members of the Legislature—not to accept our arguments or the argument of our opponents but to behold the proof firsthand." Trotter publicly assailed the tactic; a resolution his literary group adopted that Monday "deplored the visit to the Tremont Theatre" by lawmakers. Attorney Wilson chimed in with the accusation Griffith was using a free film perk to buy support, citing the other private screening Griffith had held earlier in the controversy—the one for Mayor Curley in early April—after which the filmmaker had thrown a tantrum at Hallowell, the invitee who had later denounced the movie. Wilson said, "Obviously those invited to a private view of the play were expected, *nolens volens*, to approve it." He called the free showing scheduled for Monday tantamount to an accused offering a judge a gratuity to drop criminal charges. "Is not such an invitation to the Massachusetts Legislature from such a host both an insult and a plain attempt to bribe?" he asked.

Those who did attend certainly seemed to enjoy the film, although many were careful in interviews afterward to restrict reactions to the film's "artistic quality" and avoided commenting on its portrayal of Negroes and Reconstruction. During the actual screening, however, instances when the audience was swept away by the action did not go unnoticed. "There was general and vigorous applause when the Ku Klux Klan galloped to the rescue," observed the reporter for the *Boston Evening American*. Despite the huge turnout at the Tremont, noticeably missing were the state's three most powerful elected officials: Governor David I. Walsh; the Republican House Speaker, Channing H. Cox; and another prominent Republican from the western part of Massachusetts, Senate president Calvin Coolidge.

Even with the special screening, the Trotter forces and the Boston NAACP seemed to have gained real traction in the legislative roller-coaster ride that had marked their campaign against Griffith at the State House. Starting the week of May 3, as legislators mulled the "three-headed board" proposal, the protesters staged a series of rallies and filled the lawmakers' mailboxes with antifilm resolutions and letters. No one captured the buzz better than one of the Boston Bookerites, a man named Jesse H. Harris. "We are still fighting and the best thing to my mind is that for the first time during my 27 years in Boston the entire Negro population is a unit," he wrote in a letter to Booker T. Washington that reads like field notes from the front lines. Harris observed hundreds of Negro protesters turning out daily for the State House hearings, and he said, "This thought came to me; this is a united people, though in the minority, they are going to win." He gushed to his mentor about a dream he had had, inspired by the antifilm movement: "I saw in my mind a meeting in this city in the Old Liberty Hall—the speakers Washington, Walters, Du Bois—Trotter and others—where all things of the past would be buried. And a race of Ten Millions of Negroes would be united. A Nation would *really* be born."

To be sure, there was always the hint of violence accompanying the protests. Irksome to the Trotter forces was one marketing stunt the Griffith team used on occasion to promote the film—a horse decorated in KKK regalia that was led around the Theatre District. "That Ku Klux horse parading around the streets to advertise the show is a terrible thing to tantalize us with," Thornton warned. "I've got something to hand that horse when I meet it." The evening performance on May 10 at the Tremont Theatre was halted when two men—one white, the other Negro—began a fistfight. The lights went up, the film flickered and went silent, and the velvet curtain dropped over the screen, as police descended upon the combatants and another forty officers were summoned for fear a larger disturbance might erupt. Patrons screamed and some rushed in a panic for the exits, but no further trouble occurred and the movie resumed without additional interruption.

For the most part, however, Trotter called for a truce on militant agitation, committed to working the system to win the censorship authority to run Griffith out of town. He took to praising Curley in public, even as many continued to bitterly condemn the mayor's initial rulings to allow the film. "It is not seemly that the name of Mayor Curley should be attacked here today," Trotter said, as he interrupted another speaker on the rostrum during one of the May rallies. Then, during a May meeting of the Boston Literary and Historical Association, Trotter had members adopt his resolution urging lawmakers that the "motion picture censorship bill be amended to call for a majority instead of the unanimous approval of the censors." In addition to winning passage, this was the final challenge—to make it easier for the censoring board to rule against a film. Having heartily endorsed the change, the group then approved "that $1.50 be appropriated for the purpose of presenting each representative a copy of the resolution."

The protest's focus on the State House paid off. The Massachusetts House of Representatives easily passed the bill on Monday, May 10 by a vote of 175–43. Prior to voting, a legislator from the neighboring town of Brookline who was both loyal to Walsh and a supporter of the protesters tried to change the Boston panel's voting requirement from unanimous to a majority. The amendment was defeated, in a 116–104 vote, but the margin was so narrow that it fueled film protesters' optimism they could get the change adopted once the bill moved on to the state Senate. For the next week the Senate then debated "the Boston triple-censor bill," as lawmakers backing Griffith sought to kill it and those backing the Trotter forces sought to modify the panel's voting requirements.

Trotter and the Boston NAACP continued showing up and lobbying their cause, although the legislative wrangling fell off the front pages of the Boston daily newspapers. The news raging in Boston and across the country was the sinking of the *Lusitania* ocean liner by a German U-boat on May 7 off the coast of Ireland, leaving nearly 1,200 dead, including more than one hundred Americans. While President Wilson and other US leaders condemned the German strike and debated the country's response, Thomas Dixon was moved to write his friend another of his notes voicing loyal support. "I have been unable to work since the Lusitania horror," Dixon began, before offering some advice and adding his thanks that Wilson was in charge "of this supreme hour in our history." Upon its receipt on May 13, the president dashed off a short reply: "My dear Dixon, Thank you with all my heart for your letter. It helps." In Boston, reflecting war fever and fear, the *Globe* published a magazine spread on Sunday, May 16, on the city's exposure to a submarine attack. "Boston Open to Sea Attack," screamed the headline of the story, which included a map showing where military experts were advising that new fortifications be built in various Boston harbor islands to defend the city.

The very next day, on Monday, May 17, the Trotter forces finally got what they were after from the state senators, who voted 20–18 to amend the censorship bill, striking the language "acting unanimously" and inserting "by a majority vote." Better still, the Senate adopted the newly modified bill by a vote of 15–14. That vote should have sent the bill back to the House for its final consideration, but on Tuesday those senators who had been against the bill, backed by the Griffith team, moved that the Senate reconsider the Monday vote. It suddenly seemed as if the bill might get derailed, as those against the measure rounded up what appeared to be enough votes for the stalling tactic. In a roll call vote, sixteen senators voted in favor of reconsideration, while fifteen were opposed.

But that was when Senate president Calvin Coolidge came to the rescue. In a moment of legislative high drama, Coolidge, who ordinarily did not vote, called out once he realized the direction of the roll call. "The clerk will call the name of the President of the Senate," he bellowed. Everyone looked his way, and he then voted a succinct "No" against reconsideration of the Boston censor bill. With his vote, the tally was now tied at 16–16—and a tie, in official vernacular, meant the "motion to reconsider is negatived."

The room buzzed at the suspenseful turn of events, as reporters scribbled down notes about Coolidge's unusual intervention—casting his first vote of the year—to kill reconsideration and send the amended censorship bill back to the House for concurrence. In the Senate gallery, the Trotter crowd in attendance was jubilant, while *The Birth of a Nation* lobbyists were crestfallen. The following day, Wednesday, the House approved the bill, which the press was quick to characterize as yet "another big victory" for the opponents of the photoplay *The Birth of a Nation.* The voting was not even close, 136–71, as Walsh, a Democrat, had joined with Republicans, the party of Lincoln, in the hand-to-hand combat for House votes: His staff was spotted in the lobby lining up the Democrats, while the Republican leaders cracked down on their party's members, literally pulling them away from "the theatrical men" fighting to get their attention. The successful lobbying coalition carried over into the next day, when the bill went back to the Senate for final review. Despite last-ditch efforts to stall the measure again, the bill passed the Senate. Then, on Friday, May 21, or four weeks after hearings first began on the initial Sullivan Bill, the new "three-headed censorship bill," having been endorsed by the Massachusetts Senate, was presented to the governor for his approval. Walsh signed the bill into law as soon as he received it, and he awarded the pen he used to his chief lobbyist.

The editorial opposition to the new law from the press was quick. "If it be right to censor moving picture films," said the *Boston Advertiser*, "why not newspapers? Why not books? Why not speeches? If not, where shall the line be drawn, logically, and why?" The Trotter forces and the Boston NAACP, meanwhile, were emboldened. The same day the governor signed the bill, each group drew up requests that Curley convene a new hearing. Writing for the Boston NAACP, Butler R. Wilson, William H. Lewis, and J. Mott Hallowell said they "respectfully petition your honorable board, constituted under Chapter 384 of the Acts of 1915, for a hearing to hear the protestants against the further production in Boston of the film entitled, *The Birth of a Nation.*" There was almost a celebratory feel, after so much tireless work against the film. "We are delighted with Boston's energy and success," May Childs Nerney wrote from NAACP headquarters in New York City. For his part, Trotter huddled Friday night in the office of the *Guardian* with his followers, drawing up their petition and finalizing plans to send a delegation to see the mayor in person.

Handicapping the new board, Trotter was brimming with confidence. Curley, he believed, could be counted on, not only because of flattery and a cessation of criticism, but mainly because the new bill provided the very "arbitrary power" he had sought to be able to ban the movie. Hadn't Curley said he sided with their view the film was hateful to the Negro race? The new law now allowed censors to act against a movie "at their pleasure," and Trotter fully believed one of the mayor's pleasures would be to reward his longtime and loyal Negro supporters. The press had even picked up on protesters' expectation that Curley was now firmly in their corner, with one reporter writing that the "leaders of the colored people" believed "Mayor Curley has no longer the excuse that there is no sufficient law to back up his prohibition of the movie play." Then there were the other two members of the panel. Commissioner Stephen O'Meara? He owed his job to Walsh, and so could be expected to fulfill the governor's mandate to oppose the film. Chief Justice Wilfred Bolster of the Boston Municipal Court? Who knew, but if he could be persuaded, perhaps they could roll the table in the panel's vote to ban the film.

Victory was at hand, finally.

"Every performance heaps new undeserved ignominy upon the Negro race," Trotter said within hours of the bill's signing into law. "We think it should be stopped at once. We hope to let not a day elapse before we request to censors to act."

16

The Curtain Falls

Throughout the spring, as the battle over *The Birth of a Nation* raged in Boston, plenty of other civil rights controversies, large and small, were percolating around the state and country, highlighting the very issue at the center of the film protest: how Negroes were treated, or more accurately, mistreated in America—and not just in the South. For example, civil rights activists celebrated when the New York state legislature voted to ban a popular game from summer fairs, carnivals, and resorts in the lake and mountain regions. It was called "Hit the Nigger," or "Hit the Coon." Customers paid to throw balls at a Negro or, if a live target was unavailable, a cartoon of a Negro face. Sometimes a carnival operator provided the live target with a helmet, but often not. To stir up the crowd and add to the "fun," thrower and target were encouraged between tosses to hurl racial epithets at each other. The New York ban was a small victory, to be sure; the game, or variations on it, such as "Dunk the Nigger" a.k.a. the "African Dip," was played at carnivals in other states for decades. But forbidding such "amusements" was progress nonetheless.

In Boston, too, attention was not on *Birth* all of the time. The last week of April, just days before lawmakers began to debate the Sullivan Bill, a young woman named Jane R. Bosfield went to interview for a position as stenographer at the Medfield State Hospital, or the Medfield Insane Asylum as it was commonly known. Bosfield was in her early twenties and lived with her family in the city's Allston neighborhood. She had graduated from the Cambridge High and

Latin School and then trained at Boston Evening High School in bookkeeping, stenography, and typewriting. She could write shorthand at one hundred words per minute and her fingers were known to "fly over double or single keyboards." Her father, Samuel, formerly a newspaper editor in the Bahamas, worked for a Cambridge printing company, the Riverside Press, which published the *Atlantic Monthly* magazine, among other prestigious books and publications.

Bosfield had passed the state civil service examination with honors, but despite these credentials, she had not been able to secure a stenography job with either the city or the state. "I tried for positions, tried desperately hard, and always I was refused," she said at one point. "For three years I was forced to work in a factory for half the money I could get at the work for which I had been trained." Then she learned about the opening at the Medfield hospital, a job that seemed to fit her talents perfectly, and after submitting her application she was invited to an interview with the hospital's superintendent, Dr. Edward French. Accompanied by her mother, Bosfield made her way to Medfield, located about twenty-five miles southwest of Boston, for the April 24 appointment. In appearance, the young woman made a fine impression. Thinly built and tallish for a woman, she liked to keep her hair pushed back and favored conservative outfits, such as a dark serge skirt with a dotted swiss shirtwaist and low-heeled oxfords. But her credentials, her professional look, and demeanor—none of this mattered to French, because the interview was over the moment she walked into his office.

"I couldn't think of hiring you," the hospital superintendent said.

When Bosfield asked why not, French said, "Because you are a colored girl."

Hadn't he known her race? Bosfield asked.

"No," French replied, "I had no means of knowing."

The young applicant and her mother were then escorted out of the office. The doctor later denied Bosfield's account that he had rejected her because she was dark-skinned, but conceded he did not want a Negro working on his staff "on account of harmony." Soon after, he filled the position with a young white woman.

For Bosfield, the setback was her tipping point. She began to complain, especially after hearing Governor Walsh, in support of protesters against D. W. Griffith's film, talk publicly about fighting for a fair chance for all Massachusetts citizens. In an interview with a Boston newspaper, she said, "In the North you fought hard for us not very long ago, but you aren't—you aren't living up to the contract you made. We pay equal taxes—we do not have equal rights." Soon enough, Monroe Trotter heard about Bosfield's struggles—hers was the very kind of pointed, personal discrimination he had crusaded against over the years in the pages of the *Guardian*, and he somehow found the time in the spring of 1915 amid the film protest to take up the Jane Bosfield matter. By summer's end, Walsh was also brought into the employment dispute; his secretary wrote to Bosfield that "the Governor is indeed willing to interest himself in your behalf." It was the kind of commitment Walsh had made to Trotter and film protesters at the massive State House rally that had proven so crucial—a promise that seemed to make all the difference in the world, what with the governor's May 21 signing of the law overhauling the Boston censor board and providing protesters with the weapon, finally, to pull down the curtain on Griffith's blockbuster film.

The Sunday after Walsh signed the bill, Negro clergy sermonized throughout the city about the apparent victory at hand, petitions were circulated for signatures to submit to the new board, and Monroe Trotter was the keynote speaker at a Sunday night rally at the Twelfth Baptist Church in the city's South End. The new "three-headed" board held a brief plenary session over the weekend in Mayor Curley's City Hall office, at which Curley was selected chairman and members decided they all needed to view *The Birth of a Nation* prior to deliberations. Griffith lawyer John F. Cusick released a statement exuding confidence the board would not interfere with the film. "While I sincerely believe that this new law is one of the most dangerous pieces of legislation in recent years," he said, "I trust implicitly the sane judgment of the three men who are named as censors."

Trotter and his forces matched Cusick's statement with one of their own. During the Sunday night church rally, the editor had introduced a resolution for the "honorable Board of Censors"; it declared that Griffith's movie, "by racial slander and evil design, seeks and tends to create, excite and augment prejudice against colored Americans, and thereby to deprive them of equal opportunity." Therefore, he said, "Our appeal is for the removal of this play from Boston right speedily."

But the Curley board was in no particular hurry. Protesters continued to meet during the week of May 24 to beat the drum of censorship, with Trotter speaking at the A. M. E. Zion Church on Monday night, but the board did not hold any further sessions that week. More than six thousand signatures were gathered in support of a ban, and the petition was submitted to City Hall for the board's review. Clergy calling themselves the Boston Congregation of Ministers wrote to the board urging a ban, saying the film had "aroused the entire Negro population of Boston and created a most unfavorable impression upon many fair minded persons irrespective of race or color."

For more than a week the suspense continued to build, until Curley finally convened a hearing on Wednesday, June 2. It was midafternoon on the warm spring day when the mayor opened the door to his outer office in City Hall and found about one hundred Negroes waiting. The crowd had come together quickly, having just learned about the hearing Curley had scheduled hastily earlier in the day. Trotter was not present; he later said no one had told him the starting time. But the Boston NAACP was well represented— Butler R. Wilson, William H. Lewis, and J. Mott Hallowell. Cusick was there on behalf of Griffith.

The mayor told the crowd he would only admit lawyers representing each side—meaning the NAACP threesome and Cusick— and no one else. No spectators, no stenographer (the NAACP had brought its own), and no newspaper reporters. The hearing would be held in secret in his inner chamber. He said each side would be given a half-hour to present its case, and the panel would then deliberate. The lawyers stepped inside, and Curley shut his door. The waiting began. Within minutes Trotter hurried in, dismayed at missing the beginning of the hearing. "I did not learn that this meeting was to be held until 3:30 this afternoon," he said. Without addressing whether he thought Curley had snubbed him, Trotter demanded admission, arguing he had every right as a protest leader to be included, especially "as the three lawyers from the National Association were already in there."

But the mayor's secretary blocked his way, telling Trotter the session was closed per her boss's orders. The afternoon dragged on. Within the inner sanctum, each side ended up taking about an hour to deliver its respective argument, which, in summary, was a rehash of the hate-speech versus free speech arguments that had been made throughout the Boston protest in all its venues, whether in City Hall, the Municipal Court, the State House, Boston Common, or the city's streets. The mayor's office closed officially at five p.m., at which time the crowd was moved from the mayor's outer office into the second-floor corridor—and at this point its numbers dwindled, as many took the opportunity to leave, tired of the wait. Ninety minutes later, the three NAACP officials emerged from the office, followed shortly afterward by Cusick. The Curley panel, they said, was in executive session.

Finally, at about seven p.m.—after only about a half-hour of private discussions—the mayor opened the door to face Trotter, the NAACP officials, and what remained of the crowd. The other censors, Commissioner Stephen O'Meara and Chief Justice Wilfred Bolster of the Municipal Court, were not with him. They had already left the building, Curley said, and he alone would announce the outcome. He held in his hands a seventy-three-word statement the panel had prepared. "The officials designated by Chapter 348, Acts of 1915, having received a petition . . . ," he began, and delivered a blur of bureaucratic-sounding legalese before arriving at what everyone was waiting for—the triumvirate's ruling on the fate of *The Birth of a Nation*. The panel, Curley said, having seen the film and heard the arguments, had "decided the license of the theatre should not be revoked or suspended."

The headline in the *Boston Post* the next morning said it all:

"BIRTH OF A NATION" WINS

Trotter and the others, expecting triumph, were flat-out stunned. But with the benefit of hindsight, should they have been surprised?

The antifilm protesters—so caught up in their legislative victory—
had grossly miscalculated Curley and his role on the new panel. In
thinking, wishfully, that the Boston mayor was on their side—the
"Jim Curley of old"—they ignored the plethora of signals he had sent
that he was no friend of theirs anymore, especially when it came to
Monroe Trotter, despite Curley's paying lip service early on to their
views that the film was an outrage. The mayor's smug reaction to
Judge Dowd's ruling back on April 21 should have been their first
major clue, a reaction that was so full of anger at the protesters for
continuing to press their grievances and for attacking him bitterly
as a traitor to their race. The statement alone was proof enough that
no amount of flattery after such attacks could possibly bring Curley
back into the fold. This was Boston, after all, where the idea of never
forgetting a slight was a deeply embedded tradition, past and future.

But if that was not enough, the mayor had also showed his ire
when, prior to the formation of the new board, he had sent city
lobbyists to the State House to fight the Walsh-sponsored legislation to change the Boston censor law. Curley favored the status
quo—where he was in charge rather than one voter on some "three-
headed" panel. The reform bill was an affront to him. Then there
was the most basic of political calculations. By the time of the ruling
in early June, *The Birth of a Nation* had proven itself a box-office
smash, viewed by thousands. Curley was no dummy when it came
to counting votes. "He can hardly have been unaware that by the
end of May, 100,000 or so white Bostonians had watched (and often expressed enthusiasm for) the movie," wrote one historian, "and
that African Americans still made up only small percentage of the
total population of the city." Finally, a rumor of foul play swirled
around the mayor's actions during the film controversy—that he
was bribed along the way by the Griffith team. "Curley was not
money-honest," writes Jack Beatty, author of the definitive Curley
biography. "There is no getting around that fact."

Curley certainly provided no explanations for the panel's swift
verdict. Beyond his formal reading of the ruling, he had nothing
more to say to the journalists and protesters still remaining in City
Hall, waving off the flurry of reporters' questions, saying only that
the board had decided not to discuss its reasoning or even to reveal

whether the decision was unanimous or not—although one newspaper did report the vote had been unanimous, with the powerful
Curley in complete command of the proceedings. Instead, after five
minutes the mayor left abruptly and headed downstairs, where his
chauffeur was waiting to drive him to New Bedford, Massachusetts, to attend a christening. Curley was the baby's godfather, and
he was running late.

After the curtain fell at City Hall on the Boston protest, it rose a
few minutes later at the nearby Tremont Theatre for the eight p.m.
showing of *The Birth of a Nation*, the fifty-sixth consecutive evening performance since the movie's Boston premiere on April 10—
and the first without some sort of legal review pending against it.
Settling into their seats, patrons could hear musicians tuning their
instruments in the pit, a clear sign that this feature film was a long
way from the nickelodeon. No single pianist running his fingers up
and down a keyboard or, worse, the white noise of a projector whir-
ring, but a fully equipped, forty-piece orchestra. Many ticketholders at this point had some idea of what to expect, and perhaps were
even back to the see the film again, but as was the case ever since
its first night at the Tremont. The largely white audience braced
for the cinematic experience of a lifetime.

The lights dimmed, the conductor raised his baton, and the
house exploded in music as the title card for *The Birth of a Nation*
flickered and then boldly appeared on the big screen to announce
the start of the epic tale of the Civil War and Reconstruction. Opening shots quickly showed the arrival of slavery in America, with the
ominous intertitle "The bringing of the African to America planted
the first seed of disunion." Moviegoers were then introduced to
the two star-crossed families—the Stonemans—whose patriarch,
Austin Stoneman, had been modeled after Thaddeus Stevens, the
radical Republican congressman from Pennsylvania whom many
southerners, including Griffith, regarded as the South's arch enemy overseeing Reconstruction—and the Camerons, living in the
fictional community of Piedmont, South Carolina. The audience
got to know the Stoneman children—Elsie and her brothers, Phil
and Tod—as well as the five Cameron siblings—Ben, his younger

brothers, Wade and Duke, and his two sisters, Margaret and Flora. Moviegoers learned that Phil Stoneman and Ben Cameron were friends already, and watched intently as other friendships and romances start when the Stoneman boys visit the Camerons in Piedmont. Tod Stoneman and Duke Cameron become fast friends; Phil Stoneman falls in love with Margaret Cameron; and Ben Cameron, taking a photograph of Elsie Stoneman from Phil, falls head over heels for Elsie and begins carrying her photograph with him from that point on.

The Civil War breaks out, and the boys from both families are in uniform. The battle of Atlanta is waged, Sherman marches to the sea, and Lee surrenders at Appomattox. Tod Stoneman and both Wade and Duke Cameron die in combat. Near the Confederacy's final days, Ben Cameron, known as the "Little Colonel," is seriously wounded while leading a charge in the Siege of Petersburg against Union soldiers commanded by his former friend Phil Stoneman, who saves him. Throughout the Griffith's screen depiction of war, the mesmerizing action captivated the Boston audience—the puffs of cannon fire, the armies fighting across sweeping panoramic shots of battlefields—and the musical score made the sounds of bombs' exploding seem real. Men cheered at certain parts; women wept at others. The injured Ben Cameron is taken to a hospital in the North, where his love interest, Elsie Stoneman, nurses him. Lincoln is assassinated at Ford's Theatre, Ben Cameron returns home to a ravaged South. Here the curtain falls on the film's extravagant first part.

Reconstruction in a defeated South is the focus of the remainder of the movie. The audience watched Ben Cameron and other soldiers return to shattered homes and try to begin anew, only to be confronted with freed slaves, radical Republican carpetbaggers, and "Negro domination—the most terrible punishment inflicted upon a proud white race," as reviewer Frederick Johns wrote for the *Boston American*. Leading the way is the radical northern Republican leader Austin Stoneman, who makes Piedmont, South Carolina, his headquarters and works tirelessly to "put the White South under the heel of the Black South," as the film's intertitle based on Woodrow Wilson's book, notes. Stoneman ensures the election of a Negro-dominated legislature and the victory of a mulatto named Silas

Lynch in a race for lieutenant governor, all the while blind to the
fact Lynch wants his daughter, Elsie, as his prize. In another story
line of Negro lust, Flora Cameron tragically jumps to her death
rather than submit to the advances of ex-slave Gus. Meanwhile Ben
Cameron, forlorn at rising black supremacy, has come up with an
idea "to protect the Southern country" after seeing white children
using bedsheets to scare Negro children. He creates the Ku Klux
Klan and, after holding his dying sister Flora in his arms as she
manages to name Gus as her pursuer, not only leads the Klan in
avenging her death but, in a series of climactic clashes between the
races, rescues Camerons and Stonemans from Negro danger. The
Klan night riders "look like a company of avenging spectral crusad-
ers sweeping across the moonlit roads," another critic had noted.
They were filmed as if galloping straight toward the audience, in
such a convincing way that some moviegoers ducked, while others
shrieked, worried the riders would leap off the screen at them. The
movie's final takeaway is clear: the KKK had saved the South, and
a nation is reborn.

While the film's action and excitement had left many Boston viewers breathless, Negroes in attendance likely held their breath.
Their experience of Griffith's *The Birth of a Nation* was vastly different, focusing on aspects white moviegoers tended to skip over
unhesitatingly—and what the Negroes saw stopped them in their
viewing tracks. They studied, dissected, and then churned in anger
at the grotesque distortions Griffith had presented of their race.
The smears started right away; when in the opening sequences
during a meeting of abolitionists, set before the Civil War, a white
woman who is an antislavery activist flinches in disgust at the
smell of a Negro who has moved closer to her. In the antebellum
South, meanwhile, slaves are shown living among benevolent slave
owners in a kind of plantation paradise; they work and sing, are
deeply suspicious of Yankees and cheer when Confederate soldiers
head off to defend the Old South. The horror of war is first seen
when Negro bluecoats attack the Camerons' hometown, introduced
with an intertitle that reads, "Piedmont scarred by the war; an
irregular force of guerillas [sic] raids the town." The information

includes an audience reminder that South Carolina was the state where Negro troops from Boston entered the war. The historical annotation was a device Griffith used throughout the movie to claim his work was fact-based, but it actually stood as a prime example of something in the drama that, while accurate, was not true. In the film, rifle-firing Negro soldiers are shown raiding Piedmont's streets, vandalizing everything in their way, shooting at white southerners, and chasing after white women—but nothing in the historical record about Trotter's 55th, or any other Negro unit, for that matter, suggests such savagery was ever committed against South Carolina's civilians.

The worst from the Negro's perspective, however, was the film's second part. The opening intertitle reads, "This is an historical representation of the Civil War and Reconstruction, and is not meant to reflect on any race or people of today." Negro audiences did not buy that line for a second, not when freed slaves, exercising their new voting power, were shown as ignorant, slovenly, and bullying whites, and the newly elected Negro lawmakers who took over the South Carolina legislature turn the assembly room into a free-for-all, rollicking party. The Negro audience watched as Austin Stoneman's maniacal mulatto sidekick Silas Lynch ogles, stalks, and ultimately overpowers a struggling Elsie Stoneman in a wild-eyed bid to force her to marry him. Reacting with similar revulsion, they watched the character Gus play out his obsession for the young Flora Cameron, climaxing with the chase scene that protesters most often cited as symbolic of the film's racism, and which such officials as Mayor Curley and Judge Dowd had even found objectionable. "You see, I am a Captain now—and I want to marry," reads the intertitle when Gus, looking crazed, confronts a hand-wringing, frightened Flora. When Flora slaps Gus and runs, he gives chase, yelling, "Wait missie, I won't hurt ya!" Griffith, demonstrating his trademark editing, cuts back and forth between the girl and the predatory Gus who, while running, adopts a hunkering form that unmistakably resembles an ape. "Stay away or I'll jump," Flora screams, having arrived out of breath at a cliff's edge. Using another technique to heighten the tension, the camera zooms in on a close-up of Gus's wild expression as he steps toward Flora, who jumps to her death.

A film still from *The Birth of a Nation.*
COURTESY OF THE MUSEUM OF MODERN ART, NEW YORK.

This was the scene that D. W. Griffith would, time and again, promise Boston officials that he would trim, most notably after Judge Dowd's April 21 ruling, but Negroes watching the film—whether on opening night or any subsequent screening—saw what the Boston NAACP's William H. Lewis had seen when he went to check on whether Griffith had honored the court order with substantive changes. "Gus remains a character in the photo-play," Lewis had complained. "He is seen skulking about the neighborhood where the girl lives. The girl starts for the spring and then the picture abruptly shifts to the scene where the child dies, and the Ku Klux Klan start on the hunt for Gus." Griffith had made only token changes, Lewis charged. "I don't consider that the management has acted in good faith."

Finally, there was the film's romantic portrait of the Ku Klux Klan, seen as the brainchild of Ben Cameron, the "Little Colonel," to save the South from Negro anarchy. The Klan captures Gus, executes him after a "trial," and dumps his corpse on Silas Lynch's porch. The white force rises in power and rides to the rescue of the film's key characters and, through them, a nation.

But Klan heroism stood in stark contrast to the historical record, a taste of which one Boston newspaper, the *Traveler*, gave in a story published during the movie's run and which was based on court records from criminal trials of actual Klansmen in the Carolinas. The newspaper, noting that South Carolina was the state Dixon and Griffith had chosen for dramatizing Klan activities "at their noblest," found a chasm between the Klan in the movie and in court records. In the movie, the Klan was portrayed as being organized "to protect women from the degenerate Negroes," whereas the true Klan was formed "to deprive Negroes of their votes and hang white men who tried to protect freedmen in the rights of citizenship." The Klan in Griffith's film protected whites' property, but in real life Klansmen were convicted and sent to prison "for burning buildings and robbing the country treasury." In the film, the paper said, the Klan's depiction amounted to "figments of filmland, as free from the bondage of historic truth as Alice's Wonderland." Even the defense attorneys, seeking leniency for Klansmen they represented, conceded the worst, arguing their clients had been seduced into joining a group that was guilty of "inhuman atrocities."

In the end, the movie was a tale of two viewpoints, and of the disconnect between them. By the time the evening's screening at the Tremont Theatre was over, its Negro attendees were mostly repulsed; to be sure, it was not the first time they had been shown on-screen in an unflattering light, but never before had insult occurred amid such cinematic magnificence. Meanwhile, most white viewers cheered and applauded, some standing in ovation. From their vantage of white privilege, they were clueless about the race complaints. The film, after all, reflected conventional thought that the Negro race was inferior, and to think otherwise required a paradigm shift in the media, the public's mind, and in much of the history and science of the time. The enthusiastic reaction had become the film's hallmark ever since the start of the Boston run, a Saturday kick-off that had included the director himself appearing onstage at intermission. Griffith was delighted at the film's reception but was also so nervous that he could hardly speak. He finally managed to, and profusely thanked the audience. "I feel that you appreciate my efforts."

Griffith had experienced similar triumph in Los Angeles at the Clune's Auditorium premiere back in February 1915 once the two words "The End" had flashed on the screen and the audience had stood up and cheered until the director finally emerged from the left side and stepped out onto the stage. The filmmaker had been literally speechless that night, not even taking a bow or raising his hand to acknowledge the outpouring but just standing there, "a tiny figure against the backdrop of the great proscenium arch, as wave after wave of cheers and applause engulfed him," as one Griffith biographer described.

"It was quite possibly the greatest moment of his life."

That same evening at around nine o'clock, just as the Civil War was ending in the fifty-sixth showing of *The Birth of a Nation* and moviegoers were about to watch Lee surrender to Grant at Appomattox Courthouse, Trotter walked into the St. Mark Congregational Church in Roxbury where an anxious crowd of about 250 followers awaited him. He was late arriving at the church hall, located on Tremont Street about two and a half miles south from the Tremont Theatre's downtown location. The scene resembled an election night, the way everyone stood around. But instead of tensely awaiting poll results the crowd was awaiting the fate of the Griffith film.

"This is a serious meeting," Trotter said. "We have come to a marking place in the fight against *The Birth of a Nation*." His manner was grave, his tone grim, but instead of announcing the Curley panel's ruling right away, he kept his audience in suspense. He delivered an impromptu speech, a sweeping overview of the "long struggle to stop the photo-play," a step-by-step recounting of the eight-week campaign that had included demonstrations at City Hall hearings, in court, at legislative sessions at the State House, in Boston Common and outside the Tremont Theatre.

In all, since early April, there had been some eighteen mass rallies and direct action protests, involving between 500 and 2,500 protesters at each, or many thousands of agitators in total, and resulting in more than twenty arrests—an outpouring of black power no one, not Trotter, not the NAACP's Wilson or Lewis, not anyone from the various Boston Negro factions, had ever witnessed before. Trotter recalled for his audience the near-riot at the Tremont on Saturday, April 17, where he had been arrested, and the other disturbances at the theater, including the night when a fistfight broke out between a white man and a Negro. "What happened?" Trotter asked about that incident. "People in the audience arose and cried, 'Hit the nigger!' 'Strike the nigger!' 'Look out for razors!'"

Trotter's simmering anger was becoming evident as he next described being rebuffed earlier in the day when he tried to gain entry to the Curley panel's hearing. "Our people who were there to attend the meeting were forced into the mayor's outer office," he said. When he at last reached the point of disclosing the panel's decision, he furiously attacked Curley first, calling the mayor a traitor, and then said the panel, after meeting in secret, had "sent out its verdict that *The Birth of a Nation* can stay and play in Boston, just as long as the management wants it to." Trotter announced that "the voices raised, and the petitions signed by the several thousands of persons, at the eighteen meetings of colored citizens, held in the last eight weeks in Greater Boston, have met with deaf ears."

The crowd hissed at the verdict. "Dynamite!" someone yelled. "Blow it up," called another. Others shouted out their determination, "There's a way!" In a moment of cynicism, perhaps even self-pity, Trotter complained that their agitation had only resulted in lining the pockets of Griffith and his team with money, along with getting the filmmaker "Boston's official endorsement for the continuance of this instigation of race hatred." But he recovered quickly enough. To calls for dynamite and violence, he urged caution—the idea of blowing up the Tremont Theatre was out of the question. He was no anarchist—rather, a civil rights agitator who promoted direct action to confront racism and demand that a democracy live up to its promise.

"The case now rests in the hands of you people. I, as one of you, can only warn you to be very, very careful what you do," he advised. Trotter was upset, to be sure, by the panel's decision, but he also understood that as far as censoring the film was concerned the bid to ban the movie from Boston had run its course. It was game over. *The Birth of a Nation* played that night, June 2, and the night after, and the night after that—and continued to play every night in Boston until late October when it finally closed after thirty weeks and a record of 360 performances in that city.

But this did not mean Monroe Trotter was done, or defeated. He encouraged further protest rallies and picketing against the film in the days that followed, and for the next week Boston police dispatched a total of more than three hundred officers as a precautionary measure. He continued the fight for months to come—not with explosive materials but with explosive words, through his speeches and as the crusading editor of the *Guardian*. This way the public record would always show that while the legendary movie director D. W. Griffith may have produced a technical marvel he had also created a lasting artifact of anti-Negro propaganda, and that a titanic clash between protester and filmmaker had reignited America's Civil War.

EPILOGUE

"The miracle happened," Thomas Dixon said about the stunning victory the Curley panel had handed him and D. W. Griffith on June 2, 1915, the decisive round in the long Boston protest against *The Birth of a Nation.* "Months of frantic agitation, scheming and shouting and feeble rioting had gone for nothing except to advertise the picture." Before the battle royal, Griffith and his team had always said that if they could get their film launched successfully in Boston, they could take it anywhere, and that largely bore out. During the remainder of its first year, the movie played in Massachusetts, New York, California, and, despite occasional trouble spots, elsewhere around the country, earning millions for Griffith and his investors.

By the autumn of 1915 *The Birth of a Nation* headed south. In anticipation, Atlanta's newspapers ran long features to promote the movie and to excite viewers. Many Atlantans had already seen the picture in their travels and were sending word home about its wonders. The timing coincided neatly with a true-to-life version of the epic's major story line, of young Ben Cameron's creating the Ku Klux Klan to save the South and start a new nation: On a cold late November night a dozen or so Georgians gathered to jump-start the long-defunct Klan on Stone Mountain sixteen miles outside of Atlanta. The group used flashlights to find its way through the dark, led by William J. Simmons, a veteran of the Spanish-American War, who had worked as a traveling preacher and salesman before

settling in Atlanta. Griffith's film was later said to have inspired
the men into action, but Simmons said that growing up in Alabama as the son of a proud Klansman had made him always want
to revive the KKK. He and his followers on that night gathered
stones to build a makeshift altar. They used pine boards soaked in
kerosene to make a cross. Then they lit it. "Under a blazing, fiery
torch," Simmons said later, "the Invisible Empire was called from
its slumber of half a century to take up a new task and fulfill a new
mission for humanity's good."

A week after the Simmons incident Griffith traveled to Georgia
to meet with reporters before *The Birth of a Nation* opened on Monday, December 6, at the Atlanta Theatre. The movie drew huge audiences and rave reviews. "Ancient Greece had her Homer, modern
America has her David W. Griffith," wrote critic Ned McIntosh in the
Atlanta Constitution. McIntosh observed, as had other reviewers,
the audience's frenzy near the end when new Klan leader Ben Cameron rode a galloping horse, clutching a cross of fire. Viewers stood
and cheered thunderously. "Freedom is here; Justice is at hand;
Retribution has arrived," he wrote. "The scene is indescribable."

By early 1916, Simmons, Imperial Wizard of the real-life
Knights of the Ku Klux Klan, would have about ninety followers;
and, within four years, his Klan would have several thousand
members. By 1921, the nation's Ku Klux Klan adherents would
number nearly a hundred thousand.

D. W. Griffith, who turned forty when *The Birth of a Nation* toured
the country, never made another moving picture that matched the
success and power of his 1915 blockbuster. He certainly tried. He
followed it in 1916 with a feature film titled *Intolerance*, a costly,
complex project alternating between four story lines across history that included the Persian attack in 539 BC on the kingdom of
Babylon and the sixteenth-century persecution of the Huguenots
in France. Griffith showed off his mastery once again—composing
panoramic battle sequences crackling with action that was heightened by his quick cuts—but the reviews were tepid at best, and at
more than three hours in length, the movie never established mass
appeal. Its director, who had poured more than a million dollars of

his own money into the production, lost most of it. He seemed unable to adapt to the industry takeover of "talkies" in the late 1920s and ended his filmmaking career in 1931 with *The Struggle*, which one critic described as "the lugubrious tale of a drunkard's downfall." Griffith was fifty-six.

Following its release Griffith remained defensive about the attacks made against *The Birth of a Nation*, resentful of the charges of racism and historical manipulations. He always insisted he had gotten his facts right and that the story did no harm to Negroes. But in at least one interview conducted when he had reached his midsixties, a 1941 session with a would-be biographer, Griffith expressed regrets for the intense discord his movie had caused. Most surprisingly, he said he now thought the film should be kept from the general public. Not through government restriction—nothing like that, he being a vocal proponent of free speech and expression—but through self-censorship, or the voluntary withholding of the movie from public consumption. "It should not be shown to general audiences," he said. "It should be seen solely by film people and film students. The Negro race has had enough trouble, more than enough of its share of injustice, oppression, tragedy, suffering, and sorrow. And because of the social progress which Negroes achieved in the face of these handicaps, it is best that *The Birth of a Nation* in its present form be withheld from public exhibition."

After the Los Angeles hotel that had been his favorite residence, the Alexandria, went bankrupt and closed, Griffith spent his final years in the Knickerbocker Hotel, located at Hollywood and Vine—living at the epicenter of a flourishing film industry in which he had pioneered but where he went practically unnoticed by the late 1940s. Divorced for a second time, he lived alone, his suite filled with remnants of his career. His library contained books, monographs, and a massive collection of newspaper and magazine articles about him and his movies. In the kitchen, a rare print of his sixteen-reel, 1921 silent *Orphans of the Storm*, which starred Lillian and Dorothy Gish, was stored in two large cans; and in the living room stood several trunks of memorabilia. When a reporter visited him in early 1948 he found the director dressed in pajamas and a maroon dressing gown. Griffith settled into an easy

The older D. W. Griffith.
COURTESY OF THE MUSEUM OF MODERN ART, NEW YORK.

chair, sipping a double martini and ready to take questions. "I am seventy-three years of age," he said. "I can say anything I want about Hollywood. You can print anything you please. What's the difference? I don't give a hoot what anyone says about me." During the rambling exchange that followed, Griffith mixed tart remarks about the film industry with nostalgia. "Too much today depends on the voice," he said, complaining about the "talkies." Newer films, he continued, lacked "beauty—the beauty of moving wind in the trees, the little movement in a beautiful blowing on the blossoms in the trees." He also reminisced of his New York days. "I would love to be again at 44th and Broadway and love again to see George M. Cohan walking down the street," he said. "Most of all I would love to see John and Lionel Barrymore crossing the street as they used to be, when they were young and full of youth and vitality."

It went unsaid, but Griffith likely had in mind a time when he had been full of ambition and vitality, too, when he stepped out from behind the curtain of anonymity and, with the release in 1915 of *The Birth of a Nation*, became a nationally celebrated artist admired for his technical innovations and sophistication and the envy of future directors because of the hard-won freedom he had earned—the result of the success of his controversial masterpiece— to make the movies he had wanted to make.

Within days of the Boston victory that Thomas Dixon called a miracle, members of the Boston NAACP came up with an idea to help others resist Griffith's epic as it continued to open around the country during the remainder of 1915. They gathered their "accumulated literature and evidence" into a playbook that protesters could use in new campaigns to win over the public's mind or before a censor board. "It will however take some little time to get this matter in shape, as we are only just recovering from the strain of our eight-week fight," a local NAACP official told New York headquarters in mid-June. The booklet, titled *Fighting a Vicious Film*, featured speeches, editorials, and detailed critiques of the movie that could be resourced as an opposition how-to manual. Calls for it soon began arriving at the NAACP's New York headquarters, once *The Birth of a Nation* was on the move. "Can you help us by furnishing at once the argument or reasons set forth by the Boston people?" asked an NAACP organizer from West Virginia named P. A. Goines, reporting that the film was soon to arrive in his city of Bluefield near the end of summer. Later in the year, a request for help arrived from none other than William Warley, a postal clerk in Louisville who was already involved in another major NAACP cause, as a party in *Buchanan v. Warley*, the legal test case against residential segregation ordinances pending before the US Supreme Court. "*The Birth of a Nation* is booked for this city," Warley wrote to New York, asking for "as much matters as you can spare in opposition to the play, any arguments, statistics or other matter that will help us create sentiment against it."

The NAACP remained uncomfortable about using censorship as its weapon of choice. W. E. B. Du Bois, now the most recognized Negro leader in the organization—continued to be defensive about seeking to limit free speech and expression in the name of civil rights, making clear he would have much preferred a competing film to counteract Griffith's. "If Negroes and all their friends were free to answer in the same channels, by the same methods in which the attack is made, the path would be easy," he said. "But poverty, fashion and color prejudice preclude this." Much more achievable— and cleaner, in principle—were the NAACP's legal initiatives to achieve advances in civil rights through the courts, such as in *Buchanan v. Warley*, which the Supreme Court decided in its favor in late 1917, ruling that the Louisville residential ordinance was indeed unconstitutional, and which culminated famously in 1954 when the court voted unanimously to end school segregation in *Brown v. Board of Education*, a landmark case that also overturned *Plessy v. Ferguson* and the "separate but equal" doctrine that had been the law of the land since 1896.

The censorship campaign of 1915, in addition to its philosophical baggage, was a mixed bag of results—with losses in Boston, New York, Los Angeles, and many other cities and towns. The NAACP did claim victory when the states of Ohio and Kansas banned the movie, and when permits were denied or substantial deletions in the film were ordered in several dozen locales, from Providence, Rhode Island, to Denver, Colorado, and even elsewhere in Massachusetts, such as Lynn and West Springfield. Bans were usually short-lived, however, as either Griffith or local exhibitors appealed to the courts and eventually won with their First Amendment arguments. Ultimately, censorship was seen as a dead end, a "negativistic assault" so at odds with civil liberties that it constituted "a rearguard action rather than a direct assault on racism in American life."

Even so, for a fledgling organization still seeking to establish itself, its 1915 campaign against Griffith's film was a boon like no other since the NAACP's inception six years earlier. Rather than harping on wins or losses, its protest against *The Birth of a Nation* became a rallying cry at a pivotal moment in its early history, just when it needed one in terms of establishing a national presence and infrastructure and recruiting members.

"The colored people are comparatively new to the matter of organization," said Du Bois in early 1916 to emphasize the size of the NAACP's enormous growth spurt that had largely resulted from its pulling together to challenge Griffith's movie. In 1914, membership had been at three thousand; now, he estimated, it was nearly ten thousand, distributed among fifty-four branches around the country. Taking stock of the film protest, the organization's chairman, Joel E. Spingarn, said nothing in the NAACP's brief history had done more to "unloosen the energy and to stimulate the support of the colored people of this country as this attack on their character and their place in history."

An overworked Booker T. Washington would die of heart failure at the age of fifty-nine on November 14, 1915. In addition, that year saw the demise of another national figure emblematic of the era, also from health problems aggravated by stress and overwork. Legendary vice fighter Anthony Comstock died at age seventy-one after a brief illness on September 21, just eleven days after he had testified in a New York City court featuring another of the year's free speech spectacles—the trial of artist William Sanger on a charge of obscenity for giving away a single copy of his wife, Margaret Sanger's pamphlet on birth control, *Family Limitation.*

Sanger's day in court turned into a circus, the 1915 equivalent of tumultuous political trials later in the century—the Chicago Seven case in the late 1960s, for example, when radical Yippies Abbie Hoffman, Jerry Rubin, and others disrupted proceedings to the point where the judge ordered some defendants bound and gagged. William Sanger, representing himself, regularly interrupted the three-judge panel and got into shouting matches with the government's key witnesses—Comstock himself and the agent he had sent into Sanger's studio in the sting designed to have Sanger produce his wife's publications. It was a case that had attracted considerable public interest, from socialists and free speech advocates who denounced Comstock's decades-long suppression of art and expression to a general public that increasingly considered birth control a matter that was not obscene but worthy of a wider discussion. Sanger, his unruly head of hair flying as he spoke, announced he did not dispute the facts and insisted it was the law, not him, on trial. "This self-appointed censor of our morality," he yelled at Comstock, whose muttonchops shook as his face vibrated in irritation, "did not hesitate to use criminal methods to make a criminal out of me."

In the overflowing courtroom sat an all-star cast of anarchists—including Alexander Berkman, Carlo Tresca, Elizabeth Gurley Flynn, and Leonard D. Abbott—who hooted at Comstock; at one point he shouted back at them that he had received death threats warning him to drop the case or else. Finally a gavel-pounding judge summoned extra court officers to quell the outbursts. When the court found Sanger guilty of one count of distributing material deemed immoral and obscene and fined him $150, the defendant was on his feet again, saying he would never pay the fine. The judges modified his penalty to include incarceration, and officers hauled Sanger out a side door to serve thirty days in the notorious city jail known as the Tombs. "This court can't intimidate me," he yelled over the shouts of support from the gallery.

The next day, Comstock came down with a fever, which then developed into pneumonia, and in ten days, the crusader against immorality in books, pictures, and plays was dead.

The Sanger trial joined the protracted film protest as dramatic exhibitions of the disharmonies of liberty, played out in a year that also saw such major events as Alexander Graham Bell's first transcontinental telephone call and the US invasion of Haiti—which became swept aside, and to varying degrees overshadowed, by the nation's slide into world war. In October 1915 Woodrow Wilson announced a long-term national security "preparedness program," which he promised would result in the United States' having the most powerful navy in the world and a reorganized army that would include a reserve force of 400,000 men. By year's end, Wilson had escaped *The Birth of a Nation* controversy—the statement he had made in the spring having worked to disentangle him—so that his legacy would be dominated by his record as a war president and an economic progressive rather than for being a racist.

But just because he managed to divorce himself from Griffith's film did not mean he cut his ties with old loyalist Thomas Dixon. Once *The Birth of a Nation* became a nonissue in their relationship, Dixon continued to write letters to him, this time about the war. He urged Wilson to allow him to politick against William Jennings Bryan and others who opposed the president's arms buildup.

"I saw Bryan address 3,000 traitors," Dixon reported, "amid the wildest enthusiasm for peace at any price. Every man in that organization should be in jail in my opinion." Dixon's subject had changed from bigotry to war-mongering, his target shifting from Negroes to opponents to US involvement in the European War, but the overheated prose was all too familiar. He believed "with every beat of my heart" that Germany was planning to attack the United States. "The Country is *not* awake to its danger," Dixon wrote. "Ten million Germans in America are now busy allaying our fears. Our Peace Cranks are their tools."

William Monroe Trotter, meanwhile, forged on. In July 1915, at the unveiling of a monument of Wendell Phillips in the Public Garden, he was one of five speakers honoring the famed Boston abolitionist—and the only Negro chosen to do so. Later in the year, on December 19, he and his followers placed wreaths at the foot of the statue to mark the fiftieth anniversary of the adoption of the Thirteenth Amendment abolishing slavery. The celebration included a parade to Faneuil Hall, where a civil rights rally was held. The gathering unanimously passed a resolution Trotter had helped draft and that included a jab at a favorite target, President Wilson. It said, in part, "We shall use our voices, our pens, our patronage, our votes, our money, and every resource that God has put in our power for the abolition of segregation, disenfranchisement, and lynching on the color line, undismayed that a President rules in the White House unwilling, despite his pre-election pledge, to rise above the narrow, provincial color prejudice."

Although an arch-foe of Booker T. Washington, even Trotter joined in the grieving for Washington, devoting nearly an entire issue of the *Guardian* to his sudden death and including, of course, his own commentary. "Booker T. Washington is dead," he wrote. "By the Colored race he was both ardently supported and strenuously opposed with regard to his industrial and political propaganda." He said, however, that "this hour of grief for his family and admirers" was no time for "adverse criticism. The controversy may well subside on both sides. This is a time for the race to unite in defense of its rights."

The venerated educator's death created a void in the upper ranks of civil rights leaders but Trotter was not one to fill it, not the way Washington had when he stepped up in 1895 after Frederick Douglass's passing and bowled over the nation with his "Atlanta Compromise" speech. Trotter's national fame had largely petered out by the close of 1915. The key role he played in fighting *The Birth of a Nation* turning out to be, in effect, his last hurrah. The start of the year had seen the crusading editor suddenly thrust into the limelight after his confrontation with President Wilson in the White House. He had soaked up the notoriety, and his trajectory only continued to climb during the long and militant campaign against Griffith's movie. But in the months, and then years, following the dramatic film protest, Trotter never really found his way back onto the big stage. The reasons were many, beginning with his personality. He was individualistic, refusing to make concessions when working with leaders of like-minded organizations. In addition, he was preoccupied with the financial struggle to keep his newspaper afloat. And finally, there was the long shadow of the always-growing NAACP, with which Trotter, at best, had an uneven, contentious relationship, and its rise as the dominant civil rights organization in the United States interfered with his ever sustaining prominence.

Trotter certainly never gave up, especially not on the local front, where he continued agitating for Boston constituents facing race discrimination—such as young stenographer Jane R. Bosfield, whose cause he had taken up during the spring film protest. By October 1915, and as a result of the governor's intervention, Bosfield had been appointed to fill another position at the hospital. Her superintendent, Dr. Edward French, however, only reluctantly allowed her to have a room on hospital grounds and barred her from eating in the dining room. Her meals were served on a tray at her desk, where she ate alone. "It was very humiliating," she said. She consulted with her family and an attorney, and then, in mid-January 1916, she marched into the dining room at suppertime and sat down. "Everybody was very pleasant."

Everybody but French, who only grew emboldened. Bosfield's guardian, Governor Walsh, had lost his bid for a second term to the Republican challenger despite Trotter's campaign support, and

French now ordered Jane Bosfield never to eat in the dining room again. She did the next day, however, taking all three meals there, and so the following day French fired her for insubordination.

Bosfield appealed, but lost on February 16, 1916, when a single justice of the state Supreme Judicial Court ruled that Massachusetts's civil service laws permitted employers to dismiss new workers for any reason during the initial six-month probationary period. Three days later, Trotter's lead editorial in the *Guardian*, devoted to "The Bosfield Case," called on the new governor to reverse the decision. Trotter's Boston Literary and Historical Association passed a resolution "deploring the prejudice displayed at the Medfield State Hospital"; and on Sunday, February 20, he organized a rally at the Twelfth Baptist Church, which drew more than five hundred protesters. "It was the largest meeting of protest held by the colored people of the city since they arraigned the Government for permitting the film drama, *The Birth of a Nation*, several months ago," noted one reporter.

The public pressure worked. In April the governor's council ordered Jane Bosfield reinstated and that she "be accorded equal privileges." The stenographer was satisfied with the victory, but regretted having to fight so hard. "We are given an education, but not a chance to apply that education," she told a reporter. "Is this fair?"

Trotter's agitation had once more made a difference, and he kept busy with these and other smaller causes. Visiting Philadelphia a few years later he went to get a trim, but the barber refused to cut his hair. The moment was a throwback to his days at Harvard in the early 1890s when a Cambridge barber twice refused service to then football star and future NAACP official William H. Lewis. Unlike Lewis, who left the shop after each rejection, Trotter would not budge from the barber's chair—an action some later cited as perhaps the first sit-in—and the proprietor eventually had to call the police to remove him. But over time, such causes notwithstanding, Trotter was steadily relegated to the margins of a civil rights movement writ large and eventually a virtual unknown even in his hometown of Boston.

A major factor, too, was the sudden death of his wife in 1918 at the age of forty-six. Deenie was a victim of the influenza epidemic that, by the end of that year, had killed an estimated fifty million people worldwide. Deenie fell ill, seemed to rally, but died on the evening of October 8 at her marital home at 97 Sawyer Avenue in Dorchester, which, despite their constant money problems, the Trotters had returned to in late 1914. Nearly a dozen clergy and civil rights leaders, including Moorfield Storey, William D. Brigham, and Monroe Trotter's longtime compatriot, Rev. M. A. N. Shaw, offered remembrances at a memorial service the next month. The "Geraldine Louise Trotter Memorial Fund" was created in her memory, established "for the maintenance of *The Guardian*." Everyone signed a letter to President Wilson, "in the name of Mrs. Trotter, making an appeal for the justice to the race she represented."

Trotter was never the same: the loss a "crushing blow," as he wrote in a December issue of his newspaper. From then on he ran her photograph on the editorial page along with a dedication that read, in part, "To My Fallen Comrade, Geraldine L. Trotter, My Loyal Wife, who is no more." Early in 1919 he published articles honoring her work at the paper and for Negro rights, a package that included the chart she had drawn by hand in 1913 for him to take to his first meeting with President Wilson, showing which federal agencies in the Wilson administration had begun practicing Jim Crow.

Trotter's sister Maude did her best to fill Deenie's role in putting out the newspaper, but her brother's struggles worsened. Yielding to the *Guardian*'s money woes, Trotter began accepting advertisements he had always so vehemently rejected—such as those for lotions to straighten a Negro's hair or lighten skin—although he did continue to refuse lucrative liquor ads. By the mid-1920s the *Guardian*'s following was diminishing, as readers noticed a falloff in the paper's editorial crispness. "This nationally known agitator undoubtedly has done some splendid things for his people," Eugene Gordon, a Negro journalist and reporter at the *Boston Post*, commented in 1926, but the *Guardian*, he continued, "is one of the most poorly-written Negro sheets in America." One young man who began working for Trotter that same year immediately noticed the inefficient "hit-and-miss office methods" and thought the editor seemed burdened by the idea "that he had failed, that there would be no brilliant victory in his lifetime."

William Monroe Trotter in his early fifties.
COURTESY OF THE BOSTON PUBLIC LIBRARY.

By the late 1920s, or a decade after Deenie's death, Trotter began boarding in a series of rooming houses, and in 1932 he quietly
celebrated his sixtieth birthday. By outward appearances he was
simply an older version of his old self, still making his rounds along
Newspaper Row in downtown Boston in a rumpled suit and derby
hat, and never bothering with an overcoat. But his hair and mustache were flecked with gray—"old Mon," had replaced "Mon," as
a nickname—and for all his sociability he was a lonely man. "Still
acute is the pang of her going," he wrote in the fall of 1930, "still
saddened is life by daily remembrance of her."

The nation's Depression was his depression, too, as he became
obsessively anxious about the *Guardian*'s survival and, in the summer of 1933, contracted a leg infection that hobbled him. He took
to pacing, or limping, while in conversation, in a room or on the
street. When Maude's husband, his brother-in-law Dr. Charles
Steward, asked him why he paced so much, Trotter replied, "To
think where I'm going next." In January 1934, the editor scribbled a fund-raising note that illustrated his desperation, pleading

with "Dear Bro' Floyd," to "come to my rescue" with a donation to "save *The Guardian*." On the same day, Maude Trotter Steward wrote to another of her brother's longtime friends, asking for a donation and expressing worry about his declining health. "Monroe collapsed last week and we are all frightened," she said. Friends tried to rally him. "Cheer up, old Boy," urged one from New York on April 3 in a note that included a ten-dollar money order. "You are the greatest race champion since the day of Moses, the greatest our day has ever had."

Five days later, in the early morning hours of Saturday, April 7, other boarders in the triple-decker in Roxbury where Trotter was living heard him pacing on the flat rooftop above. They were used to it. When Trotter could not sleep, he would go up and walk back and forth inside the sixteen-inch-high barrier that rimmed the roof's perimeter. The previous evening, Maude and her husband had visited him in his second-floor room, bringing with them the new edition of the weekly *Guardian* that was freshly printed and ready for sale on Saturday.

Then just before dawn, one of the residents was startled by a crashing noise. He got up to inspect the premises and found that Trotter was not in his room, and that the door to the roof was open. When he looked down from the roof, he saw Trotter lying motionless on the sidewalk below, his skull crushed. There was a rush to assist him and a call for an ambulance. William Monroe Trotter, the great civil rights agitator who had mentored W. E. B. Du Bois and whom historians later credited with doing more than anyone in the early 1900s to keep the protest tradition alive, was pronounced dead on the way to the hospital.

No one ever knew exactly what happened. His family believed he had sat on the barrier to rest and slipped off, falling tragically to his death. Others were convinced he had committed suicide, which was how nearly every newspaper reported the death. "Roxbury Negro Editor Killed in 45-Ft. Dive," was the *Boston Herald* headline. It was Trotter's sixty-second birthday.

More than 1,500 people filled the People's Baptist Church in the South End for the funeral two days later, and Trotter was buried in Fairview Cemetery in Hyde Park, the Boston neighborhood where his father had trained to serve in the Civil War and where the younger Trotter had grown up. Never able to experience a free and equal America that his father had fought for, he had taken up his own call to arms—a fiery track record of agitation and protest actions that set the stage for future civil rights activism. Du Bois went to work and wrote a lengthy appreciation of the lone crusader for the next issue of the *Crisis*. "Monroe Trotter was a man of historic proportions," Du Bois wrote. "Ready to sacrifice himself, fearing nobody and nothing, strong in body, sturdy in conviction, full of unbending belief."

William Monroe Trotter died in 1934; David Wark Griffith, of a cerebral hemorrhage, on July 23, 1948—each long out of the national spotlight at the time of their respective deaths. The epic film that was at the center of their protracted fight, however, was another matter. During subsequent engagements and reissued versions, protesters and pickets often accompanied the film. For a while the NAACP continued to seek bans, and, teaming up with Trotter once again, succeeded to briefly stop it in Boston in 1921. But despite chasing after it the way a police agency might a fugitive from justice, the chimerical effort to stamp out *The Birth of a Nation* ultimately failed. The movie endured—a cornerstone of American filmmaking and a milestone, if an ugly one, in American race relations. It has staying power, anchoring most any college class today on the history of film, with 2015 marking its centennial. In 1947, the year before Griffith died, a festival of film classics began in Los Angeles, and *The Birth of a Nation* was selected to open the event. Announcing the choice, movie historian and organizer Raymond Rohauer honored *Birth* as "one of the earliest films of any consequence that is still worth seeing and discussing," a statement still true today, with one caveat: that any such discussion be taken expansively and include race in America. That's the complete legacy of D. W. Griffith's *The Birth of a Nation*—a masterpiece that, due to its bigoted slant, became a dramatic flash point in 1915 for a changing America in mass media and marketing, civil rights, and civil liberties.

ACKNOWLEDGMENTS

The 1915 clash between Monroe Trotter and D. W. Griffith is a story that cuts across the fields of journalism, film, and mass marketing, and I'd like to acknowledge my friends and colleagues at Boston University's College of Communication who work in departments in each of those three fields. Tom Fiedler, a journalist, editor, and now COM's dean, supported the idea for this book from its start, and even recommended readings that proved crucial in my research, most notably Paul Starr's *The Creation of the Media*. I'd also like to thank Mitch Zuckoff for his friendship and for always being ready to brainstorm anytime, anyplace. Thanks, too, to Susan Walker; Michelle Johnson; Lou Ureneck; Bill McKeen, chair of the Journalism Department; Chris Daly; and Ken Holmes. During my research I benefited from the assistance of a number of BU undergraduate and graduate students in journalism, namely Samantha Pickette, Molly Connors, Max Lewontin, Jason Lind, and photographer Justin Saglio.

The Trotter Papers are held at the Gotlieb Archival Research Center at Boston University, and the folks there went far beyond the call of duty when it came to helping me with the center's holdings and tracking down materials elsewhere. I'd like to acknowledge Vita Paladino, the Gotlieb's director; Sean Noel, associate director; Katherine Kominis, assistant director for rare books; Alex Rankin, assistant director for acquisitions; Charles Niles, archivist; Ford Curran, archivist; and Laura Russo, manager of public service. In BU's Mugar Library, I'd like to thank Donald Altschiller and Diane d'Almeida for their research assistance, along with Rhoda Bilansky in the interlibrary loan department and Mary Bowen at the Krasker Film Library.

Beyond Boston University, I received vital help at archives and libraries around the country. I'd specifically like to thank Henry Scannell at the Boston Public Library; Margaret Sullivan, archivist for the Boston Police Department; and Jennifer Brathovde, a librarian at the Library of Congress, Manuscript Division.

I'd like to thank my past collaborator, Gerry O'Neill, for introducing me to Jim Vrabel, who has assembled a most amazing chronology of Boston history. I'd like to thank my friend Larry Tye for his guidance along the way, and I'd especially like to thank Dave Holahan for his careful reading of the book's first draft. My brother, John Lehr, is always there, and always asking how's it coming, and I'd like to acknowledge him and his family—Kellie, Julia, and Nate—for their love and support.

Most writers have agents, but not all writers have agents as wise, diligent, and supportive as Jill Kneerim. I thank her and her team; in particular, I'd like to thank Katherine Flynn for her input in shaping the original book proposal.

This is my third book with PublicAffairs, a house with a proven track record for its commitment and care for the books it publishes. I'd like to thank my editor Clive Priddle, as well as Maria Goldverg, Melissa Raymond, Sandra Beris, Susan Weinberg, and Peter Osnos.

Nothing keeps me going like family—my sons, Nick and Christian, each of whom read parts of this book and made it better with their feedback; my daughters, Holly and Dana, who sometimes found their way upstairs to work alongside me on their own writing projects; and my wife, Karin, who inspires me in every way. I could not do this without her.

NOTES

PROLOGUE

xiii **new medium of film:** *Riverside Press-Enterprise*, December 4, 2010, 1.

xiii **Henry B. Walthall:** Advertisement, *Riverside Daily Press*, January 1, 1915, and "'The Clansman' Is Wonderful," *Riverside Daily Press*, January 2, 1915.

xiii **of a death scene:** Cuniberti, 24.

xiv **"complete product":** *Collier's*, April 24, 1926, 8.

xiv **230 separate titles:** Cuniberti, 25.

xv **"in the production":** *Riverside Daily Press*, January 2, 1915.

xvi **"forever be White":** *Hartford Courant*, December 31, 1979, 1.

xvi **"the splendid individualist":** Stephen R. Fox, *The Guardian of Boston*, 187.

xvii **"restraints of organization":** Bay, 9; Wells, 377.

xvii **managed to block him:** *Chicago Tribune*, January 3, 1915, 1.

CHAPTER 1

3 **south of Vicksburg:** Most sources list James Trotter's birth date as February 7, 1842, but some, including Stevenson, who cites Virginia Trotter's 1908 Civil War widow's pension application in the National Archives, say he was born on November 8, 1842.

4 **a career in education:** Stevenson, 379–91; Forbes Papers, George W. Forbes, "James Monroe Trotter," unpublished article, n.d., 2.

4 **the foot of the hills:** Fairlie Papers, Monroe Trotter letter, August 10, 1893.

4 **wit and hospitality:** William H. Dupree's obituary, *Guardian*, July 7, 1934, 1, 4.

4 **Hemings and Jefferson:** Dorman, 442, cites the groundbreaking work by historian Annette Gordon-Reed in her book *Thomas Jefferson and Sally Hemings: An American Controversy*, 25, which provides the most direct connection between Monroe Trotter and Thomas Jefferson. The first account—and variations of it linking the two families—can be found in Stephen R. Fox, 8, and nearly every biographical summary of Trotter's life and ancestry.

5 **to spread the word:** Trudeau, 9–10.

5 **would eventually settle:** Stevenson, 391.

5 **"bleak and cheerless" mudflats:** Trudeau, 12.

5 **comprising Negro recruits:** The 54th, commanded by Colonel Robert Gould Shaw, is the better known of the two Massachusetts regiments, for its courageous but failed assault on Confederate Fort Wagner on July 18, 1863, the subject of a PBS documentary and a feature film titled *Glory*, and written about extensively in articles and books.

5 **that made up the 55th:** Trudeau, 13.

6 **"their peculiar hymns":** Ibid., 12.

6 **"a certain refinement":** Stevenson, 93.

6 **"this fighting parson":** Trotter article, quoted in Wilson, 507.

6 **three letters home:** Trotter letter, August 2, 1864, in Trudeau, 142.

7 **Confederacy: Charleston:** Ibid., 15.

8 **"to save the Brigade":** Trotter letter, July 18, 1864, in Trudeau, 119.

9 **"our brave fellows":** Ibid., 122.

10 **back on duty:** Trotter letter, December 18, 1864, in Trudeau, 163.

11 **a general said:** Trotter letter, August 2, 1864, Trudeau, 141.

11 **"Manhood and Equality":** Trotter letter, June 2, 1864, Trudeau, 106.

11 **"less than the soldier's pay":** Coddington, 4, quoting a soldier in Company I in an article from the *Christian Recorder*, March 3, 1887.

11 **"by the Government":** Trotter letter, November 21, 1864, in Trudeau, 155.

11 **"feeling of insubordination":** Trudeau, 21.

11 **from his regiment, executed:** Ibid.

11 **"excitement was made":** Trotter letter, November 21, 1864, in Trudeau, 56.

12 **wrote in July 1864:** Trotter letter, July 18, 1864, in Trudeau, 123.

12 **"might be his character":** Trotter letter, August 2, 1864, in Trudeau, 140.

12 **"painful and burning wrong":** Trotter letter, November 21, 1864, in Trudeau, 155.

12 **the editor's son Franky:** Trotter letter, August 2, 1864, in Trudeau, 140.

12 **"among the Georgians":** Trotter letter, January 29, 1865, in Trudeau, 180.

13 **"manifest any Colorphobia":** Trotter letter, May 27, 1865, in Trudeau, 181.

13 **"service of their country":** Forbes article, 7.

13 **"They began the Rebellion":** Trotter letter, July 1, 1865, in Trudeau, 183.

CHAPTER 2

15 **"in its truest sense":** Forbes Papers, George W. Forbes, "James Monroe Trotter," unpublished article, n.d., 12.

15 **"complete and glorious victory":** *Christian Recorder*, December 14, 1882.

16 **registry section:** Worthy thesis, 6. James and Virginia Trotter had a third child, daughter Bessie, born in 1883 when the family lived in Hyde Park.

16 ***Outlook* in its review:** Simmons, 837.

16 **years of its release:** Stevenson, 395. Trotter's book was so highly regarded that later histories of Negro music, into the 1930s, plagiarized from it.

17 **"in rank and ability":** Forbes article, 8.

18 **"on death's door":** Stevenson, 398, quoting the *Washington Bee*, April 2, 1887, and Forbes article, 11.

18 **at one such event:** *Boston Globe*, August 18, 1887, 4.

18 **"one to a white boy":** *Guardian*, May 24, 1952, "A Little Boy Named Munroe [*sic*]." The story covered Monroe's fighting as a boy, including, "the father told him if he ever came home having suffered a whipping by another boy he would get another whipping"; Carl Senna, *Bay State Banner*, September 24, 1966: "William Trotter: A Black Hero." Monroe Trotter's brother-in-law, Dr. Charles G. Steward, was the source for the anecdote about James Trotter's fighting instructions to Monroe.

19 **attend Harvard College:** Worthy, 4–8; Forbes article, 11; Stephen R. Fox, 14–15.

19 **silk topper, and cane:** Harvard College Class of 1896, Fiftieth Anniversary Report, 1.

20 **"present. Your Friend":** Fairlie Papers, Trotter letter, February 26, 1892.

20 **"interesting personality":** *Boston Globe*, March 2, 1892, 8.

21 ***All Its Phases:*** Goldsby, 43–46, 73.

21 **beach with family:** Fairlie Papers, Trotter letter, August 18, 1892.

22 **"magnificent and grand":** Fairlie Papers, Trotter letters, August 10 and September 5, 1893.

22 **flocking into Chicago:** Wells, *Crusade for Justice*, 115–19.

22 **leave the premises:** Stephen R. Fox, 18.
23 **"I had no chance":** Du Bois, *Crisis*, 1934; Du Bois, *Massachusetts Review*, 1960.
23 **north of Boston:** Stephen R. Fox, 22.
23 **"affectionate and merry":** Worthy, 9, from April 8, 1947, interview with Maude Steward.
23 **"straight for Hell":** Ibid.
23 **"years of fellowship":** Fairlie Papers, Trotter letter of September 8, 1895.
23 **"real democracy":** Trotter's entry his class's 1923 alumni report.

CHAPTER 3

25 **filmmaker said later:** Griffith unpublished autobiography, 4.
25 **"true Kentucky estate":** Henderson, 26; Griffith unpublished autobiography, 10.
25 **bourbon barrel:** Henderson, 17.
26 **for the eager boy:** Ibid., 25.
26 **upon a worshiper:** Griffith unpublished autobiography, 4.
26 **barroom swashbuckler:** Henderson, 17.
26 **"into my memory":** Lang, 25; Henderson, 28.
27 **one way or another:** Schickel, 612n6.
27 **Washington, DC:** Henderson, 19; Schickel, 17.
27 **proof for the claim:** Henderson, 18; Schickel, 18.
28 **so much money again:** Schickel, 19; Henderson, 22.
29 **according to one account:** Schickel, 19.
29 **"belligerent parties":** Coulter, 56n84.
29 **staged theatricals:** Ibid., 3.
29 **Griffith biographer:** Schickel, 19.
30 **on April 9:** Jackman, 1–2.
30 **in war records:** Schickel, 23.
31 **existed to support it:** Henderson, 24; Schickel, 22, 612n17; Judge Charles Kerr (ed.), *History of Kentucky*, Chicago and New York: American Historical Society, 639. Note: Griffith cites as proof a Kentucky history that never existed, then relies on Kerr's history, but Kerr offers no source and citations, so the claim remains unproven.
31 **"*carte* and *tierce*":** Long, 25.
32 **who got the haircut:** Griffith Papers, 4.
32 **"world," he said later:** Long, 25.
33 **"the carpetbagger":** Coulter, 439.
33 **"secede from the Union":** Ibid.
33 **"nursed and nurtured":** Ibid., 387.
33 **he wrote later:** Griffith unpublished autobiography, 10.
33 **"catechetic instruction":** Long, 24.
33 **"lots of pets around":** Griffith unpublished autobiography, 2.
33 **a hard exterior:** Ibid., 6.

34   **rotted and broke:** Ibid., 8.
34   **"another nearby barrel":** Schickel, 31.
34   **"ever loved in my life":** Griffith unpublished autobiography, 8.
34   **Confederate veteran:** Schickel, 31.
35   **"family now," he recalled:** Griffith unpublished autobiography, 6.
35   **cash and a mortgage:** Schickel, 31–32; Griffith unpublished autobiography, 6–7.
35   **"villainous gentleman":** Ibid., 11. Note: Griffith seems to have mixed up homes, and biographers have concluded Lofty Green was the home he was actually referring to here.
36   **they shouted:** Schickel, 36.
36   **US Supreme Court:** *Buchanan v. Warley*, 245 U.S. 60 (1917).
36   **on the wall:** Henderson, 55.
37   **"The District":** Schickel, 37, and 37n2.
37   **full-time wage:** Griffith unpublished autobiography, 12.
37   **"companies played":** Mayer, 61.
37   **"indeed," he said:** Griffith unpublished autobiography, 13.
37   **"something to say," he said:** Ibid.
37   **legitimate options:** Schickel, 40.
37   **"become an actor":** Griffith unpublished autobiography, 15.
38   **north to Cincinnati:** Henderson, 58; Schickel, 42–43; Mayer, 57, 60.
39   **"and beak-nosed":** Schickel, 39.
39   **"fame and glory":** Griffith unpublished autobiography, 15.
39   **"were excellent":** Schickel, 47, quoting *New York Dramatic Mirror*, May 27, 1896.

CHAPTER 4

40   **impressive features:** *New York Times*, September 17, 1895.
41   **"the great South":** *New York Times*, September 18, 1895.
41   **Booker Taliaferro Washington:** Ibid.
43   **"delirium of applause":** Rogers, excerpting the *New York World*; *New York Times*, September 17 and 18, 1895.
43   **where he was staying:** Rogers, 394.
43   **opening-day ceremony:** *Washington Post*, Sunday, September 22, 1895, 8.
43   **Greek and Latin:** Washington Papers, Du Bois letter of September 24, 1895.
43   **newborn sons "Booker T.":** Norrell, 4.
45   **"decorations thus far":** Fairlie Papers, Trotter letter of September 8, 1895.
46   **"use of *You People*":** Forbes Papers, George W. Forbes, "James Monroe Trotter," unpublished article, n.d., 12.
46   **"not have to hinder them":** Fairlie Papers, Trotter letter of September 8, 1895.
47   **"to my future plans":** Ibid.

47   **"her to the floor!":** *Atlanta Constitution*, in *Washington Post*, April 23, 1899, 3.

47   **by souvenir seekers:** Bay, 242–44; *Washington Post*, April 25, 1899, 3.

48   **"murdered and starved":** Du Bois, *Autobiography*, 221–22.

48   **"nearly all our troubles?":** *New York Times*, April 10, 1899.

49   **"assaulting a woman":** *New York Times*, April 26, 1899.

49   **against Jim Crow:** Bay, 242–44.

49   **marketing Tuskegee:** Ibid.

49   **"car be abolished":** Wells, 265.

50   **countryside beyond:** 97 Sawyer Avenue; information comes from author visit; Suffolk County Registry of Deeds, Boston City Assessors records; Fox, 23.

51   **"twenty-five story buildings":** E. L. Doctorow, *Ragtime*. New York: Random House, 1975, 168.

51   **35 Court Street:** Trotter's entry in Harvard, 1895, Second Report; Worthy, 14.

51   **property's tenants:** Suffolk County Registry of Deeds; Boston Assessors Office.

52   **"make out of college":** Fairlie Papers, Trotter letter, March 30, 1897.

52   **"their pigmentation":** Trotter's entry in Harvard, 1895, Seventh Report.

52   **equality on all fronts:** Cathcart thesis, 230; Worthy thesis, 15.

52   **Garrison Jr.:** Stephen R. Fox, 28; minutes of the Boston Literary & Historical Association, Trotter Papers.

52   **typed pages:** Forbes article.

53   **"position in the nation":** Cathcart thesis, 225.

53   **"color were concerned"** Trotter's entry in Harvard, 1895, Fourth Report.

54   **"what has occurred":** *New York Times*, October 19, 1901, 1.

54   **"colored men is absurd":** *New York Times*, October 20, 1901, 6.

54   **"the whites wish":** *Boston Globe*, October 24, 1901, 2.

54   **"that set of idiots":** Washington Papers, Courtney letter of October 27, 1901.

55   **censure of Booker T. Washington:** Trotter Papers, *Guardian*, November 9, 1901.

55   **"from its columns":** Trotter Papers, *Guardian*, May 17, 1902.

56   **"unasylumed maniac":** Trotter Papers, *Guardian*, November 29, 1902.

56   **"small attendance":** Trotter Papers, *Guardian*, September 20, October 4, December 20, 1902.

57   **"civil and political rights":** Trotter Papers, *Guardian*, July 11, 1903.

58   **"lives from lynching":** *Washington Bee*, July 11, 1903.

58   **"He will turn and fight":** *Guardian*, July 18, 1903, quoted in Stephen R. Fox, 232.

58   **not even mentioned:** *New York Times*, July 2, 1903, 1.

62   **"large jar of cream":** the account of the July 30, 1903, "riot" is a distillation of coverage the next day by Boston newspapers, most notably the *Boston Post* and the *Boston Globe*; also the *New York Times*, the *Los Angeles Times*, the *Atlanta Constitution*, and the *Guardian*, August 1, 1903; *Boston Globe*, August 6, 1903; Fox, 51–54.

CHAPTER 5

64   **"finite acting prowess":** Mayer, 2, 57.

64   **"look hawk-like":** Merritt, 7.

64   **Victorian novel:** Ibid., 19.

64   **former Masonic hall:** Mayer, 65.

65   **the show closed:** Ibid., 67.

65   **an acrobatic team:** Mayer, 71; Merritt, 6.

65   ***In Washington's Time:*** Mayer, 75–76; Schickel, 66.

68   **huge financial losses:** "Testimonial to Nance O'Neil," *Boston Globe*, May 22, 1906, 11.

68   **by the Red Cross:** see Stokes, 64, for summary of tour.

69   **"office every day":** telegram exchange with Wood Detective Agency, July 1906, in Booker T. Washington Papers, vol. 9, 45.

69   **"of theatre goers":** "Testimonial to Nance O'Neil," *Boston Globe*, May 22, 1906, 11.

69   **"her Boston friends":** "Miss O'Neil's Farewell," *Boston Globe*, May 16, 1906, 2.

70   **"bit of character work":** *Boston Globe*, May 8, 1906, 11.

70   **"one-night stands":** Merritt, in *Cinema Journal* 21, no. 1 (Fall 1981): 7.

70   **out of his fortune:** "At the Local Theatres," *Washington Post*, October 1, 1907, 11.

71   **Doubleday, Page and Company:** Schickel, 75–76.

71   **to press Washington:** "Choate and Twain Plead for Tuskegee," *New York Times*, January 23, 1906, 1.

71   **"of the races":** Dixon, letter to Booker T. Washington, January 22, 1906, Booker T. Washington Papers, vol. 8, 508.

71   **"advertise his book":** Letter to Washington from Ralph Waldo Tyler, dated January 27, 1906, Booker T. Washington Papers, vol. 8, 512.

72   **years 1775 and 1781:** Mayer, 83.

72   **around the country:** Starr, 305.

73   **from the White House:** Henderson, 3.

73   **out of the theater:** Stokes, 66.

73   **"far below par":** *New York Dramatic Mirror*, October 12, 1907.

73   **historian described it:** Mayer, 60.

CHAPTER 6

77   **"and safe leader":** Emmett Jay Scott letter, July 31, 1903, Booker T. Washington Papers, vol. 7, 244.

78   **"lamentable episode":** *Buffalo Courier*, August 2, 1903; *New York Times*, August 1, 1903.

78   **"related to his race":** Villard letter to W. E. B. Du Bois, August 18, 1905.

78   **"made them mad?":** [*Indianapolis*] *Freeman*, August 8, 1903.

78   **"importance to the Negro":** *Washington Bee*, August 8, 1903; *Chicago Broad Ax*, August 8, 1903.

78   **"night all over again":** *Boston Evening Transcript*, July 31, 1903.

78   **"me as his guest":** Du Bois, *Crisis* 41 (1934): 134.

79   **"the way backward":** Du Bois letter to George Foster Peabody, December 28, 1903.

80   **"influenced by it":** Du Bois, *Dusk of Dawn*, 73.

80   **"and submission":** Du Bois, *Souls of Black Folk*, 87.

80   **"for many a year":** Parini, 209.

80   **"on B.T. Washington":** Fairlie Papers, Trotter letter, August 12, 1903.

81   **disparage Trotter:** Booker T. Washington Papers, Lewis letters, September 5, 1903; September 16, 1903.

81   **"wise counselors":** *Boston Evening Transcript*, September 3, 1903.

81   **effort rattled Forbes:** Stephen R. Fox, 65.

82   **"criticize in any way":** Du Bois Papers, letter to Villard, March 24, 1905.

82   **"and for Trotter":** *Guardian*, August 15, 1903, 3.

82   **advocacy journalism:** Worthy, 20; Stephen R. Fox, 64.

83   **in December 1903:** Du Bois letter to George Foster Peabody, December 28, 1903.

83   **fined $25:** *Boston Globe*, August 6, 7, 8, 1903; *Boston Evening Transcript*, August 5, 6, 7, 1903; *Boston Traveler*, August 8, 1903; *Guardian*, August 8, 1903; Worthy, 68.

83   **wrote to a friend:** Fairlie Papers, Trotter letter, August 2, 1903.

84   **"government control":** Starr, 267.

84   **home of Victorianism:** Ibid.

84   **"prizefight pictures?":** *Boston Globe*, July 9, 1910, 4.

85   **Newton Newkirk:** *Boston Globe*, July 21, 1910, 1.

85   **a few blocks away:** Superior Court Criminal Record Book, vol. 471, 1903; Commonwealth of Massachusetts; *Boston Globe*, October 2, 7, 9, 1903; *Boston Traveler*, October 8, 1903; *Boston Post*, October 8, 1903; *Guardian*, October 10, 1903.

86   **"strengthened our forces":** Towns Collection, Trotter letter of October 28, 1903.

86   **his political hall:** Beatty, 77–91; *Boston Globe*, June 28, 1903, 10; *Boston Globe*, August 19, 1903, 4; *Boston Globe*, October 3, 1903, 9.
86   **"have entered his soul":** *Guardian*, April 23, 1904, 4.
87   **"our political spokesman":** Cathcart, 253.
87   **"his race in the world":** Ibid.
87   **"possession of the ballot":** Towns Collection, Trotter letter, January 19, 1904.
87   **another in his group:** *Boston Globe*, August 18, 1903, 10.
87   **"national forward movement":** Du Bois Papers, Niagara Movement Archive.
87   **"can pay expenses":** Cathcart, 254.
88   **society at large:** Du Bois Papers, Niagara Movement Archive; Cathcart, 255–56; Stephen R. Fox, 91.
88   **establishing local chapters:** Cathcart, 257.
88   **Boston detective agency:** Washington Papers, vol. 9, 45. James R. Wood Jr. letter, July 19, 1906.
89   **"Trotter's gang":** Washington Papers, vol. 8, 189. Charles Alexander letter, February 6, 1905.
89   **"perhaps fatal":** *New York Age*, October 26, 1905; 4; *Freeman*, November 11, 1905.
89   **man behind it:** Washington Papers, vol. 8, 182. Bradley Gilman letter, January 25, 1905.
89   **"make-up of his son":** Washington Papers, Garrison letters: May 17, 1905; December 3, 1907.
89   **"crazy man like Trotter":** Washington Papers, vol. 8, 531, letter to Timothy Thomas Fortune, February 21, 1906.
89   **"Trotter and Trotterism":** Washington Papers, vol. 8, 383. E. J. Scott, draft editorial for the *New York Age*, ca. September 1905.

CHAPTER 7

91   **"singularly exhilarating":** "Edison's Vitascope Cheered," *New York Times*, May 24, 1896, 5.
91   **holes in the front:** Ibid.; "Edison's Latest Invention," *New York Times*, May 26, 1896, 10.
92   **in the film industry:** Starr, 299–300.
92   **sixteen million patrons:** Ibid., 305.
92   **"calculus perfectly":** Ibid., 301.
93   **delinquency and crime:** Ibid., 305.
93   **crude and disgusting:** Ibid., 301.
93   **twenty-first century:** Barbas, 672–74.
94   **1900, for example:** Starr, 248.
94   **"or the flag":** Beatty, 176.
95   **"request of the mayor":** Massachusetts Legislature, Acts of 1908, chap. 494.

95 **"corrupt public morals":** Barbas, 676.

95 **"could be improved":** Slide, *Griffith Interviews*, 42–43 (the 1916 interview with Henry Stephen Gordon that appeared as part one in the six-part series in *Photoplay*).

96 **the former ballroom:** Mayer, 87–88; Stokes, 66.

96 **of lesser quality:** Mayer, 60; Slide, *Griffith Interviews*, 43 (the 1916 interview with Henry Stephen Gordon that appeared as part one in the six-part series in *Photoplay*).

96 **promote the movie:** Mayer, 1.

96 **"Biograph Company":** Griffith interview, *Pictures and the Picturegoer* (London), April 28–May 5, 1917, 102–4, reprinted in Slide, *Griffith Interviews*.

97 **physical naturalness:** Mayer, 89–90.

97 **not to do it again:** Bitzer, 63.

97 **"flock of geese":** Ibid., 6.

97 **Griffith's scripts:** Mayer, 90.

98 **box office earner:** Stokes, 67–68.

98 **minutes or less:** Mayer, 70; Merritt, 6.

99 **"I won the argument":** Sara Redway, *Motion Picture Classic*, October 1924, 39–40, in Slide, *Griffith Interviews*, 161.

100 **"my millions, anyway":** Frederick James Smith, *Photoplay*, December 1926, 30–31, in Slide, *Griffith Interviews*, 180.

100 **"his films reside":** Fred Camper and Jonathan Shimkin, "Griffith's Composition and Recent American Cinema," in University Film Study Center, Cambridge, MA, Newsletter Supplement, vol. 5, no. 2 (1974): 7.

100 **told one journalist:** Robert E. Welsh, *New York Dramatic Mirror*, January 14, 1914, 49, in Slide, *Griffith Interviews*, 6.

100 **"see what happened":** Richard Barry, ed., in *Editor*, April 24, 1915, 407–10, in Slide, *Griffith Interviews*, 26.

102 **"destinies in the film":** Tom Gunning, "Griffith, Biograph, and the Development of Film Language," in University Film Study Center, Cambridge, MA, Newsletter Supplement, vol. 5, no. 2 (1974): 1–4.

103 **"what he would like":** Billy Bitzer letters/writings on Griffith and *The Birth of a Nation*, reel 2, Griffith Papers, Library of Congress. This quote is from a typed page with heading "The Birth of a Nation."

103 **Kentucky values:** Mayer, 3; Stokes, 68.

103 **"along those lines":** in Slide, *Griffith Interviews*, 16; *New York Dramatic Mirror*, July 1, 1914, 21.

104 **Packard touring car:** Schickel, 167, 175.

104 **"or other publications":** Slide, *Early American Cinema*, 88–89.

104 **formula films:** Schickel, 185.

105 **"been seen here":** "'Quo Vadis?' at Astor: Moving Pictures of Famous Story of Rome Shown for First Time Here," *New York Times*, April 22, 1913, 11.

105 **"in his direction":** Gish, 95–96.

CHAPTER 8

106 **"a poor general":** William H. Ferris in letter to *New York Age*, November 11, 1907.

106 **"mistakes or weaknesses":** Cathcart, 258.

106 **"with organizations":** Du Bois, *Dusk of Dawn*, 94–95.

107 **"risk-all-to-win courage":** Du Bois Papers, Correspondence, 1920–1929. Clement G. Morgan letter, May 31, 1927. Trotter's personality generally: Worthy, 88–91; Cathcart, 257–59; Stephen R. Fox, 103, 109–13.

108 **"William Monroe Trotter":** Wells, 323.

108 **found Trotter unbearable:** Villard Papers, Villard letter to Francis J. Garrison, June 4, 1909.

108 **scrutiny of studio bosses:** Henderson, 24–26.

109 **"bursting over a rock":** Karl Brown, 5; Wagenknecht and Slide, 21–23; Mayer, 110; Schickel, 189.

109 **"costumes we will use":** *Photoplay*, September 1916, 85–86, in Slide, *Griffith Interviews*, 53.

109 **Charlie Chaplin:** Seymour Stern, November 25, 1947, in Slide, *Griffith Interviews*, 210.

109 **"is his recreation":** *Movie Weekly*, January 7, 1922, 11, in Slide, *Griffith Interviews*, 140.

110 **acknowledge his talents:** Mayer, 110; Schickel, 190–94; Stokes, 73–74.

111 **"for a livelihood":** Fairlie Papers, Trotter letter, September 6, 1906.

111 **the paper's printer:** Forbes Papers, George W. Forbes bankruptcy papers; Fox, 65.

111 **"a free press":** Towns Collection, box 2, folder 46, Trotter letter, February 2, 1904.

111 **Trotter said:** Russell Papers, Trotter letter, January 1915.

111 **"rights and freedom":** *Guardian*, December 19, 1914, 1.

112 **"condition financially":** Washington Papers, vol. 12, 446; letter to Ralph Waldo Tyler, February 20, 1914.

112 **"twentieth century civilization":** Stephen R. Fox, 206, citing the John E. Bruce Papers, letter from (unknown first name) Franklin to Bruce, ca. 1911.

112 **"against my principles":** *Bay State Banner*, October 8, 1966, quoting 1913 Trotter letter.

112 **"the race any good":** Murray Papers, Trotter letter, September 23, 1913.

112 **he told a friend:** Fairlie Papers, Trotter letter, June 15, 1902.

112 **"Garrison's Old Stand":** *Guardian*, 1910 issues and after.

113 **Long Island, New York:** Cathcart, 272–74; *Guardian*, July 25, 1908, 1; August 22, 1908, 4.

113 **"through his efforts":** Puttkammer and Worthy, 307.

114   **devoted to each other:** Information about the Trotters' marriage and daily life: Russell Papers, Trotter letter, January 18, 1916; Fox, 212; Trotter Papers, Fox's 1965 interviews with: Monroe Mason (August 31); Ernest G. O'Banyoun (September 2, 1965); Rev. St. Clair Kirton (September 1, 1965); Mrs. Malcolm Banks (September 1, 1965); Ralph J. Banks (September 4, 1965); and Dr. Charles Russell (December 3, 1912); Worthy, 16–18. Waldorf Lunch and trend in lunchrooms: John A. Jakle and Keith A. Sculle, *Fast Food; Roadside Restaurants in the Automobile Age* (Baltimore and London: John Hopkins University Press, 1999), 27–29.

114   **"results of their effort":** Harvard, '95 Fourth Report, 1910, 199.

115   **"abruptly to an end":** Stokes, 74.

116   **accomplished that:** Mayer, 111; Schickel, 196; Henderson, 138; Stokes, 75.

116   **"of the screen":** *Moving Picture World,* January 3, 1914, 52, in Slide, *Griffith Interviews,* 3.

116   **"gird the earth":** *New York Dramatic World,* January 14, 1914, 49, in Slide, *Griffith Interviews,* 6.

116   **about 490 films:** Mayer, 2, 119; Schickel, 202–4; Stokes, 78–79.

117   **"my very being":** *Photoplay,* October 1916, 90–94, in Slide, *Griffith Interviews,* 58.

117   **he said later:** Hart, 88.

118   **"watch 1914 and see":** *New York Dramatic Mirror,* January 14, 1914, in Slide, *Griffith Interviews,* 10.

119   **inferior and incapable:** Cathcart, 262–64; Sullivan, 13–16; Stephen R. Fox, 136–37.

119   **"socially ostracized":** Grimké Papers, letter from Albert E. Pillsbury, November 26, 1913.

120   **"by the colored people":** Stephen R. Fox, 140, citing Trotter before Congressional Antilynching Hearings Before the Committee on the Judiciary, January 29, 1920.

120   **"our people":** Wilson Papers, two letters from William T. Ferguson of Trotter's National Independent Political League: July 22, 1910; August 9, 1910.

120   **of New Jersey:** Wilson Papers, Trotter letter, November 15, 1910.

121   **"campaign of 1912":** Wilson Papers, W. C. Payne letter, November 9, 1910.

122   **"in their place":** Chace, 43.

122   **the twentieth century:** Chace, 238. The voting breakdown: Wilson: 6,293,454; Roosevelt: 4,119,538; Taft: 3,484,980; Debs: 901,873. Debs's total was more than twice his total in the 1908 election, and it was the largest share—6 percent—of the popular vote ever won by a Socialist candidate for president before or since. Wrote Chace: "The 1912 election thus marked the apogee of the Socialist movement in America." Wilson carried forty states and 435 electoral

votes. Chace: "Wilson's sweeping victory allowed the Democrats to take control of the Senate for the first time in 20 years."

122 **"employees work":** Wilson Papers, Library of Congress, reel 47, Trotter letter, February 26, 1913.

122 **federal departments:** *Guardian*, February 15, 1919, ran a picture of Deenie Trotter's chart; see Wilson Papers, vol. 28, 1913, for a copy of Trotter's statement and petition.

122 **three weeks away:** *Boston Globe*, November 7, 1913, 13.

122 **"solution to the problem":** *Boston Globe*, November 14, 1913, 10.

123 **"straight to my heart":** Wilson Papers, Wilson letter to Dixon, December 3, 1912.

123 **"your brilliant conduct":** Wilson Papers, Dixon letter to Wilson, January 1, 1914.

123 **"cockles of my heart":** Wilson Papers, Dixon letter, January 1; Wilson reply, January 5, 1914; Slide, *Griffith Interviews*; *Photoplay*, October 1916, discusses Griffith's initial talks in 1913 about adapting *The Clansman*; see Stokes, 81, for start of 1914 and Dixon's considering Griffith's adaptation.

CHAPTER 9

127 **"to tell its story":** Gish, 131.

128 **one more film:** Gish, 131; Mayer, 145; Henderson, 146; Schickel, 207; Stokes, 78–79.

128 **"something worthwhile":** Bitzer's writings, Griffith Papers, Library of Congress, reel 2.

128 **"to save a nation":** Hart, 89.

129 **mighty impressive:** Mayer, 157–58.

129 **his battle scenes:** Stokes, 89–91.

130 **Bertha Watson:** Margaret Sanger, 109–120.

131 **pictures got shown:** MacGregor, 163–74; National Board of Censorship, http://encyclopedia.jrank.org/articles/pages/2054/The-National-Board-of-Censorship.html.

131 **"as the press":** *PM*, May 19, 1948, in Slide, *Griffith Interviews*, 215.

132 **Supreme Court:** Barbas, 676–81.

132 **"stage actress":** *Pictures and the Picturegoer*, April 28, 1917, in Slide, *Griffith Interviews*, 75.

132 **"anywhere else":** *Theatre Magazine*, June 1914, 312, in Slide, *Griffith Interviews*, 12.

132 **he once said:** Ibid., 76.

133 **"we have shown that":** *New York American*, February 28, 1915, 9, in Slide, *Griffith Interviews*, 20.

133 **"It served a purpose":** Walter Huston interview with Griffith, 1930, in Slide, *Griffith Interviews*, 188.

133 **from his studio:** Schickel, 225. Note: The area today is near where Universal City is located and is part of Forest Lawn Memorial Park, a famous cemetery.

134 **his massive cast:** Ibid., 226.

134 **leaping overhead:** Stokes, 95.

135 **"surrender were signed":** *New York American*, February 28, 1915, 9, in Slide, *Griffith Interviews*, 20.

135 **one observer noted:** *Pictures and Picturegoer*, April 1917, in Slide, *Griffith Interviews*, 73.

135 **director was satisfied:** *Movie Weekly*, January 7, 1922, 11, in Slide, *Griffith Interviews*, 104; *Photoplay*, September 1916, 85–86, in Slide, *Griffith Interviews*, 56.

135 **"a beautiful statue":** *Motion Picture Magazine*, August 1922, 21–25, in Slide, *Griffith Interviews*, 147.

135 **"my big game":** Hart, 92; Stokes, 97–98.

135 **film of its time:** Mayer, 145; Stokes, 98.

135 **shot 140,000 feet:** Cuniberti, 21; *Los Angeles Times*, February 19, 1915, 1, in "Myth and Fact: The Reception of 'The Birth of a Nation'" by Arthur Lennig, *Film History* 16.2 (April 2004): 117.

136 **"music and spectacle":** *Boston Herald*, July 18, 1915, review by Harlow Hare.

136 **sound of horses' hooves:** Ibid.; *Los Angeles Times*, February 19, 1915, 1, in Lennig.

136 **"rest of the night":** *Motion Picture Magazine*, August 1922, in Slide, *Griffith Interviews*, 148.

136 **"world is a stage":** *The Theatre of Science*, 1914, in Slide, *Griffith Interviews*, 18.

137 **"personal prejudice":** Franklin P. Mall, "On Several Anatomical Characters of the Human Brain, Said to Vary According to Race and Sex, with Especial Reference to the Weight of the Frontal Lobe," *American Journal of Anatomy* 9, no. 1 (1909): 1–18.

138 **"enjoyed by whites":** NAACP Papers, Proceedings of 1909 Conference, Wilder talk, 22–66.

138 **"without a dollar":** Burt G. Wilder, *The Fifty-Fifth Regiment of the Massachusetts Volunteer Infantry, Colord*, 3rd ed. (Brookline, MA, The Riverdale Press, 1919), 2–8.

138 **"or 2 weeks":** Murray Papers, Trotter Letter, January 20, 1914.

138 **rate of 18 percent:** Suffolk County Registry of Deeds, Trotter deeds for Robinson Place properties.

138 **a $100 pledge:** Stephen R. Fox, 210, citing the diary of John Milholland from the Milholland Papers.

139 **"lighthearted again":** Murray Papers, Deenie Trotter letter, July 13, 1914.

139 **"important to work on":** Wilson Papers, Library of Congress, Manuscript Division, Trotter letter, December 5, 1913.

139 **"bonds of segregation":** Ibid., Trotter telegram, December 22, 1913.

139 **twenty-seven thousand:** NAACP Fourth Annual Report, 1913, 36–38; Sullivan, 23–33.

139 **"as an equal":** Du Bois Papers, Letter to Mary W. Ovington, April 9, 1914.

140 **"a child race still!":** Stephen R. Fox, 142; Villard Papers, Villard letter to Francis J. Garrison, March 14, 1913.

140 **"almost racial":** Stephen R. Fox, 142; Storey Papers, Storey letter to Villard, October 17, 1911. Note: Storey backtracked on this statement after Villard challenged him, writing to Villard in an October 19, 1911, letter, "I have no doubt you are right, and the weakness of which you speak is common to human nature and not the property of any particular race."

140 **"a good many weeks":** Washington Papers, vol. 12, 417; Letter to Emmett Jay Scott, January 16, 1914.

140 **"its colored members":** NAACP Fourth Annual Report, 1913, 36–38; Sullivan, 23–33.

140 **color line was erased:** NAACP Papers, NAACP Annual Conference, Baltimore, MD, May 1914; Second Session, Boston branch report by Butler R. Wilson, 18, 2–7.

141 **"Oh! Susanna!":** Boston Public Library, Rare Books and Manuscripts, Boston School Committee Records, Board's vote of Nov. 16, 1914; McLaughlin, James M., *Forty Best Old Songs*, Ginn and Company Publishers, Boston, 1914.

142 **wouldn't end there:** *Buchanan v. Warley*, 245 U.S. 60 (1917); Sullivan, 46–47.

142 **"Federal departments":** Wilson Papers, Villard letters to Wilson, September 23, 1913; January 6, 1914.

142 **"in the departments":** Wilson Papers, Wilson letters to Villard, September 23, 1913; August 29, 1913.

143 **"walking on air":** *Washington Post*, November 16, 1914, 2.

143 **"nomination Roosevelt":** Trotter Papers, Trotter telegram to Addams, August 6, 1912.

143 **"common justice":** Wilson Papers, Trotter letter to Gallivan, October 17, 1914.

143 **"a date in October":** Ibid., Trotter letter to Peters, October 19, 1914.

144 **"matter of this sort":** McAdoo Papers, DLC, McAdoo letter to Frank I. Cobb, November 26, 1914, also copied in Wilson Papers, McAdoo letter to Wilson, November 28, 1914.

144 **the clerk fired:** *Chicago Defender*, June 20, 1914, 6.

144 **"President this week":** Wilson Papers: Walsh letter to Wilson, October 26, 1914; Thacher letter to Tumulty, October 28, 1914.

145 **"in that direction":** Ibid., Dixon letter of November 21, 1914; Wilson's reply, November 24, 1914.

145 **"Mrs. Wilson's death":** Stephen R. Fox, 180, citing diary of Edward M. House, November 6, 1914.
145 **"fortunes of a nation!":** Wilson Papers, Wilson letter to Nancy Saunders Toy, November 9, 1914.
147 **"entirely disappointing":** *New York Times*, November 13, 1914, 1; Wilson Papers, Transcript of White House meeting, vol. 31, November 12, 1914.
148 **"a just cause!":** Stephen R. Fox, 185, citing Villard Papers, Villard letter to Francis J. Garrison, November 18, 1914.

CHAPTER 10

149 **in the White House:** Grace Kingsley, "At the Stage Door," *Los Angeles Times*, February 18, 1915; *Los Angeles Times*, February 19, 1915, 4–5, in "Myths and Fact: The Reception of 'The Birth of a Nation'" by Arthur Lennig, *Film History* 16.2 (April 2004): 117. In his article, Lennig notes that a film, *Cabria*, was screened the previous June outdoors on the White House grounds; Griffith's was nonetheless the first film screened inside.
150 **"a powerful weapon":** Dixon, *Southern Horizons*, 297–99; Wilson Papers, Dixon letter to Tumulty, January 27, 1915.
150 **"exhibition of the picture":** Kingsley, *Los Angeles Times*, February 7, 1915, section 3, 4.
150 **"made to look hideous":** NAACP Papers, Los Angeles branch letter to Los Angeles City Council, February 2, 1915.
151 **face value of $0.75:** *Los Angeles Times*, February 19, 1915, 5, in Lennig.
151 **in formal attire:** Stokes, 111; Dixon, *Southern Horizons*, 298.
152 **as Wilson put it:** Woodrow Wilson, *A History of the American People, Volume 5: Reunion and Nationalization* (New York and London: Harper & Bros., 1902), 58.
152 **"to startle the world":** Kingsley, *Los Angeles Times*, February 7, 1915, section 3A, 10.
153 **North Sea:** *New York Times*, February 24, 1915, 2.
153 **a lopsided 50–7:** *New York Times*, January 3, 1915, 8.
153 **in Chicago, Illinois:** *Chicago Tribune*, January 11, 1915, 6; *Chicago Tribune*, January 4, 1915, 4.
153 **not always the enemy:** *Boston Globe*, January 29, 1915.
154 **the screen heroism:** Karl Brown, 88–89.
154 **freedoms of Negroes:** Silva, 6.
154 **"you do to my people":** Beatty, 175.
154 **candidly admitted:** The film; NAACP Papers, Los Angeles Branch letter, February 2, 1915, 1–2.
155 **"most sincere gratitude":** Wilson Papers, Dixon letter, February 20, 1915; Griffith letter, March 2, 1915.
155 **expansive banquet hall:** Cripps, 52.

155 **remaining seats:** *Washington Herald*, February 20, 1915; *New York City American*, February 23, 1915.

156 **February 20:** *Washington Post*, February 20, 1915, 5.

156 **"from David Griffith":** *Los Angeles Times*, February 18, 1915, section 3, 4.

156 **"at the White House":** *Washington Post*, February 21, 1915.

156 **"written in lightning":** Thomas Cripps, "The Reaction of the Negro to the Motion Picture, Birth of a Nation," in *Historian* 26 (1963): 344–62.

156 **"history by lightning":** *New York American*, February 28, 1915, in Slide, *Griffith Interviews*, 21.

157 **"other periodicals":** Brief of Appellants at 32, *Mutual Film Corporation v. Industrial Commission of Ohio*, 236 U.S. 230 (1915).

157 **"liberty of opinion":** *Mutual Film Corporation v. Industrial Commission of Ohio*, 236 U.S. 230 (1915), 243–44.

157 **the court said:** Ibid., 244.

157 **"used for evil":** Ibid.

157 **"insidious in corruption":** Ibid.

157 **"manner of exhibition":** Ibid.

158 **"mid-twentieth century":** Barbas, 666.

158 **"incite to crime":** MacGregor, 164; *Variety*, "Rigid Movie Censorship Bill Before Albany Legislature," 1914.

158 **at the Cort Theatre:** Stokes, 133; Griffith Papers, "Sheets," 1, showing opening intertitles.

160 **to get him fired:** *New York Call*, February 3, 1915, 3; *New York Times*, February 6, 1915, 12; *Modern School*, February–March, 1915, 15; *Chicago Tribune*, March 19, 1915, 9.

160 **the journalist afterward:** *New York American*, February 28, 1915, in Slide, *Griffith Interviews*, 20–22.

160 **epic proportion:** Griffith Papers, Liberty Theatre and other programs for *The Birth of a Nation*.

161 **entered the room:** NAACP Papers, Nerney letter to Mrs. Max Morgenthau, March 16, 1915.

161 **in a 12–9 vote:** Ibid.

161 **"dangerous film":** NAACP Papers, Nerney letter to National Board of Censorship's Rev. Charles S. McFarland, March 26, 1915.

162 **smashing success:** Stokes, 134–40.

162 **"allowed it to be shown":** Hart, 95. Note: The quotation was edited slightly for brevity.

162 **"ever conceived":** *New York American*, February 28, 1915, in Slide, *Griffith Interviews*, 20–22.

CHAPTER 11

163 **Edward M. House:** *New York Times*, November 14, 1914, 1.

163 **"President to the press":** *Boston Globe*, November 17, 1914, 1.

163   **"insulting to the President":** *Washington Herald*, November 16, 1914, 1.

164   **headline the next day:** Ibid.; *Boston Traveler*, November 16, 1914.

164   **of the United States:** Trotter Papers, Boston Literary and Historical Society minutes, November 16, 1914.

164   **"at the White House":** Ibid.

165   **he said emphatically:** *Boston Globe*, November 18, 1914, 9; *Boston Traveler*, November 18, 1914; *Boston Herald*, November 18, 1914; *Guardian*, November 28, 1914.

165   **"in this connection":** Wilson Papers, Anderson letter to Tumulty, December 22, 1914; Booker T. Washington Papers, Anderson letter to Washington, December 29, 1914.

166   **"Boston as a hub":** Wells, *Crusade for Justice* 376–77.

166   **"rights of his race":** Ibid., 376.

166   **"cheap notoriety":** Washington Papers, George Cleveland Hall letter to Washington, January 6, 1915.

166   **Negro Fellowship League:** *Chicago Defender*, January 9, 1915, 2–3.

166   **"'Insult President Wilson?'":** Ibid.

167   **"cordially" and left:** *Chicago Tribune*, January 3, 1915, 1; *Chicago Defender*, January 9, 1915, 8.

167   **defeat the Senate bill:** *Chicago Tribune*, January 4, 1915, 4; *Chicago Defender*, January 9, 1915, 1.

167   **"upheld his hands":** Wells, 376–77.

167   **"I had promised," she said:** Ibid.

167   **"come to the rescue":** *Guardian*, November 21, 1914, 4.

168   **"fixed badly":** Russell Papers, 1915, date unknown.

168   **"members of this race":** Wilson Papers, Rosenwald letter of November 13, 1914.

168   **"played the fool":** Ibid., "A News Report," November 12, 1914, footnote 9, citing Daniels's letter to F. D. Roosevelt, June 10, 1933.

168   **ran the gamut:** *Evening Mail*, New York, November 13, 1914, which wrote: "It is hard to discover any sufficient reason for the President's resentment of the efforts of Mr. Trotter to dissuade him to abandon the office policy of several cabinet officers in drawing the color line in the federal departments."

169   **"elective official's conduct":** *New York Evening Post*, November 13, 1914.

169   **"'race equality'":** *Crisis*, January 1915, 125, quoting the newspapers.

169   **"denounced by the South":** *Boston Globe*, November 18, 1914, 9.

169   **"Negroes of this country":** *Crisis*, December 1914, 82.

169   **"attitudes and words":** Wilson Papers, Moton letter, November 16, 1914.

169   **"temper and disposition":** Ibid., Wilson reply to Moton, November 18, 1914.

170 **Moton wrote:** Washington Papers, vol. 13, 181, Moton letter of November 23, 1914.

170 **"being taken from us:"** *Chicago Defender*, January 9, 1915, 9.

171 **"against the measure":** Washington Papers, vol. 13, 216, Hall letter to Washington, January 6, 1915.

171 **"a grave injustice":** *Crisis*, January 1915, 129.

171 **to the Negro race:** *New Republic*, March 1915.

172 **"3 hour entertainment":** NAACP Papers, Cobleigh-Dixon letters, March–April 1915; Library of Congress, Collection of Books, *Fighting a Vicious Film: Protest Against "The Birth of a Nation,"* published by the NAACP Boston branch, 1915; Cobleigh, in *Fighting a Vicious Film*, 12–17.

172 **"heartfelt endorsement":** Joseph P. Tumulty Papers, Library of Congress, Manuscript Division, Harriet Blaine Beale letter to Tumulty, March 29, 1915.

173 **"anywhere else in the country":** Library of Congress, Collection of Books, *Fighting a Vicious Film: Protest Against "The Birth of a Nation,"* published by the NAACP Boston branch, 1915; Cobleigh, 17.

173 **opponents there:** NAACP Papers, Boston branch letters; Stokes, 118–22.

173 **at one point:** Ibid., Nerney letter to Joseph P. Loud, May 21, 1915.

173 **"they keep it up!":** NAACP Papers, *Fighting a Vicious Film: Protest Against "The Birth of a Nation,"* published by the NAACP Boston branch, 1915; Cobleigh portion, 12–17.

174 **"not played on them":** Washington Papers, vol. 13, page 277. Letter to Courtney, April 23, 1915.

174 **"control of thought":** William L. Chenery, *Chicago Record Herald*, April 13, 1915, in Stokes, 133.

175 **"period of Reconstruction":** *Crisis*, October 1915, 292.

175 **"the B.T.W. influence":** NAACP Papers, Nerney letter to Joseph P. Loud, May 6, 1913; May 17, 1915; Elaine Sterne letter to Nerney, August 1915; Nerney letter to Dr. Charles E. Bentley, May 11, 1915; Russell Papers, Nerney letter to Russell, with confidential pitch document, June 9, 1915.

176 **wrote in 2003:** *Chaplinsky v. New Hampshire* (315 U.S. 568, 1942); *Brandenburg v. Ohio* (395 U.S. 444, 1969); *R.A.V. v. St. Paul* (505 U.S. 377, 1992); *Virginia v. Black* (538 U.S. 343, 2003).

177 **separate YMCAs:** *Peoria Star*, April 2, 1915, cited in *Guardian*, April 17, 1915, 1.

178 **"any such distortion":** *Boston Herald*, letters to the editor, Tuesday, April 6, Wednesday, April 7, 1915.

178 **"grounds of immorality":** Trotter Papers, Boston Literary and Historical Society minutes, meetings of March 22 and April 5, 1915.

179 **all forms of bigotry:** *Guardian*, April 17, 1915.

179   **"Post Office Department":** Wilson Papers, Curley letter to Tumulty, August 12, 1913.

180   **"obscene or immoral":** Massachusetts Legislature: Chapter 494 of the Acts of 1908.

180   **"immoral exhibition":** *Boston American*, March 30, 1915.

CHAPTER 12

183   **the previous year:** *Crisis*, September 1915, 220.

183   **"peculiarly barbarous," he said:** Baker, *World's Work* 32, no. 1 (1916): 232–36.

183   **cities and towns:** *Fort Worth Record*, July 31, 1915, cited in *Crisis*, January 1915, 145.

184   **"a woman is his prey":** Stephen Phillips, "The Black Peril," cited in *Crisis* 10, no. 1 (May 1915): 38.

185   **"boldness of tone":** Baker, *World's Work*, 1916, 234.

185   **"the last two days":** *Boston Globe*, March 28, 1915, 4.

185   **a striking iron gray:** Worthy, 38.

187   **case against the film:** Sources for the City Hall hearing of April 7, 1915, include: *Boston (Evening) American*; *Boston Traveler*, 1; *Boston (Morning) Journal*, 1; *Boston Post*, 1; *Boston Herald*; *Boston Globe*—all on April 8, 1915; *Guardian*, April 17, 1915 (found in Storey Papers); *Moving Picture World*, April 24, 1915; NAACP Papers, Mary White Ovington letter to Joel Spingarn, April 9, 1915, and Joseph P. Loud letter to May Nerney, April 15, 1915; Grimké Papers, Howard University, Elizabeth Putnam letter to Grimké, April 10, 1915; Beatty, 180–83.

188   **"barb from the Bard":** Beatty, 59, 33, 233.

191   **historical record:** *Guardian*, April 17, 1915.

197   **"Saturday night":** NAACP Papers, Ovington letter to Joel Spingarn, April 9, 1915.

197   **"play is presented":** *Guardian*, April 17, 1915.

197   **"riot and violence":** Ibid.

197   **"a Few Opponents":** *Boston Post*, April 9, 1915.

198   **in the *Congregationalist*:** *Congregationalist*, May 13, 1915.

198   **"to the country by them":** NAACP Papers, Loud letter to May Childs Nerney, April 15, 1915.

199   **found in the house:** *Boston American*, April 9, 1915.

199   **"colored population of Boston":** *Boston American*, April 10, 1915.

199   **to art critic:** In five years she would move to New York City, where she would work at the *Tribune* and meet the writer Janet Flannery. Eventually the couple would move to Paris and join Gertrude Stein's literary circle.

199   **"so insidious," she wrote:** *Boston Traveler*, April 10, 1915.

200   **"certain of the public":** *Boston Herald*, April 11, 1915.

200   **venues in the city:** Today the Loew's Boston Common Theatre multiplex occupies the site.
200   **the Blue and Gray:** *Boston Herald*, April 9, 1915.
201   **the first screening:** *Boston Globe*, April 12, 1915.
201   **"history upside down":** *Boston Herald*, Pillsbury letter to the editor, May 5, 1915.
201   **"assassination of a race":** *Boston Post*, April 10, 1915.
201   **the filmmaker said:** *Boston Post*, April 11, 1915.
201   **including the captain:** Ibid., 1.
203   **the morality test:** *Boston Herald, Boston Post, Boston Journal*— all April 13, 1915.

CHAPTER 13

204   **"approve the show":** Wilson Papers, vol. 33, White letter to Joseph Tumulty, April 5, 1915.
205   **European War:** Wilson Papers, Remarks to the Associated Press, April 20, 1915; *New York Times*, April 19, 1915, April 20, 1915, 1.
205   **"old acquaintance":** Wilson Papers, vol. 33, Wilson to Tumulty, April 24, 1915, and April 28, 1915.
205   **approval for the movie:** *Boston Post*, May 1, 1915.
205   **"race prejudice":** *Boston Herald*, Peabody letter to the editor, April 15, 1915.
206   **promote the school:** *Boston Post*, MacMahon letter to the editor, April 23, 1915; Washington Papers, Allston letter to Washington, April 10, 1915.
207   **alleged film fans:** *Boston Post*, MacMahon letter to the editor, April 17, 1915.
207   **"colored traitors":** Trotter Papers, Literary and Historical Association minutes, April 19, 1915.
207   **"National Meeting":** Washington Papers, Courtney letter to Washington, April 19, 1915.
207   **"will be successful":** Ibid., Washington letter to Courtney, April 23, 1915.
207   **with the director:** *Boston Post*, April 24, 1915, 6.
208   **hailed the *Boston Globe*:** *Boston Post*, April 18, 1915, 26, advertisement quoting reviews.
208   **"fighting race calumny":** *Crisis*, June 1915, 87.
208   **Phillies, 3–0:** *Boston Globe*, April 15, 1915, 1.
209   **often at odds:** Polgar, 94.
209   **"in these pictures":** *Boston Globe*, April 16, 1915, 7.
209   **"their public career":** *Boston Post*, April 16, 1915, 22.
210   **"considered harmful":** *Guardian*, April 17, 1915.
210   **city's police commissioner:** Chapter 323 of the 1885 Massachusetts Acts and Resolves. The power to appoint the police commissioner

did not return to the city until the 1960s, and the governor still holds appointing authority for Boston's liquor licensing board.

210 **over the production:** *Boston Post*, April 15, 1915; *Boston Globe*, April 15, 1915.

210 **"not more than $500":** Chapter 367 of the 1910 Massachusetts Acts and Resolves.

211 **"hate their neighbors":** *Boston Globe*, April 23, 1915.

211 **state criminal statute:** *Boston Globe*, April 20, 1915; *Boston Herald*, April 20, 1915.

212 **"Union was secure":** *Boston Post*, April 17, 1915, 1.

212 **join their cause:** *Guardian*, April 17, 1915.

212 **"assented to," he wrote:** *Boston Herald*, April 18, 1915, 5.

213 **still available:** *Boston Globe*, April 18, 1915.

213 **certainly was not:** *Boston Post*, April 18, 1915.

213 **whatsoever against it:** NAACP Papers, Nerney letter to Charles Bentley, April 17, 1915.

214 **"happen [*sic*]," she said:** *Boston Globe*, April 18, 1915.

214 **at the Boston Theatre:** *Boston Evening Transcript*, May 1, 1915, *Boston Evening American*, May 4, 1915.

215 **up to ten officers:** Ibid.; Tremont Theatre photographs, Bostonian Society.

215 **milling about:** *Boston American, Boston Post, Boston Globe, Boston Herald*, April 18, 1915.

215 **"William Monroe Trotter":** *Boston Globe*, April 18, 1915.

216 **one of hers to Moore:** *Boston Globe*, April 30, 1915.

216 **"Nothing doing":** *Boston Herald*, April 18, 1915.

216 **he barked:** *Boston American*, April 18, 1915.

216 **ushered inside:** Ibid.

216 **he roared:** *Boston Herald, Boston American*, April 18, 1915.

217 **shoving began:** *Boston American*, April 18, 1915.

217 **getting to Trotter:** *Boston Herald, Boston American*, April 18, 1915.

217 **"Don't you hurt him!":** *Boston Globe*, April 30, 1915; *Boston Herald*, April 18, 1915.

217 **cries of "Nigger":** *Boston Post*, April 18, 1915, in Puller's statement.

218 **into custody:** *Boston Post, Boston American*, April 18, 1915.

218 **turned up a movie ticket:** *Boston Post*, May 3, 1915, *Boston Globe*, May 5, 1915.

218 **in the works:** *Boston Herald*, April 18, 1915.

219 **excessive force:** *Boston American, Boston Post, Boston Globe, Boston Herald*, April 18, 1915.

220 **"odiferous bombs":** *Boston Globe*, April 30, 1915.

220 **police presence:** *Boston American, Boston Post, Boston Globe*, April 18, 1915.

221 **"the police officers":** *Boston Post*, April 18, 1915.

221 **charge of profanity:** *Boston Herald, Boston Globe*, April 18, 1915.

222   **the film's screening:** *Boston Herald*, April 18, 1915.
222   **its front-page story:** *Boston Post, Boston Globe*, April 18, 1915.
223   **"ran for their lives":** Dixon, *Southern Horizons*, 306.
223   **"who live here":** *Boston Globe*, April 18, 1915.
223   **"best sentiment":** *Boston American*, April 18, 1915.
223   **he could not:** *Boston Herald*, April 18, 1915.
224   **"will be responsible":** *Boston Globe*, April 18, 1915.
224   **"outrageous film":** *Boston Herald*, April 19, 1915.
224   **"the mayorality":** *Boston Globe, Boston Post, Boston Journal, Boston Advertiser, Boston Herald*, April 19, 1915.

CHAPTER 14

225   **"drive it out of Boston":** Washington Papers, vol. 13, 274, Courtney letter to Washington, April 19, 1915.
226   **"during the performances":** *Boston Globe* advertisement, April 19, 1915.
226   **May would be 94:** Annual Report for the Police Commissioner for the City of Boston, 1916.
228   **"I'm a sinful man!":** Joseph P. Tumulty Papers, Manuscript Division, Library of Congress, Dixon letter to Tumulty, May 1, 1915. Dixon's misspelling of *asininity* has been corrected.
228   **one reporter observed:** *Boston American*, April 19, 1915.
229   **resting and waiting:** Ibid.
229   **the prospects ahead:** *Boston Globe, Boston Herald*, April 19, April 20, 1915.
229   **"nervous from the start":** *Boston Transcript*, April 19, 1915.
230   **"Boston police authorities":** *Boston American, Boston Traveler*, April 20, 1915.
230   **and entered, too:** *Boston American, Boston Herald*, April 20, 1915. Trotter Papers, Literary and Historical Association, minutes of the April 19, 1915, meeting.
231   **film "extraordinary":** *Boston American, Boston Herald, Boston Traveler*, April 20, 1915.
232   **"you're good looking":** *Boston Globe, Boston Herald, Boston Transcript, Boston Traveler*, April 20, 1915.
233   **"of the United States":** *Boston Transcript*, April 19, 1915.
234   **"God bless our governor!":** *Boston Globe, Boston Journal, Boston Post, Boston Traveler*, April 20, 1915.
235   **"religious prejudice":** *Boston Globe, Boston Herald, Boston Traveler*, April 20, 1915.
235   **to speak for him:** Ibid.
235   **found guilty and fined:** *Boston Journal, Boston Globe, Boston Herald, Boston Traveler*, April 20, 1915.
236   **"hung on," wrote one:** *Boston Globe, Boston Journal, Boston Post*, April 20, 1915.

236　*"The Birth of a Nation"*: *Boston Herald*, April 20, 1915.

236　**"the fight was won"**: Trotter Papers, Literary and Historical Association, minutes of the April 19, 1915, meeting.

236　**"take time," he said**: *Boston Herald*, April 15, 1915.

237　**"their case to date"**: *Boston Post*, April 21, 1915, *Boston Traveler*, April 20, 1915.

237　**"are badly advised"**: *Boston Post*, April 21, 1915, *Boston Herald*, April 22, 1915.

238　**"covered by the statute"**: *Boston Globe, Boston Herald*, April 22, 1915.

238　**"and a vilification"**: *Boston Post*, April 22, 1915.

239　**"obeyed to the letter"**: *Boston Globe*, April 22, 1915.

CHAPTER 15

244　**"violent emotions"**: *Boston Globe*, April 22, 1915.

244　**"censorship of plays"**: Ibid.

245　**never before in Boston**: *Boston Herald*, April 22, 1915.

245　**might be trouble**: *Boston Post*, April 22, 1915.

245　**attorney Wilson said**: *Boston Herald*, April 22, 1915.

246　**"rid of it by foul"**: *Boston Globe*, April 26, 1915.

246　**the others facing trial**: *Boston Traveler*, April 26, 1915.

246　**"morals of the young"**: *Boston Post*, April 26, 1915.

246　***Boston Post* observed**: *Boston Post*, May 1, 1915.

247　**"just what happened"**: *Boston Globe*, April 30, 1915.

247　**50-cent tickets**: *Boston Globe*, May 1, 1915.

248　**none in March**: Ibid.

249　**"or the courts"**: *Boston Herald, Boston Traveler, Boston Post, Boston Globe, Boston Journal, Boston American*, May 5, 1915.

250　**disenfranchising Negroes**: *Guinn v. United States*, 238 U.S. 347 (1915); *New York Times*, June 22, 1915; Sullivan, 47–48.

250　**a total of 764**: NAACP Papers, *Crisis*, NAACP Sixth Annual Report, 1915, 256.

250　**"liberty becomes anarchy"**: *Boston Globe*, April 19, 1915.

251　**"horrible fear of rape"**: *Boston Journal*, April 28, 1915.

251　**"conclusions," he said**: *Boston Traveler, Boston Globe*, April 27, 1915; *Boston Journal*, April 26, 1915, Dixon letter to the editor.

252　**"by Mr. Sullivan"**: *Boston Herald*, April 26, 1915, containing its editorial and that of the *Boston Transcript* in a paid advertisement titled "Kill The Sullivan Bill."

252　**"think it over, Mr. Trotter"**: *Boston Herald*, April 26, 1915.

253　**palatable politically**: *Boston Advertiser*, April 26, 1915.

253　**(italics added)**: Journal of the Massachusetts House of Representatives, Friday, April 30, 1915, House Bill 2127, an act to amend Chapter 494 of the Acts of 1908; *Boston Post, Boston Journal, Boston Globe*, May 1, 1915.

254 **"they say 'Nigger'":** *Boston Post,* May 3, 1915.

255 **"proof firsthand":** *Boston Globe,* April 30, 1915, *Boston Evening American,* May 4, 1915.

255 **by lawmakers:** *Boston Traveler,* May 4, 1915.

255 **"to bribe?" he asked:** NAACP Papers, Butler R. Wilson letter to the editor, April 27, 1915.

255 ***Boston Evening American:*** *Boston Evening American,* May 4, 1915.

256 **Calvin Coolidge:** *Boston Herald,* May 4, 1915.

256 **"would *really* be born":** Washington Papers, Jesse H. Harris letter to Washington, May 3, 1915. Note: Errors of spelling and grammar were corrected in this letter.

256 **"when I meet it":** *Boston Post,* May 3, 1915.

257 **without additional interruption:** *Boston Post,* May 11, 1915.

257 **one of the May rallies:** *Boston Post,* May 24, 1915.

257 **"copy of the resolution":** Trotter Papers, Minutes of the Boston Literary and Historical Association, May 17, 1915.

257 **to the state Senate:** Journal of the Massachusetts House of Representatives, May 10, 1915, 1158–59; *Boston Post,* May 11, 1915.

258 **"It helps":** Wilson Papers, Dixon letter, May 12, 1915; Wilson reply, May 14, 1915.

258 **to defend the city:** *Boston Globe,* May 16, 1915.

259 **were crestfallen:** Journal of the Massachusetts Senate, May 18, 1915, 1048; *Boston Globe, Boston Evening American,* May 18, 1915.

259 **get their attention:** *Boston Post,* May 20, 1915.

259 **his chief lobbyist:** Journal of the Massachusetts House of Representatives, May 19, 1915, 1234–39; Journal of the Massachusetts Senate, May 20, 1915, 1067; May 21, 1915, 1075; *Boston Post, Boston Globe,* May 22, 1915.

259 **"logically, and why?":** *Boston Advertiser,* May 22, 1915.

259 ***"The Birth of a Nation":*** *Boston Globe,* May 22, 1915.

259 **in New York City:** NAACP Papers, Nerney letter to Joseph Loud, May 21, 1915.

260 **"of the movie play":** *Boston Post,* May 22, 1915.

260 **"censors to act":** Ibid.

CHAPTER 16

261 **progress nonetheless:** *Crisis,* July 1915, 114; Jim Crow Museum, Ferris State University, February 2007 response by curator David Pilgrim to a question about the carnival game.

262 **books and publications:** *Boston Traveler,* April 27, 1916.

262 **"I had been trained":** *Crisis,* April 1916, 296, quoting the *Boston Evening Record,* January 1916.

263 **Massachusetts citizens:** *New Era Magazine,* March 1916, 119.

263 **"not have equal rights":** *Boston Traveler,* April 27, 1916.

263   **"in your behalf"**: *Guardian*, February 19, 1916, printing the Walsh letter to Bosfield of August 27, 1915.

263   **"named as censors"**: *Boston Journal*, May 23, 1915.

264   **"right speedily"**: *Boston Post*, May 24, 1915.

264   **"of race or color"**: NAACP Papers, pamphlet *Fighting a Vicious Film*, 47.

265   **per her boss's orders**: *Boston Traveler*, *Boston Globe*, June 3, 1915.

265   **"revoked or suspended"**: Ibid.

265   **"BIRTH OF A NATION' WINS"**: *Boston Post*, May 24, 1915.

266   **"population of the city"**: Stokes, 149.

266   **"getting around that fact"**: Beatty, 185–86.

267   **command of the proceedings**: *Boston Traveler*, June 3, 1915.

267   **forty-piece orchestra**: Arthur Lennig, "Myth and Fact: The Reception of 'The Birth of a Nation,'" *Film History*, 16.2 (April 2004), 13.

268   **the *Boston American***: *Boston American*, April 9, 1915.

269   **another critic had noted**: *New York Times*, March 4, 1915.

269   **a nation is reborn**: Wagenknecht and Slide, 46–48.

271   **"acted in good faith"**: *Boston Post*, April 23, 1915.

272   **through them, a nation**: Wagenknecht and Slide, 46–48; Slide, *Griffith Interviews*, 169–70; Cripps, 46–51, for material on black perspective viewing film; author's viewing.

272   **"inhuman atrocities"**: *Boston Traveler*, April 29, 1915.

273   **"appreciate my efforts"**: *Boston Globe*, *Boston American*, April 10, 1915.

273   **"moment of his life"**: Stokes, 25.

274   **he advised**: *Boston Traveler*, *Boston Post*, *Boston Globe*, June 3, 1915.

275   **in that city**: *Boston Globe*, October 24, 1915.

EPILOGUE

277   **"advertise the picture"**: Dixon, *Southern Horizons*, 306.

277   **about its wonders**: *Atlanta Constitution*, October 24, 1915.

278   **"for humanity's good"**: Chalmers, 28–38.

278   **"The scene is indescribable"**: *Atlanta Constitution*, November 28, December 7, 1915.

278   **nearly a hundred thousand**: Chalmers, 28–38.

279   **"a drunkard's downfall"**: Schickel, 373.

279   **"from public exhibition"**: Silva, 8, quoting from an interview Griffith biographer Barnet Bravermann had with Griffith at the Robert Treat Hotel in Newark, New Jersey, in 1941.

280   **"youth and vitality"**: Slide, *Griffith Interviews*, 212–17 (a reprint of a 1948 interview between Griffith and the writer Ezra Goodman, originally published in *PM*, in Slide, *Griffith Interviews*, May 19, 1948).

281   **he had wanted to make:** Schickel, 12, 300.
281   **headquarters in mid-June:** NAACP Papers, Library of Congress, Joseph P. Loud letters to May Childs Nerney, June 4, June 15, 1915.
281   **end of summer:** Ibid., P. A. Goines letter to W. E. B. Du Bois and the NAACP, August 12, 1915.
281   **"sentiment against it":** Ibid., William Warley letter to May Childs Nerney, December 12, 1915.
282   **"prejudice preclude this":** NAACP Sixth Annual Report: 1915, *Crisis*, March 1916, 251.
282   **the land since 1896:** *Buchanan v. Warley*, 245 U.S. 60 (1917); *Brown v. Board of Education*, 347 U.S. 483 (1954).
282   **First Amendment arguments:** For a more complete list, see NAACP Sixth Annual Report: 1915, *Crisis*, March 1916, 256; Sullivan, 48–50; Stokes, 157–59.
282   **"racism in American life":** Cripps, 64.
283   **around the country:** NAACP Sixth Annual Report: 1915, *Crisis*, March 1916, 254–55; Schickel, 299–300.
283   **"their place in history":** NAACP Papers, report of Joel Spingarn, NAACP chairman, to the board of directors, January 3, 1916.
283   ***Family Limitation:*** *New York Times, Boston Globe, Chicago Tribune,* September 22, 1915.
284   **from the gallery:** *New York Times,* September 11, 1915.
285   **"are their tools":** Wilson Papers, Dixon letter to Wilson, September 10, 1915.
285   **"provincial color prejudice":** *Boston Globe,* December 20, 1915.
285   **"defense of its rights":** *Guardian,* November 20, 1915.
287   **probationary period:** *Boston Globe,* February 16, 1916, citing Judge William Loring's ruling.
287   **"Medfield State Hospital":** Trotter Papers, Literary and Historical Association minutes, January 31, 1916.
287   **noted one reporter:** *Boston Globe,* February 20, 1916.
287   **"Is this fair?":** *Boston Traveler,* April 27, 1916.
287   **police to remove him:** Jillian Sim, "Monroe Trotter, Profile in Protest," *American Legacy* (summer 2003): 73–82.
288   **"race she represented":** *Boston Globe,* October 9, October 17, November 17, 1918.
288   **"who is no more":** *Guardian,* December 28, 1918, and selected issues afterward.
288   **practicing Jim Crow:** *Guardian,* February 15, 1919.
288   **"Negro sheets in America":** Eugene Gordon, "The Negro Press," *American Mercury,* 1926, 214; Stephen R. Fox, 268.
288   **"in his lifetime":** Worthy, 151.
289   **"remembrance of her":** Stephen R. Fox, 269–70.
289   **"where I'm going next":** Worthy, 166.
290   **"save *The Guardian*":** Trotter Papers, Trotter letter of January 23, 1934.

290 **"all frightened," she said:** Ibid., Maude Trotter letter to George A. Towns, January 23, 1934.

290 **"our day has ever had":** Ibid., Thomas S. Harten letter to Trotter, April 3, 1934.

290 **reported the death:** Worthy, 167–68; Stephen R. Fox, 272; *Boston Transcript*, April 7, 1934; *Boston Herald*, April 8, 1934.

291 **"unbending belief":** *Crisis*, 41 (1934).

291 **"seeing and discussing":** Raymond Rohauer, in postscript to Dixon's *Southern Horizons*, 324.

SELECTED BIBLIOGRAPHY

PAPERS AND ARCHIVES

James Michael Curley Papers, Library of College of the Holy Cross.

W. E. B. Du Bois Papers, Special Collection and University Archives, W. E. B. Du Bois Library, University of Massachusetts, Amherst.

John Archibald Fairlie Papers, University Archives, University Library, University of Illinois at Urbana-Champaign.

George W. Forbes Papers, Rare Book and Manuscript Department, Boston Public Library.

D. W. Griffith Papers, Manuscript Division, Library of Congress.

Archibald Grimké Papers, Moorland-Spingarn Research Center, Howard University.

James Weldon Johnson Memorial Collection, Beineke Rare Book and Manuscript Library, Yale University.

Freeman H. M. Murray Papers, Moorland-Spingarn Research Center, Howard University.

National Association for the Advancement of Colored People Papers, Manuscript Division, Library of Congress.

Dr. Alfred E. Russell Papers, Gotlieb Archives, Mugar Library, Boston University.

Arthur Spingarn Papers, Manuscript Division, Library of Congress.

Joel E. Spingarn Papers, Moorland-Spingarn Research Center, Howard University.

Moorfield Storey Papers, Manuscript Division, Library of Congress.

George A. Towns Collection, Archives Research Center, Robert W. Woodruff Library, Atlanta University Center.

William Monroe Trotter/Guardian Papers, Gotlieb Archives, Mugar Library, Boston University.

Tumulty Papers, Library of Congress.

Oswald Garrison Villard Papers, Houghton Library, Harvard University.

David I. Walsh Papers, Library of College of the Holy Cross.

Booker T. Washington Papers, University of Illinois Press.

Woodrow Wilson Papers, Manuscript Division, Library of Congress.

BOOKS AND MATERIALS: WILLIAM MONROE TROTTER

Abramowitz, Jack. "A Civil War Letter: James M. Trotter to Francis J. Garrison." *The Midwest Journal*, 4 (1952), 113–122.

Brown, Lois. *Pauline Elizabeth Hopkins: Black Daughter of the Revolution.* Chapel Hill: University of North Carolina Press, 2008.

Cathcart, Dolita Dannet. *White Gloves, Black Rebels: The Decline of Elite Black National Political Leadership in Boston, 1870–1929.* PhD thesis, Boston College, Boston, MA, 2004.

Coddington, Ronald S. "We Will Not Degrade the Name of an American Soldier." *The Civil War News,* December 30, 2012.

Cromwell, Adelaide M. *The Other Brahmins: Boston's Black Upper Class, 1750–1950.* Fayetteville: University of Arkansas Press, 1994.

Daniels, John. *In Freedom's Birthplace: A Study of the Boston Negroes.* Boston: Houghton Mifflin Co., 1914.

Dorman, Franklin A. *Twenty Families of Color in Massachusetts, 1742–1998.* Boston, MA: The New England Genealogical Society, 1998.

Fox, Charles Bernard. *Record of the Service of the Fifty-Fifth Regiment of Massachusetts Volunteer Infantry.* Cambridge, MA, 1868.

Fox, Stephen R. *The Guardian of Boston: William Monroe Trotter.* New York, NY: Atheneum, 1970.

Harrison, William. "William Trotter–Fighter." *Phylon Profile IX,* vol. 7 (1946), 236–45.

Hayden, Robert C. *Boston's NAACP History 1910–1982.* Boston: Boston NAACP, 1982.

Kountz, Mabe. *Monroe Trotter, Monroe Mason and the Guardian.* Boston: unpublished, June 1965.

———. *A History of the Early Colored Press in Massachusetts and a Second Sketch of the Boston Guardian Weekly.* Boston: unpublished, July 1967.

O'Connor, Thomas H. *Boston A to Z.* Cambridge, MA: Harvard University Press, 2000.

Polgar, Paul. "Fighting Lightning with Fire: Black Boston's Battle Against 'The Birth of a Nation.'" *Massachusetts Historical Review* 10 (2008): 84–113.

Pride, Aaron Noel. *Black Leadership and Religious Ideology in the Nadir, 1901–1916: Reconsidering the Agitation/Accommodation Divide in the Age of Booker T. Washington.* MA thesis, Miami University, Oxford, OH, 2008.

Puttkammer, Charles, and Ruth Worthy. "William Monroe Trotter, 1872–1934." *Journal of Negro History* 43, no. 4 (October 1958): 298–316.

Reid, Richard M., ed. *Practicing Medicine in a Black Regiment: The Civil War Diary of Burt. G. Wilder.* Amherst: University of Massachusetts Press, 2010.

Schneider, Mark R. *Boston Confronts Jim Crow: 1890–1920.* Boston: Northeastern University Press, 1997.

Simmons, Rev. William J. *Men of Mark: Eminent, Progressive and Rising.* New York: Arno Press and *New York Times,* 1968. Originally published in 1887.

Stevenson, Robert. "America's First Black Music Historian." *Journal of the American Musicological Society* 26, no. 3 (Autumn 1973): 383–404.

Trotter, James M. *Music and Some Highly Musical People.* Boston: Lee and Shepard, Publishers, 1880; New York: Charles T. Dillingham, 1881.

Trudeau, Noah Andre. *Voices of the 55th: Letters from the 55th Massachusetts Volunteers, 1861–1865.* Dayton, OH: Morningside House, 1996.

Worthy, Ruth. *A Negro in Our History: William Monroe Trotter, 1872–1934.* MA thesis, Columbia University, New York, 1952.

BOOKS AND MATERIALS: DAVID WARK GRIFFITH

Bitzer, G. W. *Billy Bitzer: His Story.* New York: Farrar, Straus and Giroux, 1973.

Brown, Karl. *Adventures with D. W. Griffith.* New York: Farrar, Straus and Giroux, 1973.

Carter, Everett. "Cultural History Written with Lightning: The Significance of The Birth of a Nation." *American Quarterly* 12, no. 3 (1960): 347–57.

Chalmers, David M. *Hooded Americanism: History of the Ku Klux Klan.* Durham, North Carolina: Duke University Press Books, 3rd ed., 1987.

Cook, David A. *A History of Narrative Film.* New York, London: W. W. Norton, 1996.

Cripps, Thomas. *Slow Fade to Black: The Negro in American Film, 1900–1942.* New York: Oxford University Press, 1977.

Cuniberti, John. *The Birth of a Nation: A Formal Shot by Shot Analysis.* Woodbridge, CT: Research Publications, 1979.

Dixon, Thomas. *Southern Horizons: The Autobiography of Thomas Dixon.* Alexandria, VA: IWV Publishing, 1984.

Dixon, Wheeler Winston, and Gwendolyn Audry Foster. *A Short History of Film.* New Brunswick, NJ: Rutgers University Press, 2008.

Gish, Lillian, with Ann Pinchot. *The Movies, Mr. Griffith and Me.* Englewood Cliffs, NJ: Prentice-Hall, 1969.

Grieveson, Lee. *Policing Cinema: Movies and Censorship in Early-Twentieth-Century America.* Los Angeles: University of California Press, 2004.

Hart, James, ed. *The Man Who Invented Hollywood: The Autobiography of D. W. Griffith.* Louisville, KY: Touchstone, 1972.

Henderson, Robert M. *D. W. Griffith: His Life and Work.* New York: Oxford University Press, 1972.

Lang, Robert, ed. *The Birth of a Nation (continuity script).* New Brunswick, NJ: Rutgers University Press, 1994.

Long, Robert Edgar. *David Wark Griffith: A Brief Sketch of His Career.* New York: D. W. Griffith Service, 1920.

MacGregor, Ford H. "Official Censorship Legislation," *Annals of the American Academy of Political and Social Science* 128 (November 1926): 163–74.

Mayer, David. *Stagestruck Filmmaker: D.W. Griffith and the American Theatre.* Iowa City: University of Iowa Press, 2009.

Merritt, Russell. "Rescued from a Perilous Nest: D. W. Griffith's Escape from Theatre into Film," *Cinema Journal* 21, no. 1 (Autumn 1981): 2–30.

Schickel, Richard. *D. W. Griffith: An American Life.* New York: Simon & Schuster, 1984.

Sifakis, Stewart. *Compendium of the Confederate Armies: Kentucky, Maryland, Missouri, the Confederate Units and the Indian Units.* New York: Facts on File, 1995.

Silva, Fred, ed. *Focus on The Birth of a Nation.* Englewood Cliffs, NJ: Prentice-Hall, 1971.

Slide, Anthony. *Aspects of American Film History Prior to 1920.* Metuchen, NJ: Scarecrow Press, 1978.

———. *Early American Cinema.* Metuchen, NJ: Scarecrow Press, 1994.

———, ed. *D. W. Griffith Interviews.* Jackson: University of Mississippi Press, 2012.

Stokes, Melvyn. *The Birth of a Nation: A History of "the Most Controversial Film of All Time."* New York: Oxford University Press, 2007.

Wagenknecht, Edward, and Anthony Slide. *The Films of D. W. Griffith.* New York: Crown Publishers, 1975.

BOOKS AND MATERIALS: GENERAL

Aptheker, Herbert, ed. *The Correspondence of W. E. B. Du Bois: Volume I: Selections 1877–1934.* Amherst: University of Massachusetts Press, 1973.

Baker, Ray Stannard. *Following the Color Line: American Negro Citizenship in the Progressive Era.* New York: Harper & Row, 1964. Originally published in 1908 by Doubleday, Page & Company.

———. "An Ostracized Race in Ferment: Story of the Conflict of Negro Parties and Negro Leaders over Methods of Dealing with Their Own Problems." *American Magazine* 66 (May 1908): 60–70.

———. "Gathering Clouds Along the Color Line." *The World's Work* 32, no. 1 (1916): 232–36.

Barbas, Samantha. "How the Movies Became Speech." *Rutgers Law Review* vol. 64, no. 3 (Spring 2012): 665–745.

Bay, Mia. *To Tell the Truth Freely: The Life of Ida B. Wells.* New York: Hill and Wang, 2009.

Bean, Dr. Robert Bennett. "Some Racial Peculiarities of the Negro Brain." *American Journal of Anatomy* 5 (1906): 73.

Beatty, Jack. *The Rascal King: The Life and Times of James Michael Curley (1874–1958).* Reading, MA: Addison-Wesley, 1992.

Beisel, Nicola. *Imperiled Innocents: Anthony Comstock and Family Reproduction in Victorian America.* Princeton, NJ: Princeton University Press, 1997.

Bennett, Lerone Jr. *Black Power U.S.A: The Human Side of Reconstruction 1867–1877.* Chicago: Johnson Publishing Co., 1967.

———. *Pioneers in Protest.* Baltimore, MD: Penguin Books, 1969.

Broun, Heywood, and Margaret Leech. *Anthony Comstock: Roundsman of the Lord.* New York: Albert & Charles Boni, 1927.

Chace, James. *1912: Wilson, Roosevelt, Taft & Debs—The Election That Changed The Country.* New York: Simon & Schuster Paperbacks, 2005.

Chesler, Ellen. *Woman of Valor: Margaret Sanger and the Birth Control Movement in America.* New York: Simon & Schuster, 1992.

Coulter, E. Merton. *The Civil War and Readjustment in Kentucky.* Chapel Hill: University of North Carolina Press, 1926.

Davis, John P. *The American Negro Reference Book.* Englewood Cliffs, NJ: Prentice-Hall, 1966.

Du Bois, W. E. B. *The Souls of Black Folks.* Chicago: A. C. McClurg & Co., 1903.

———. *Dusk of Dawn: An Essay Toward an Autobiography of a Race Concept.* New York: Harcourt, Brace and Co., 1940.

———. *The Autobiography of W. E. B. Du Bois.* New York: International Publishers, 1968.

Fighting a Vicious Film: Protest Against "The Birth of a Nation." Pamphlet published by the Boston branch of the NAACP, Spring 1915.

"First National Negro Conference Program," New York City. May 31, 1909.

Folkerts, Jean, and Dwight L. Teeter Jr. *Voices of a Nation: A History of Mass Media in the United States.* Boston, MA: Allyn & Bacon, 2002.

Forbes, George W. "The Progress of the Negro: A Study in the Last Census." *Arena* 32 (1904): 134–41.

Franklin, John Hope. *From Slavery to Freedom: A History of Negro Americans, Third Edition.* New York: Knopf, 1967.

Franklin, John Hope, and August Meier, ed. *Black Leaders of the Twentieth Century.* Urbana: University of Illinois Press, 1982.

Giddings, Paula J. *Ida: A Sword Among Lions.* New York: HarperCollins, 2008.

Goldsby, Jacqueline. *A Spectacular Secret: Lynching in American Life and Literature.* Chicago and London: University of Chicago Press, 2006.

Gordon, Eugene. "The Negro Press," *American Mercury* 8 (1926): 207–14.

Gottheimer, Josh, ed. *Ripples of Hope: Great American Civil Rights Speeches.* New York: BasicCivitas, 2003.

Grantham, Dewey W. Jr. "The Progressive Movement and the Negro." *South Atlantic Quarterly* 54 (1955): 461–77.

Grimké, Angelina. "A Biographical Sketch of Archibald H. Grimké." *Opportunity* 3 (February 1925): 44–47.

Hentoff, Nat. *The First Freedom: The Tumultuous History of Free Speech in America.* New York: Delacorte Press, 1988.

Hopkins, Pauline Elizabeth. "The Bosfield Case." *New Era Magazine* 1, no. 2 (March 1916): 119–21.

Jackman, John S. *Diary of a Confederate Soldier: John S. Jackman of the Orphan Brigade.* Columbia: University of South Carolina Press, 1990.

Jakle, John A., and Keith A Sculle. *Fast Food: Roadside Restaurants in the Automobile Age.* Baltimore and London: Johns Hopkins University Press, 1999.

Kantrowitz, Stephen. *More Than Freedom: Fighting for Black Citizenship in a White Republic, 1829–1889.* New York: Penguin, 2012.

Kors, Alan Charles, and Harvey Silverglate. *The Shadow University: The Betrayal of Liberty on America's Campuses.* New York: The Free Press, 1998.

Link, Arthur S. "The Negro as a Factor in the Campaign of 1912." *Journal of Negro History* 32, no. 1 (January 1947): 81–99.

———. *Wilson: The Road to the White House.* Princeton: Princeton University Press, 1947.

Litwack, Leon F. *How Free Is Free? The Long Death of Jim Crow.* Cambridge, MA: Harvard University Press, 2009.

Mall, Dr. Franklin P. "On Several Anatomical Characteristics of the Human Brain, Said to Vary According to Race and Sex, With Especial Reference to the Weight of the Frontal Lobe." *American Journal of Anatomy* 9, no. 1 (1909): 1–32.

Meier, August, and Rudwick, Elliott. "The Rise of Segregation in the Federal Bureaucracy, 1900–1930." *The Pylon: The Atlanta University Review of Race and Culture* 28, no. 2 (1967): 178–84.

Miller, Kelly. "Race Adjustment: Essays on the Negro in America." New York: The Neale Publishing Co., 1908.

Morrison, Joseph L. *Josephus Daniels: The Small-d Democrat.* Chapel Hill: University of North Carolina Press, 1966.

Newkirk, Pamela, ed. *Letters from Black America.* New York: Farrar, Straus and Giroux, 2009.

Norrell, Robert J. *Up from History: The Life of Booker T. Washington.* Cambridge, MA: The Belknap Press of Harvard University Press, 2009.

Odum, Howard W. *Social and Mental Traits of the Negro.* New York: AMS Press, 1910.

Ovington, Mary White. *The Walls Come Tumbling Down*. New York: Harcourt, Brace, 1947.

Parini, Jay. *Promised Land: Thirteen Books That Changed America*. New York: Doubleday, 2008.

Rogers, J. A. *World's Great Men of Color: Volume II*. New York: Simon & Schuster, 1947.

Rose, Arnold. *The Negro in America: The Class Condensation of Gunnar Myrdal's The American Dilemma*. Boston, MA: The Beacon Press, 1956.

Salem, Dorothy C., ed. *African American Women: A Biographical Dictionary*. New York: Garland Publishing, 1993.

Sanger, Alexander. *Beyond Choice: Reproductive Freedom in the 21st Century*. New York: PublicAffairs, 2005.

Sanger, Margaret. *The Autobiography of Margaret Sanger*. Mineola, New York: Dover Publications, 1971.

Silverglate, Harvey A. *The Tuskegee Machine and Civil Rights Agitation: The Role of Booker T. Washington in Suppressing Negro Militance, 1895–1910*. Senior thesis, Princeton University, Princeton, 1964.

Smock, Raymond W. *Booker T. Washington: Black Leadership in the Age of Jim Crow*. Chicago: Ivan R. Dee, 2009.

Sollors, Werner, Caldwell Titcomb, and Thomas A Underwood. *Blacks at Harvard: A Documentary History of African-American Experience at Harvard and Radcliffe*. New York: New York University Press, 1993.

Starr, Paul. *The Creation of the Media: Political Origins of Modern Communications*. New York: Basic Books, 2004.

Sullivan, Patricia. *Lift Every Voice: The NAACP and the Making of the Civil Rights Movement*. New York: The New Press, 2009.

Tye, Larry. *Rising from the Rails: Pullman Porters and the Making of the Black Middle Class*. New York: Henry Holt and Company, 2004.

Van Deusen, John G. *The Black Man in White America*. Washington, DC: Associated Publishers, 1944.

Washington, Booker T. *My Larger Education: Chapters From My Experience*. Amherst, New York: Humanity Books, 2004. Originally published in 1911.

Wells, Ida B. *Crusade for Justice: The Autobiography of Ida B. Wells*, edited by Alfreda M. Duster. Chicago and London: University of Chicago Press, 1991.

Wilson, Joseph T. *The Black Phalanx: A History of the Negro Soldiers of the United States*. Hartford, CT: American Publishing Co., 1888.

Wolters, Raymond. *Du Bois and His Rivals*. Columbia and London: University of Missouri Press, 2002.

Wright, Kai, ed. *The African American Experience: Black History and Culture Through Speeches, Letters, Editorials, Poems, Songs, and Stories*. New York: Black Dog & Leventhal Publishers, 2009.

INDEX

ABOUT THE AUTHOR

Karin Lehr

Dick Lehr, a professor of journalism at Boston University, has won numerous national and regional journalism awards. He is a former investigative reporter, legal affairs, and magazine writer for the *Boston Globe*, where he was a Pulitzer Prize finalist in investigative reporting. He is the author of *The Fence: A Police Cover-Up Along Boston's Racial Divide*, an Edgar Award finalist for best nonfiction; and coauthor of the *New York Times* bestseller and Edgar Award winner *Black Mass: Whitey Bulger, the FBI, and a Devil's Deal*, and its sequel, *Whitey: The Life of America's Most Notorious Mob Boss*. He lives outside Boston with his wife and four children.

PublicAffairs is a publishing house founded in 1997. It is a tribute to the standards, values, and flair of three persons who have served as mentors to countless reporters, writers, editors, and book people of all kinds, including me.

I. F. STONE, proprietor of *I. F. Stone's Weekly*, combined a commitment to the First Amendment with entrepreneurial zeal and reporting skill and became one of the great independent journalists in American history. At the age of eighty, Izzy published *The Trial of Socrates*, which was a national bestseller. He wrote the book after he taught himself ancient Greek.

BENJAMIN C. BRADLEE was for nearly thirty years the charismatic editorial leader of *The Washington Post*. It was Ben who gave the *Post* the range and courage to pursue such historic issues as Watergate. He supported his reporters with a tenacity that made them fearless and it is no accident that so many became authors of influential, best-selling books.

ROBERT L. BERNSTEIN, the chief executive of Random House for more than a quarter century, guided one of the nation's premier publishing houses. Bob was personally responsible for many books of political dissent and argument that challenged tyranny around the globe. He is also the founder and longtime chair of Human Rights Watch, one of the most respected human rights organizations in the world.

.   .   .

For fifty years, the banner of Public Affairs Press was carried by its owner Morris B. Schnapper, who published Gandhi, Nasser, Toynbee, Truman, and about 1,500 other authors. In 1983, Schnapper was described by *The Washington Post* as "a redoubtable gadfly." His legacy will endure in the books to come.

Peter Osnos, *Founder and Editor-at-Large*

Made in the USA
Monee, IL
30 January 2023

26783639R00215